W9-BAU-610

ANTON BRUCKNER

Anton Bruckner in the 1880's

ON BRUCKNER
USTIC GENIUS

BY WERNER WOLFF
HEAD OF MUSIC DEPARTMENT
TENNESSEE WESLEYAN COLLEGE

Introduction by WALTER DAMROSCH

NEW YORK · E. P. DUTTON & CO., INC.
1942

FIRST EDITION

S. A. JACOBS, THE GOLDEN EAGLE PRESS, MOUNT VERNON, N. Y.

DEDICATION

TO THAT DISTINGUISHED FOUNDATION, AND GENEROUS HELPER OF THE AMERICAN PROFESSOR,

THE OBERLAENDER TRUST,
PHILADELPHIA, PA.

WITHOUT WHOSE ASSISTANCE THIS BOOK WOULD NOT HAVE BEEN WRITTEN

PREFACE

I SAW him — face to face.

It was in the early 1890's that our parents told us the famous composer Anton Bruckner was coming to have dinner with us. They warned us to be on our good behavior. We did not pay an unusual amount of attention to their admonition, for we fortunate children had seen such celebrities as Tschaikowsky, Brahms, Saint-Saëns, and Anton Rubinstein in our home. Although they did not in the least resemble one another physically, they all had something in common in attitude and behavior which we young ones recognized as characteristic of celebrities. It was the cosmopolitan manner of the "grand seigneur."

Then the day came and Anton Bruckner really entered our living room. Although we had seen pictures of him, we were surprised, even startled. There was something peculiar in his appearance. It was not that his head seemed rather small (I had Brahms' powerful skull still in mind); it was not the length of his eyelids, either. It was something less personal and therefore more striking to childish eyes. It was his clothes. Certainly musicians at that time were no models of elegance; they rather distinguished themselves from their lay brothers by nonchalance in attire. This man, however, was so very different from the musicians we had seen in our house that we were perplexed. His short black jacket and his voluminous baggy trousers reminded me of the countrymen I had seen on our annual trips to the Alps. He did not say much until my little sister entered the room. Then he fell on his knees and addressed her in his Upper Austrian patois: "*Jessas, das gnaedige Fraeulein*" (Jeez, the little lady!) The poor child was scared out of her wits and fell to weeping. But that was only the beginning of our embarrassment. At dinner Bruckner picked up the fish with his fingers and broke the bones. Then we knew why we had been told to behave ourselves.

As soon as I heard the old man's music, however, I forgot the oddity of his appearance and manners. How different seemed the man who had written the *Second* and the *Fifth Symphony*, which my father later played for me! I can still see my father playing the scores on the piano, stopping now and then to shake his head at the general rests, yet going on and working out the compositions. The themes became as familiar to me as those from Beethoven's symphonies or from Bach's *Mass in B Minor*, themes which belong to my first musical memories. So I began to love Bruckner and what happened to me happens to everyone who loves Bruckner – once you love him, you love him forever. I have seen musicians converted to Bruckner's music late in their careers but I have never seen anyone, once converted, who abandoned him. Devotion to Bruckner is not a matter of taste or fashion but of character and conviction.

While I was studying law at the University of Berlin and pursuing music under the instruction of Engelbert Humperdinck, I heard the first performance of Bruckner's *Ninth Symphony* under the direction of Arthur Nikisch. I wrote in my diary: "I am overwhelmed. It makes me suffer. It works in me and on me with the power of a catastrophe of nature. The rhythm of the clarinets at the end of the First Movement over the inexorable organ point on D will never cease haunting me."

I came to a definite decision; I would make music my lifework. I opened my first concert in Berlin with Bruckner's *Eighth Symphony*. In my symphonic concerts in Hamburg I began a systematic campaign for Bruckner and had the great satisfaction of converting many concert-goers to this master of music. Even before this time I had noticed I could do much more for him – I could remove certain prejudices against him which were in danger of becoming set in the minds of the music world. I began writing explanatory notes for the Nikisch concerts and I started lecturing on Bruckner. The first public lecture ran for two and a half hours instead of the scheduled hour. Something unforeseen had occurred while I was lecturing: the "Problem Bruckner" had arisen in my mind. It has kept me busy to the present day.

When I came to this country three years ago, I wrote an article for *The New York Times* in which I pointed out my belief that Bruckner's music should become more familiar to American concert-goers. I did not need to wait very long. Interest in the composer grew strong enough to make an extended biography necessary. I was happy and honored in being chosen to write it after my half century of familiarity with Bruckner's music. It will probably be my last contribution to Bruckner's cause. May it be a helpful one!

Werner Wolff

ACKNOWLEDGMENT

For assistance in the work, I wish to express my heartiest thanks to Lorna Dietz, and to Mr. Harold Byrns, New York City, and to the Associated Music Publishers, Inc.

Silhouettes in this book are by
Dr. Otto Böhler

TABLE OF CONTENTS

INTRODUCTION

By Walter Damrosch

MUSICIANS and music lovers generally will read with great interest this full-length biography of Anton Bruckner, Austrian peasant and symphonic composer who is worthy of being included in that hierarchy beginning with Haydn and ending with Brahms.

The author, Werner Wolff, has written this book as a labor of love. For years he was a conductor of opera and symphony in Hamburg, Germany, and he has now settled in America. He was among the first to introduce the symphonies of Bruckner in Germany and to analyze and write about them sympathetically. Our own great musicologist Philip Hale of Boston wrote of Werner Wolff as follows: ". . . I am indebted in a measure for the preceding sketch of the contents of this symphony (Bruckner's *Eighth*) to the analysis by Werner Wolff, published in the program book of the Philharmonic Orchestra, Berlin, October 29, 1906. I have followed chiefly in the footsteps of Mr. Wolff."

I have known Werner Wolff for some time and am therefore familiar with his professional and family background. He was brought up in exceptional musical surroundings. The home of his parents was the very center of musical life in Berlin, which at that time was considered the musical capital of Europe. His father was the founder of the Berlin Philharmonic Orchestra, and to his hospitable house came all the great composers, singers and instrumentalists of that period.

Introduction

In Werner Wolff's fascinating and revealing Preface he tells us very vividly how, as a boy in his father's house, he first saw Anton Bruckner with his peasant clothes, speech and manners. But shortly after, his music so enthused the boy that he then and there resolved to become a musician.

To me it has always seemed one of the inscrutable mysteries that Bruckner, while retaining all his life the simplicity of peasant life, speech and customs, should have had within him a musical genius so extraordinary as to enable him to write music of such indescribable warmth, nobility and eloquence. I felt this very strongly when I first began my musical career as an orchestral conductor and when I gave his *Fourth Symphony* at a concert of the New York Symphony Society on December 5, 1885. This was the first performance of a work of Bruckner's in our country. Since then his compositions have become part of the regular repertoire of all our great symphony orchestras. Although occasionally Bruckner's mastery as a great improviser at the organ may have influenced him in his symphonies to a somewhat lengthy and rhapsodic development of his themes, this does not materially detract from the loftiness of his works.

This book in which Werner Wolff has contributed his own musical knowledge, together with an intimate study of Bruckner's life as well as his music, is a most welcome and necessary addition to the more serious biographies of the great music masters of the past.

ANTON BRUCKNER

PART I

BRUCKNER'S LIFE AND PERSONALITY

CHAPTER I

"ONLY in his works did Bruckner disclose his true nature. In comparison with his creations everything else is unimportant and carries with it the danger of making him appear in a wrong light before a public which has not yet fully recognized his grandeur." These words, recently written to me by the well-known composer and former pupil of Bruckner, Friedrich Klose, are as true as they are discouraging to the biographer. In fact, there is a one-way bridge from Bruckner's works to the man himself. Crossing that, we can recognize his true character. But the biographer who is forced to follow a detour comes, sooner or later, to the point on his journey where further progress becomes almost impossible. The man whose life he is describing and the creator of the nine great symphonies seem to be two entirely different subjects.

Interesting as Bruckner's personality is, there is nothing in his prosaic life to justify us in drawing conclusions as to its influence on the development of his genius. In following his career, one never senses a tension nor a climax leading to majestic heights, such as other great composers of the nineteenth century reached. His exterior life had no seeming effect upon his work. An immense reserve of psychic forces, originating in a realm not subject to any influence from the outside, must have been stored in the man, gifted with so great a creative power. His life itself showed no dynamic factors. The higher the artist in him soared, the more the man himself remained earthbound. It is not necessary to think of Wagner or Liszt, whose lives were so closely connected with their creations. Even Brahms, a rather bourgeois soul, and Verdi, the country baron, are more attractive than Bruckner as subjects for a biographer. And yet Bruckner was the creator of nine symphonies which many connoisseurs consider not inferior to Beethoven's.

On the other hand, Bruckner was only a poor schoolmaster's son and he himself might very readily have remained a schoolmaster in one of the wretched villages of his homeland. He had a hard struggle in making a modest living. Nothing ever came easily to him. Even the great mystery of music revealed itself to him in a slow and hesitating manner before he became its accomplished master. During the first forty years of his life nothing pointed to the man who was to become one of the outstanding exponents of European music. When finally the general opposition to his art began to fade, in the last years before his death, it was too late to alter the true direction of his life. Not one of his numerous biographers has been successful in persuading us into the belief that the great artist was also a great man.

Contrast, one of the main characteristics in Bruckner's music, is also one of the most important features in the composite picture of the man and the artist Bruckner. This contradiction between artist and man must not be concealed; any attempt to do so deprives the whole enigma of its mysterious spell. The unexplainable mystery of music is reflected in this singular man himself. To describe it is the aim of this book.

What it meant to be the son of a schoolmaster in a small village of Upper Austria in the 1800's cannot easily be conveyed to the American reader. There were, and there still are, sections in America, too, which are possibly as poor as Bruckner's homeland. However, the general conditions of life in the Austria of the years preceding the Revolution of 1848 were ruled by a reactionary trend, by a formalism and an intolerance never known to the American people.

In characterizing the atmosphere of that time and place, Ernst Decsey in his book on Bruckner says: "Bruckner springs from the epoch of Emperor Franz I (1768-1835). It is the period of deepest reaction (*Vormaerz*),* of senile middle age. It (Austria) is segregated from Europe, chained to a silence and devoid of ideas... The word 'freedom' sounds like high treason; authority weighs down all forms of life."

A vestige of this control wielded by an all-powerful caste of State functionaries was more noticeable in Austria than in Germany up to the time of the World War. It was especially discernible in the official language, which abounded in formal and stereotyped figures of speech. Bruckner's old-fashioned and sometimes servile style, as shown in his letters, is reminiscent of eighteenth-century usage, as revealed in Bach's petitions and dedications.

The other powerful factor which made itself overwhelmingly felt in the land of "His Apostolic Majesty," the Austrian emperor, was the Roman Catholic Church. The Catholic Church, although *una sancta ecclesia*, plays different parts in the various countries of Europe. In the German Rhineland, Catholicism is a deeply ingrained matter of conscience; in Italy, it is a way of life; but in Austria, Catholics are unquestioningly devoted to the authority of the Church.

So much, then, for the atmosphere in which Bruckner was born and bred.

It was on the fourth of September, 1824, that he first saw the light of day in Ansfelden in Upper Austria. This little village is situated in a lovely and peaceful region, with the Alps forming an imposing background. His grandfather, Josephus, first a cooper by trade and later a school teacher, had come to the community from Lower Austria. Josephus's son Anton, born in 1791, had married Therese Helm in 1823. She was the daughter of an *Amtsverwalter* (administrator)

* Literally, pre-March; i. e., the period preceding the Revolution of March, 1848.

and innkeeper, a man whose position gave him a social standing higher than that of a school teacher.

Eleven children were born to this union. There was nothing unusual in such prolificness. Up to the 70's of the nineteenth century it was a very natural thing in central Europe for a healthy wife to have a child every year. The financial difficulties in raising a large family were never considered, and so the great natural increase in population brought about pitiful living conditions for such underprivileged classes as school teachers and musicians.

Anton was the oldest of the eleven children. Six of them died soon after birth or in infancy, but Rosalie and Ignatz survived their brother Anton. Ignatz, who lived until 1913, was in later life a precious source of information on the composer's life after the latter's death.

According to his baptismal certificate, Bruckner's full name was Joseph Anton. Incidentally, the only way we have of knowing this is from a copy of the certificate, which was sent to the University of Cincinnati in 1885. It was accompanied by a request for an honorary doctor's degree from that institution. A swindler had promised to get him this degree and Bruckner had given him money for the purpose.

Bruckner's parents differed greatly in character. The mother was very temperamental and sometimes treated the children harshly, whereas Father Bruckner was a good-natured man who wanted peace in his home during the few free hours granted an overburdened teacher.

Anton grew up without displaying any outstanding traits of character. In common with other boys, he liked playing with comrades of his own age and disliked studying. Goellerich says: "When they played 'robbers,' he padded his pants so that he would feel the expected spanking less." The first real tendency he showed towards intellectual matters was his great liking for music. He was always delighted with the evening singing lessons and he learned to play the violin, piano, and organ. And he would grow quiet when he heard someone play the spinet. The priest of his church loved the four-year-old Anton for his ability in playing the violin. But even in music the boy did not demonstrate a striking talent. He definitely was not a child prodigy. None of Bruckner's biographers, not even those who have collected all the details of his early life, are able to point out any unusual sign of musical talent. If there had been anything of the sort, acquaintances of his early youth, who were questioned by the biographers, of course would have known of it, since especially gifted children as a rule make a distinct impression. In a small community they are quite often looked upon as odd children who do not fit into the average group. There is no record of anything to this effect. The father himself was Anton's first music teacher. He was probably just good enough in music for school and church duties. He played the fiddle, the spinet, and wind instruments, and he also sang in church. Decsey called the average Austrian school "the village conservatory."

Bruckner never received instruction from a real virtuoso. At that time, a school teacher in Austria had to be not only an instructor in academic work but also a practical musician. In the German language such musicians are called *Musikanten* as distinguished from *Musiker*, or men who have dedicated themselves to music as an art. The *Musikanten*, although of a lower musical standing, later contributed to the development of the orchestra in Germany and Austria. Orchestra players, especially those who played wind instruments, usually served their apprenticeship under these *Musikanten* before being sent to the customary conservatory. And, by the way, as far as the elementary school teacher is concerned, Austria was ahead of Germany, where the teacher was never required to do more than merely get the children to sing a simple tune or hymn.

Father Bruckner was certainly a *Musikant* of very limited

abilities and young Anton must have had a good deal of talent of his own, for his cousin, Johann Baptist Weiss, was so deeply impressed by the ten-year-old boy's organ playing that he took him into his home at Hoersching and gave him instruction in organ and thorough bass. Weiss himself was a composer of some proficiency. His works show the influence of Haydn's church music. In 1836 Bruckner wrote his first organ preludes. The introductory chords of one of these preludes display the future Bruckner inclination toward magnificent harmonies, although the lack of harmonic cadences makes us realize that his studies had reached only a very modest level.* However, they are of enough interest to be compared with the works of other composers of the same age.

Toward the end of 1836 Father Bruckner was taken sick; and when it became evident that he would not recover, Anton was called home to help in the taxing work at school. As the invalid steadily grew worse, it was finally necessary to summon the priest to administer last rites. The grief-stricken boy in attendance at the bedside, emotionally overcome, fainted at his post. The poor schoolmaster died in 1837 and Anton, not yet thirteen years old, temporarily took over the teaching.

On the very day of her husband's death, Mrs. Bruckner, with characteristic firmness, took the first step in assuring her boy's future. Armed with a letter of introduction and her own indomitable spirit, she immediately went to St. Florian, a monastery of the Augustinian canons. Anton became a chorister at St. Florian a few weeks later.

Here began a new and decisive phase of his life. He took root, and throughout his entire existence he never lost his

* I cannot agree with Gabriel Engel, who says in *The Life of Anton Bruckner* (page 6) that these organ preludes exhibit a freedom of expression which deserted Bruckner, all through his Odyssean decades of theoretical study, to return unimpaired in his ripe symphonic years.

feeling of attachment to the place. In later years, when he felt the need of a little peace, he would often return to the quietness of St. Florian. And St. Florian rewarded his faithfulness by granting him a last resting place, for his body lies forever beneath the organ of the church. Auer describes the place in these words: "The famous baroque style of the building, the sumptuous furnishing of the imperial rooms, and above all the magnificent organ exerted their spell on the sensitive boy."

In August of the same year young Bruckner entered the public school and evidently found happiness in the friendly home of the principal, Michael Bogner, with whom he lived. His organ instructor was Kettinger, the organist of St. Florian, who exerted a great influence on the boy's development. He made rapid strides in his study of the organ and was soon sufficiently advanced to play occasionally for the services in church. And he continued studying the violin, piano, and thorough bass. Carrying all this work besides his regular school lessons meant a fairly full daily schedule.

Bruckner's goal seems never to have been a matter of uncertainty. His grandfather and his father had been school teachers. What, then, could he become but a school teacher? In those days it was the custom in certain German and Austrian circles for the son to continue the father's profession. For instance, the son of an army officer was supposed to enter the army, and most of the school teachers came from teacher families. Not to take up the paternal profession constituted almost a break in family tradition, even though officers and teachers were most poorly paid.

Had Anton ever thought of any other career at the time when boys of his age usually make ambitious plans? Whether he did or not, we see him in October, 1840, entering the preparatory course for public-school teachers in Linz, the capital of Upper Austria. It is indeed interesting to learn that history and natural science were excluded from the curriculum at the time. The course of study was decidedly antiquated, having come down from the days of Maria Theresa.

Bruckner's instructor in music was the excellent organist Duernberger, for whom he had a great affection which lasted for many years. Here in Linz he heard a symphony by Beethoven for the first time. It was the *Fourth*, in B flat major. We do not know much about the standard of Beethoven performances at that time; the type of rendition to which we are accustomed was created many years later by the great conductor Hans von Buelow. However, as only a few years had passed since Beethoven's death, we can assume that the performance approximated the desires of the composer, and there may have been many men among the orchestra members who had heard Beethoven's symphony performed in Vienna as the composer wished it. They may even have participated in performing it. Nor do we know what impression the *Fourth Symphony* made on the young music student. Listening to a Beethoven symphony for the first time does not seem to have been an overwhelming experience for him, as it has so often been for other musicians. The determining event in Bruckner's life came later and from quite different sources.

In the summer of 1841 the young candidate passed his examinations and was appointed assistant teacher in Windhaag, a little settlement of a few hundred inhabitants. The important moment of taking up a profession had come. Bruckner may not have had great expectations as far as Windhaag was concerned, but the actual conditions must have been worse than he imagined. Although he had certainly not been pampered in his earlier days, he found the position at Windhaag really beneath his dignity. Thus far Bruckner, modest as he was, had never shown any sort of social pride, but being banished to the kitchen and the society of the maid-of-all-work for his meals was a bitter demand. He hated being considered her equal and the girl, for her part, may have made a fool of this peculiar fellow who was so different from all the men she knew. What a theme for a dramatist — a scene presenting a clash between the two sharply contrasting characters!

The girl was not the only one in the small village to look upon him as a rather strange apparition. The young man, totally absorbed in his musical ideas, must have aroused the curiosity of the townspeople, when in walking through the fields he would suddenly stop to jot down a theme or a thought in his notebook. They may even have distrusted him, for as an outsider he was not fully accepted by the community. Up to the end of the World War, suspicion and distrust towards musicians were generally to be found in small towns throughout central Europe. I myself will never forget the landlady in a small city who refused to rent me rooms when she learned I was the musical director of the opera house.

All in all, the position of a school teacher at that time must have been a pitiful one. Decsey thinks an assistant teacher was a person of the lowest social standing, and we know that a man in Windhaag made the following illuminating remark: "I would rather see my son a shoemaker than a school teacher." A monthly remuneration of about eighty cents, a poor little room, scanty food, and hard and even humiliating work were the earmarks of the profession. Besides his regular work in the school, Bruckner had to function as sacristan. That meant ringing the chimes at four o'clock in the morning, helping the priest dress for services, playing the organ, training the choir, and last and worst of all, working in the fields digging potatoes, making hay, and threshing grain. So when we hear that he would often play for dances after his regular day's work, we cannot fail to realize how grossly he was overworked.

Bruckner's early career was harsh and bitter. Yet music, the most spiritual and ethereal of all the arts, possesses magic power. In the first place, it rewards its follower through its very nature; it comforts him if he seriously strives in it. Second, it has a unifying, universal force; it fosters friendship. In spite of all his hardships, Bruckner was therefore in a mood to compose his first Mass, in C major.*

Friendship was offered him, for he was a welcome guest at the home of the weaver Suecka, to whose son he became both boon companion and mentor. They enjoyed playing violin duets together, with Bruckner invariably taking the second part. Sometimes Father Suecka assisted them on the trumpet. Occasionally the village doctor joined them with his flute, and once in a while other villagers came with their instruments. They are said to have done fairly well, and this is not hard to believe, as Austria has always been the country for home-music-making. Haydn, Mozart, and Beethoven had not lived in Vienna without leaving a trace of their passing. They had helped establish a musical tradition which made itself felt in private circles as well as in public performances. As a result, Austrian criticism was sharpened to a point of aggressiveness, in which it differed from the more contemplative attitude of the Germans. Anyone who has lived among Austrians knows their lack of compromise in all musical matters, but theirs is a constructive, discriminating attitude which has contributed greatly to the high standard of musical performance in their country.

In Windhaag Bruckner studied Bach's *Art of the Fugue.* If this was the first of Bach's works with which he became familiar, we shall have to assume that he was not yet mature enough for this last great work of Bach's. But then, he never thought of method in his study; rather, he seized every opportunity of ridding himself of the depressing sameness and stultifying routine of the daily treadmill.

* Goellerich's assumption that Bruckner's *Pange Lingua* was written in Windhaag has been rejected by Auer, who was the better informed of the two critics.

The principal watched his young assistant with jealous attention and had every reason for dissatisfaction when Bruckner confused the congregation by his strange improvisations, thus conjuring up a situation similar to the one in Arnstadt more than a hundred years before, when Bach had astounded his audience and superiors. And in all probability Bruckner himself contributed his share in making the position unbearable. Once when he was ordered to perform a very menial task and refused, the principal denounced him to the prelate Arneth, the supreme authority in question. But the tables were turned and the complaint proved to be a piece of good luck for the young man, for Arneth, apparently impressed by the degrading conditions about which Bruckner himself gave a report, took the opportunity of drawing the young musician closer to his own residence and transferred him to Kronstorf. Was he the first to divine Bruckner's later development? It was not often that anyone put himself out to help Bruckner along the way.

In 1843 Bruckner left the scene of his disappointing experiences. It has sometimes been said these early experiences laid the foundation for a kind of pessimism seen in the older Bruckner. Yet Goellerich has pointed out that melancholia was recurrent in the Bruckner family, and I think we had better not attribute permanent impressions to the comparatively short stay he made in Windhaag. Men easily forget the unfortunate experiences of their youth as soon as they enter a new and more favorable environment. And so, apparently, did the new teacher at Kronstorf. Living conditions were pleasanter, the work was less exhausting, and near by there were two larger towns which attracted him — Steyr with its wonderful organ and Enns, where the famous organist Zenetti lived. Bruckner did not begrudge the fatigue of walking to Enns three times a week to study organ, piano, and harmony with this musician.

At this time he was introduced to Bach's *Well-tempered*

Clavichord, that inexhaustible well-spring for everyone devoted to the study of music. He evidently enjoyed it thoroughly and was inspired by it, as can be seen from the number of compositions he wrote in Kronstorf. In 1843 he wrote a chorus for men's voices which he thought worthy of rewriting forty years later under the name of "Tafellied." There were also a "Libera Me" and a "Tantum Ergo." In 1844 he produced a Choral Mass for Maundy Thursday. Unfortunately, the singers were so terrified of the very idea that none of them appeared at the first choir rehearsal. The last work written in Kronstorf, in 1845, bears the name "Vergissmeinnicht" (Forget-me-not) for soloist, singers, chorus, and piano. There are no clues to the whereabouts of three other compositions of this period – a "Litany" and a "Salve Regina," both written in 1844, and a "Requiem" in the year 1845.

The next of the long series of examinations which Bruckner took during the first forty years of his life was one for schoolmaster. It goes without saying that his grades in music were excellent, and in 1845 he returned as a teacher to St. Florian, the place he had learned to love as a schoolboy.

Bogner's house, which he had left five years before, once more became his home. The special attraction which drew him there seems to have been Bogner's daughter Louise. He dedicated a few songs to her. But this little romance ended like so many others in his life: the girl refused his proposal of marriage. Anton's depression was as deep as a youth's could be. Goellerich thinks Bruckner's grief caused him to write the cantata "Entsagen" (Renunciation) in 1851, and other biographers assume Bruckner found a musical expression for his experiences in many of his works. But we should be careful in drawing such conclusions; it is too easy to assume that Bruckner was inspired by love affairs, as were Berlioz and Wagner in like situations. Romance is often overrated as a source of creative power in an artist, and a later examination of Bruckner's character will set us straight on this point.

Sources of information on Bruckner's second stay in St. Florian are scarce and hard to find. We see him applying himself relentlessly to organ and piano practice. In Kronstorf he had annoyed the members of the household by practicing on the piano until one o'clock in the morning, but here, at St. Florian, he began at four o'clock in the morning and carried on until six forty-five. He evidently expected the folks around him to be pretty indulgent, but the delight of playing on a beautiful grand piano was a temptation not to be resisted. His friend and protector, Franz Seiler, a copyist at St. Florian until his death in 1848, had bequeathed his brand-new Boesendorfer piano to him. A Boesendorfer was considered the best Austrian instrument and it had an exceptional tonal quality, although its mechanics demanded a strong touch. Bruckner kept this beloved piano until his death, and I do not think it an exaggeration to say that without this fortunate gift from his friend, Bruckner probably would never have had a grand piano. To the end of his days he was very economical, even parsimonious, and he avoided all large expenditures of money even after his financial conditions improved in the last years of his life. It was perhaps for this reason that he copied interesting passages from the works of Handel, Albrechtsberger, Caldara, Michael Haydn, Mozart, and Beethoven. We are reminded of Bach busily copying the music he needed for various purposes. However, times had changed since Bach's day and surely few musicians of the last century applied themselves to such trying and time-consuming tasks. Kurth, who regarded Bruckner from the mystic's point of view, thinks his religious concepts gave him the impetus for such absorbing labor. He tells us, too, that Bruckner, although in the bloom of youth, withdrew more and more from the world. It was only occasionally that he associated with people and displayed his former rustic hilarity at festivals. "While walking in the fields or in the shadow of the woods, the solemn sadness of nature greeted the future creator of the *Romantic Symphony* . . . His grave face always remained capable of a benevolent smile."

Some of the facts relating to Bruckner's sojourn at St. Florian are not very easily explained. Kettinger's post as organist should have been a desired goal for the young musician, and Bruckner actually was his temporary successor in 1849. When the position definitely became his in 1851, he seemed quite happy over the turn of affairs and expressed gratitude for the "heavenly dispensation" in his "Magnificat," written for soloist, chorus, and orchestra (1852), a work which Auer believed showed characteristics of Mozart.

But what a surprise to find him considering a new profession just after his lot had improved so considerably! We know of a petition he wrote in 1853 to the *Organisierungskommission in Linz* (Organizing Committee of Linz) wherein he asks for the post of secretary at court. The man who had spent almost three decades of his life in the approach to his art, who had written scores of compositions, and who, one would suppose, should have felt the urge of his true vocation irresistible, now tried seriously to secure a position which required nothing more than dry and conscientious work. One is tempted to believe a sudden flare-up of temper caused him to take the step. What would have become of his awakening genius if, some years later as an appointed State employee, he had been made to feel the greatness of this error? But Fate did not permit the world to be deprived of a genius such as his, even though his talent had not as yet clearly manifested itself. In tracing Bruckner's career it is often difficult to refrain from feeling compassion for him as we see his petitions and modest requests rejected again and again by his superiors and those in authority. But in this instance we rejoice over the commission's refusal to grant him the secretarial post.

Where were Bruckner's friends at this time, when they should have warned him against such a step? Was there no one sufficiently interested in his music to fear that art itself might suffer an irreparable loss? It is surprising, indeed, to find no traces of thoughtful friends at this time of his life. We know of only one letter dealing with the affair. It was written in July, 1853, by a certain Schaarschmidt, an acquaintance rather than a friend. This man, however, must have had a presentiment of what was at stake, for he advised Bruckner to give up the idea of changing his profession and at the same time he incidentally revealed the impression Bruckner's music made on him. He wrote: "You are making a mistake if you look exclusively to Mendelssohn for your instruction. In any case, you should take from the sources he did, namely Sebastian Bach, whom you should study thoroughly."

Bruckner had taken this strange step deliberately; he had even prepared himself in advance for the proposed new profession. From 1851 on, he had done service as court secretary without any remuneration. It therefore seemed quite reasonable when he said in his application for the job that he had always had an inclination toward the profession he was now trying to enter.

His actions astonish us still more when we learn that from 1850 to 1852 Bruckner attended the preparatory courses newly instituted for candidates for high-school positions. On January 25, 1855, he passed the final tests and seems to have decided definitely on a career as schoolmaster. And yet, unbelievably, at the same time he was striving for membership in the *Hofkapelle** in Vienna. In seeking to become a member, he got in contact with the famous *Hofkapellmeister* Assmayr, to whom he complained in a letter that

* Originally the *Hofkapelle* was the church in which services were restricted to the Imperial Court. This restriction was abolished before Bruckner got an appointment there.

St. Florian "is treating music and musicians with great indifference."

In 1853 he had gone to Vienna for the first time in order to get an organist's certificate. Among the judges was the famous organist and theorist Simon Sechter, who recognized Bruckner as a skilled and thorough organist. In 1855 Bruckner made his second trip to the capital and was accepted as Sechter's pupil.

Those of his biographers who look at this period as a time of crisis in Bruckner's life may not be entirely mistaken, although their theory does not completely explain the situation. In fact, it is worth noting that all of this happened when Bruckner was about thirty years old, shortly before his genius became evident. He had taken military training and served in the National Guard during the Revolution of 1848. How much of his time he spent in the service has not been reported, nor do we know what his motives were in joining the Guard. As a matter of fact, he was never interested in politics. He was naturally greatly depressed when Austria was defeated by Prussia in 1866 and was deeply concerned over the fate of the unlucky Maximilian, Emperor of Mexico. But it was mainly the sensational death of the Austrian emperor's brother which affected him emotionally.

Taking all of Bruckner's activities in review, we are inclined to assume that an apparent lack of concentration should have hampered his creative impulses. The atmosphere in which an artist produces his work is not to be defined categorically, despite the popular belief that a composer needs the utmost quiet when he is at work. Did Johann Sebastian Bach live in surroundings ideal for composing? He was not only the father of twenty children but organist, choir director, and copyist of his own and others' music into the bargain. Not every one of the great masters could afford to dedicate his life exclusively to his art, as did Richard Wagner, although most of them tried to. Absolute quiet and stillness are not what the music creator needs most of all. Richard Strauss once said the rhythm in the motion of a train often brought him inspiration. The noise of rushing water or the regular thud-thud of a machine can have a soothing effect and create an atmosphere ideal for composition.

Although Bruckner's schedule at St. Florian seemed acutely hostile to composition, he actually produced a great number of works. Auer reported about thirty pieces of music, and it is quite probable there were others which may have been destroyed by Bruckner in later years. Most of the thirty are for chorus, although some are for piano. One, called "Aequale," is for three trombones. Two organ pieces in D minor and a prelude and fugue in C minor, written in 1846 and 1847, also belong among the works composed at St. Florian. They are of no great significance when compared with Bruckner's works as a whole, and we wonder why an organist of his ability did not create more and greater music for his instrument.

Bruckner was undoubtedly an outstanding master of the "Queen of the Instruments," although he was never a virtuoso. Even his most enthusiastic admirer, Goellerich, judges him as follows: "In spite of his teachers, he remained mainly self-taught. On the other hand, he proved throughout his life that creative power and true inspiration can conquer everything." Goellerich also mentions Bruckner's elemental force in pedaling and, especially, his pedal trill. But the average listener was most deeply impressed by his improvisations, when he is said to have played with an overwhelming power of expression, transporting in effect.

The art of improvisation holds a special place in the realm of music. In earlier times, improvising was considered a natural acquirement of any musician but it fell into temporary disrepute during the nineteenth century. It disappeared from most of the courses of music study and was retained only in the classes for organ students. The opportunity of listening to improvisations by artists has now become extremely rare, and the passing of the art is indeed to be deplored. Bruckner was one of the last great masters in this very specialized art. Why, we ask again, did he not leave tangible evidence of his mastery of the organ as, for instance, did Max Reger and César Franck? Ferruccio Busoni in his clever essays on music made the remark that Bach never was greater than in those of his preludes and *fantasias* which have all the characteristics of improvisation.

It is not easy to define this type of music. In my opinion, its most significant characteristic is to be found in its very beginning. We do not feel where we are being taken, for the direction is not outlined at the start. Truly, it is this lack of direction which is the very essence of improvisation. An outstanding example of the nature of improvisation is the prelude to Bach's great *A Minor Fugue* for organ. Many of the preludes in Johann Sebastian Bach's works have all the characteristics of improvisation, especially those which are not internally connected with the following fugue. Those writers who allege the contrary have forgotten that Bach loved contrast no less than continuity. There is no contrast more interesting than the one between an opening free improvisation (in the form of a prelude) and the strict form of the following fugue.

There is another type of free style in composition also called improvisation, although the technical term *fantasia* would be better – *fantasia* in the sense in which it was used in the seventeenth and eighteenth centuries. In this period the performer developed a given theme, sometimes his own, at sight. In such improvising the player was more conspicuous than the composer, for although the player naturally had to possess a great deal of imagination, his technical ability in counterpoint was of greater importance and necessarily of the highest rank.

The report on Bruckner as an organist leads us to believe

that his improvisations were in the *fantasia* class. His eminent technical skill astounded many musicians who came to hear him. And so we can understand why he, who labored so slowly and meticulously on his greater works, looked upon his improvisations as incidental music not worthy of being included in the galaxy of his master works. This, however, does not satisfactorily explain why Bruckner the great organist did not bequeath any excellent organ music to posterity.

In recent musical history there is a similar case, the case of Gustav Mahler. An opera conductor throughout his life, Mahler never got over his fear of imperfection at the beginning of every performance. Anyone who has ever held a position of responsibility in an opera house knows these ever-present uncertainties and apprehensions. Too many factors are involved in a successful performance. For instance, even the stage-hand who raises and lowers the curtain can ruin the beginning or the end of an entire act. Mahler, suffering from the strain of these trying conditions and trying to rid himself of them, sought and finally found surcease and gratification in the realm of pure music – symphonic composition. Was Bruckner's case the same? Did he find food for his imagination in music contrasting with his daily organ work?

* * * * *

In contemplating the life of a person it is generally an idle consideration to ask what would have been the outcome if certain things had not happened. But in view of Bruckner's age and the stage of his development we cannot do otherwise, and our reason is found in the individuality of the man. We shall deal with his strange character later, but here we stress the fact that Bruckner, already some thirty years old, was not yet in possession of an insight into his own destiny. He was drifting along between the high road of his great natural gifts and a narrow path of apparently prescribed duty. Could he, the writer of almost fifty compositions,* even if they were not of great significance,** really countenance the idea of remaining a school teacher all his life? We dare not speculate on what would have become of the development of symphonic music if school teaching had been his final occupation. Yet we are tempted to believe that mere coincidence prevented this catastrophe from taking place. The year 1855 was to bring about the decision.

During the year 1855 the position of city and cathedral organist in Linz became vacant, and on the thirteenth of November a try-out was held for a temporary appointment. Because of his modesty, Bruckner had not applied for the place, but he attended the contest as a listener. When neither of the two aspirants for the position, Heinz and Lanz, was able to develop the theme into a strict fugue, Professor Duernberger, who was a member of the examining board, asked his former pupil to compete also. As Bruckner, standing a little apart, still hesitated, Duernberger called out imperiously: "Tonerl, you must!" Whereupon Bruckner seated himself at the organ and easily surpassed the others by his splendid performance. In fact, he was so good that Lanz turned to him and remarked: "You're the death of all of us!"

Goellerich tells us Bruckner would not have attended the contest at all, not even as a listener, if the organ tuner had not chanced to be at St. Florian on the very day of the try-out. It was this man's persistent urging which led him to attend.

Bruckner was chosen temporary organist but again hesitated to compete for the final permanent appointment to the position. His friends were desperate; they earnestly pressed him to take the necessary steps and pleaded with him "not to make his calls on the mayor and the vicar of the city wear-

* According to Auer.
** Goellerich, Vol. II, page 215.

ing his overcoat" on which a button was missing. And he should please "remove his shawl and galoshes before entering the room." He finally tried for the post and again won in the competition. Early in 1856 he left St. Florian, the scene of ten years' activity, and went to Linz.

This move was significant, for from then on he was rid of all school work and could devote himself to music alone. What a great moment that would have been in the life of a musician who felt his true vocation! But we seek in vain for a sign of satisfaction in Bruckner over this fortunate turn of events. And again we wonder whether or when enlightenment will come. Even if we take Bruckner's extremely slow development into consideration, we cannot help feeling it was high time for him to leave "the home of his soul," as Auer called St. Florian. He was not one of those artists who can depend exclusively upon their own resources. He needed the stimulation of new surroundings.

Generally speaking, I think Auer was mistaken when he said: "Away from great centers strong and healthy natures thrive best." Music, more than any other art, addresses itself to the masses; it needs living contact with people or it soon loses its reason for being. It must be heard, perceived, and felt. Let a great picture or a statue be in some secluded spot forgotten by the world and only rarely seen, or let a masterplay be read by only a limited number of drama lovers – neither loses any of its value. But music requires the actual presence of listeners. With the exception of those few who are able to read a score and hear it through their inner ear, it can be enjoyed only through the actual sense of hearing. Furthermore, there is some music which is out of place when the number of listeners is small. Present a symphony by Bruckner, Mahler, or Tschaikowsky to a small audience and you at once feel that it loses much of its effect. Young musicians need the competition and the criticism met only in the larger towns. And, finally, Auer's opinion quoted above can be proved wrong in the case of many composers, of whom I mention but two: Brahms and Richard Strauss. Surely Strauss could never have developed into the artist he is if he had not grown up in the music center of Munich and had not spent so much of his life in Berlin and Vienna. The fragrance of city civilization as we become conscious of it for the first time in music in the *Rosenkavalier* could not have been evoked by a man who had not himself lived in such a center. This specific atmosphere in the *Rosenkavalier* signifies a "discovery of *terra incognita*" in the realm of musical expression. And this fact means actual progress in music.

CHAPTER II

LINZ was no more important a center at that time than it is now, but it offered the young organist the benefits of a music-loving town. There was a fairly good orchestra and a theater which presented operatic performances. An opera house in a town the size of Linz may seem quite exceptional. In America only a few of the larger cities enjoy a permanent opera season; others have to be content with a few performances by touring companies. In central Europe there is scarcely a town of a hundred thousand inhabitants which does not have a ten months' opera season.

Bruckner frequently attended concerts in Linz but he avoided the theater, which religious zealots had depicted to him as "the devil's breeding place." * In his new place of residence, he won friends and patrons, the most outstanding among them being Bishop Rudigier, who evidently recognized Bruckner's value to his diocese. Rudolf Weinwurm, who in 1858 became director of music at the University of Vienna and also conductor of the academic glee club, could be called one of Bruckner's most intimate friends. There are many letters addressed to him in the collection of Bruckner's correspondence. The letters are very interesting because they show an innocence and a naïveté which one never finds in the correspondence of Wagner or Liszt. Even the self-contained Brahms revealed more of the inner life of an artist in his letters than did Bruckner.

Goellerich claims ** it was Bruckner's mastery as an improviser at the organ which astounded everyone, but he was not a very good sight reader. Whether this remark refers to the period in Linz alone or to a longer time is unimportant, but it is one of the most striking facts in the life of this thirty-

* According to Goellerich.
** Volume II, page 305.

year-old musician who possessed so great a natural gift. With good reason, playing at sight has always been considered an earmark of the true musician. In sight reading, technical ability is not the important factor. The important factor is, rather, a special presence of mind, an alertness, which enables the performer to grasp the rhythmic and harmonic structure at a glance and to bring out whatever is significant in the composition in question. The reader of an orchestra score can often see but a section of what he is reading, as two eyes cannot scan eighteen or more staffs of music at a time. It is left to his skill and musical divination to decide on what is required at the moment. Reading the melodies of many Classical compositions enables the player to find the right harmonies by himself, as he was formerly supposed to find the descant for the figured bass at sight.

That Bruckner was not a good sight reader can be explained by the psychology of the man. His individuality as a musician was evidently so strong and he was so deeply absorbed in his own train of thought that he could not find his way into the realm of another's ideas. He was always spinning his own thread. He forgot the world around him as soon as inspiration called. Bruckner, a great and powerful improviser on the one hand and a mediocre sight reader on the other, offers an interesting study in personality.

* * * * *

Bruckner's visit with Sechter in Vienna was not without fruit, for in 1856 he began studying with the famous teacher. This action shows another peculiar psychological trait in the artist. Here he was, a man thirty-two years of age, holding a respected position, living in a town of limited size where he had a certain standing as competent musician to uphold. Yet he did not hesitate to become a pupil! He as much as admitted he was not accomplished in his own line of work. At least, such was the opinion held by other people, for there are few who realize that the true artist studies and works throughout his life.

Becoming a pupil of Sechter meant not only getting advice and support from an older musician who took a special interest in his work but also giving up a good deal of his own personality and forgetting his previous ideals. He had to submit to Sechter's authority and to render unconditional obedience. It certainly was self-inflicted chastisement for a composer of Bruckner's imagination to place himself in such a position and it obviously had an effect on his creative powers.

Sechter was born in 1788 and first became assistant schoolmaster in a small place in Upper Austria. In 1804, as private tutor to the children of a socially prominent family, he went to Vienna, where his position enabled him to enjoy music instruction from the best teachers and to finish his studies by himself. He became *Hoforganist* at the Imperial Court and was appointed teacher of harmony and counterpoint at the conservatory in 1851. His chief publication, *Die Grundsaetze der Musikalischen Komposition* (*Basic Principles of Music Composition*), released in 1853-1854, is considered a model of clarity and consistency. His system was based on the principles of Rameau, who asserted: "It is harmony, not melody, which guides us, and no combination of melodies can sound well unless their movement is governed by harmonic consideration and exigencies." Cecil Gray, who quoted these words, added: "Rameau in one word was the father of modern textbook harmony and all the vices and heresies to which it gives rise." *

Rameau's ideas certainly had no appreciable effect on Bruckner. Other dogmatic tenets in Sechter's system cannot be discussed here. It is more important for us to consider what impressions Sechter's pupils carried away from his

* *The History of Music*, page 161.

teaching. Selmar Bagge made an interesting observation when he said: "Sechter's instruction consisted of digging into details to such a degree that anyone who had not reached creative heights before the lessons began necessarily lost all sense of proportion and his free point of view. His instruction was only useful to one who wanted to work thoroughly and strictly on discipline without having his ideas disturbed on the very being of artistic production."* On the other hand, this same Bagge claims Sechter's system has never been equaled in clarity. Rudolf Louis stresses the fact, and considers it an advantage, that in Sechter's system there are no exceptions to the rules, once they have been established. Louis also mentions the meticulous and pedantic method of instruction Sechter followed. He again quotes Bagge, who said practice under Sechter in the writing of fugues never resulted in the composition of a complete piece of work but only in fragmentary bits. No serious attempt was made to unite them into a harmonious whole. Louis's statement that Sechter was definitely not an artistic soul is the most important of all his remarks. This statement furnishes us with a valuable bit of information when we attempt to gauge the influence his personality had on Bruckner. Louis thinks that although Bruckner's lack of moderation and his tendency towards extravagance needed a curbing hand, Sechter was not the right teacher for him since the Sechter system neglected the architecture of music.

I have purposely quoted Louis's criticism to show how, at the beginning of this century, a musician who loved Bruckner judged him, his former master. Can anyone today seriously speak of extravagance in connection with Bruckner's music?

Bruckner's first lessons with Sechter were very peculiar. Bruckner sent his prepared assignments by mail to Sechter,

* Quoted by Rudolf Louis on page 30 of his Bruckner biography.

who then corrected them and returned them, likewise by mail. It is rather difficult to see how any helpful instruction could come out of the arrangement. But, whenever Bruckner could afford it from 1857 to 1861, he went up to Vienna and took lessons in person. His far-sighted patron, Bishop Rudigier, gave him leave especially during Advent and Lent, when the organ in church is customarily silent, and sometimes during the summer. In this way the bishop contributed his share to the glory of the Catholic Church, which can rightly boast of being the perennial protector of music.

Bruckner applied himself to Sechter's instruction with painstaking zeal. While working his way through Sechter's *Grundsaetze der Musikalischen Komposition*, Bruckner the student displayed the meticulousness of Bruckner the schoolmaster. His copy of the book is completely worn out; the pages are loose and dog-eared and filled with notations and musical examples.

Sechter's casuistic method turned music into a system of arithmetic, and to such an extent that we can but admire the power of Bruckner's imagination. It was able to resist the paralyzing effect of Sechter's method of instruction. The ideal teacher of harmony and counterpoint never forgets there is only one method: To develop in his pupil the ability of analyzing master works from a technical angle. There is no rule which cannot be proved by an excerpt from existing music. In truth, the musician who follows certain rules is in actuality applying laws from the scores of his predecessors and not from a harmony manual. Whether he accepts their work or rejects it, he is nevertheless continuing it.

Then there is another point about teaching. Even the best teacher is not necessarily the right teacher for a particular pupil. The two must fit together; they must suit one another. Now this was certainly the case with Sechter and Bruckner. Sechter even had to warn his young pupil, time and again, against overwork. For instance, he wrote him in 1860:

"I ask you to spare your health and to take necessary periods of rest. I am convinced of your diligence and zeal. I would not like you to suffer in health from excessive application to study. I feel compelled to tell you that I never had a more industrious pupil than you."

We repeatedly come across this last sentence in Sechter's letters. Perhaps he was endeavoring to calm his pupil's anxious fears. Sechter's attitude is an indication of his warm, fatherly feeling towards Bruckner and it arouses our sympathy, but it does not answer the question as to why Bruckner voluntarily placed himself in such an inconceivable situation. Later on, when we examine Bruckner's personality, we may come across a clue.

Bruckner finished his course in harmony in 1858; in counterpoint and double counterpoint in 1859; in triple and quadruple counterpoint in 1860; and, finally, in canon and fugue in 1861.

"In order to have an official statement concerning the result of his studies, Bruckner applied to the Vienna Conservatory, asking to be admitted for an examination. He received a favorable reply and was asked to submit all his written exercises in counterpoint. The examining board consisted of the prominent musicians Herbeck, Hellmesberger, Sechter, Dessoff, and the school supervisor Becker. When one of the members proposed that they ask an oral question, Herbeck declared it superfluous, since the candidate had already revealed his great knowledge in the written exercises he had submitted." *

The board then decided to ask Bruckner to develop a theme in fugue style at the organ. A few days later the examination took place.

"Sechter wrote down four measures. When Herbeck was shown the theme, he turned to Dessoff and said: 'Make the

* Auer, page 72.

theme longer.' 'No,' Dessoff replied, 'I'd rather not.' 'Well, then I will!' said Herbeck, and he extended it to eight measures. 'Ah, but you're hard-hearted!' Dessoff retorted.

"The slip was handed to Bruckner and, while he was lingering over the theme because of the *comes*, the examining board was overcome with a certain hilarity. But Bruckner quickly mastered the situation. He started with an introduction consisting of sections of the theme and then developed a brilliant fugue . . . He was heartily congratulated when he finished, and Herbeck turned to his colleagues and said: '*He* ought to have examined *us*!' Nor did Herbeck ever forget this outstanding candidate, whose patron he later became."

Sechter did not like to have his students write compositions while they were studying with him. Bruckner respected his wishes and wrote only a very few during the period between 1856 and 1861. The number increased remarkably as soon as he had finished his studies. But even then he evidently felt his technical ability as yet inadequate to cope with the richness of his imagination. Unlike his other biographers, I do not believe he attributed this deficiency in musical skill to insufficient instruction by his beloved teacher in Vienna. It was rather the pedantic trait in his nature which prevented him from considering his studies completed until he had taken essential courses in musical form and orchestration.

In importance, these two branches of music instruction differ greatly from harmony and counterpoint, in that their educational value is open to question. Orchestration, in fact, cannot be taught at all, except in a very limited sense. The elements, of course, can be taught, but the composer of the *Requiem*, the *Missa Solemnis*, and *Psalm 146* (all scored with orchestra accompaniment) knew them as well as his new teacher, the opera conductor Otto Kitzler, knew them. Beethoven's piano sonatas were chosen as subjects for Kitzler's instruction. Bruckner, whenever he discovered something not compatible with Sechter's pedantic codex, was highly elated, like a schoolboy who is delighted when his teacher makes a mistake. To explain the formal structure of those sonatas, the teacher must point to about as many digressions from the regular scheme of a sonata as there are from the fugue in Bach's *Well-tempered Clavichord.*

As to form in music, surely the man who is able to study the scores of the great masters and perceive the meaning of form can dispense with the guidance of a teacher who is no better as a musician than he is himself. This was the situation with Bruckner and Kitzler at the time. I cannot see what qualifications Kitzler had for teaching Bruckner, aside from his long experience as a worthy conductor of opera. After all, Kitzler was not the best teacher Bruckner might have chosen. Moreover, form means one thing to the conductor and quite another thing to the composer. To the composer, every note he is going to write has the same amount of importance; and, if he has a fertile imagination, he must develop enough architectonic sense to anticipate what psychological effects the distribution of weights throughout his work will have on the listeners.

The conductor, on the other hand, has a very sensitive instrument for estimating those weights. It is his arm. His arm feels their heaviness with infallible accuracy, almost as though he had to carry them. Even before the listeners have manifested any reaction, he can sense the degree of audience tension behind his back while he is conducting. But how many conductors are able to judge a composition before they have actually heard it in rehearsal? How many can practically hear what they are reading in the score? Experience tells me that even the best conductor is not necessarily the best teacher. So I rather doubt whether Bruckner was fortunate in choosing Kitzler as his new instructor. In my opinion, a real master of composition, one who would give his pupil an insight into his art, would have been the ideal instructor for Bruckner.

For one thing, however, we have reason to be grateful to Kitzler. It was he who introduced Bruckner to Wagner's music and thus caused a definite and decisive change of direction in Bruckner's development. One might say, without exaggeration, that under the impression of Wagner's music Bruckner grew to be the composer we know and love. Wagner awoke a dormant genius and gave the world not only his own immortal works but also the renaissance of symphonic music through Bruckner.

It may be that Bruckner had heard excerpts from Wagner's music in concerts given by military bands. Austrian bands have long been considered among the best in Europe. Moreover, they used to take a practical interest in contemporary music and met with great popularity and esteem. In Italy the military band contributed to Wagner's popularization early in his career. Old people in Venice have told me Wagner liked to listen to the performances of his music at San Marco Square.

It was *Tannhaeuser* which impressed Bruckner so deeply. In Linz, no Wagnerian opera had previously been performed. The manager of the opera house had little confidence in the success of a Wagnerian production and had even refused to pay the lowest royalty to the composer. Kitzler finally got personal permission from Wagner to present *Tannhaeuser* without royalty fees. Bruckner had studied this score under Kitzler's guidance and had learned modern orchestra technique from it.

"He was highly amazed to find in this tone work the technique which he, being psychologically related to Wagner, had previously divined. Bruckner's genius was freed from scholastic chains by Kitzler's performance of *Tannhaeuser* in Linz. After the performances of February 13 and 20, 1863, he thoroughly restudied the partitura. The extended use of chromatics and enharmonics, against which Sechter thundered in his chief work and which Bruckner adopted in his very first attempt at composition, were splendidly reconfirmed in the opera." *

I challenge this statement, although it is interesting in itself. In what does this "soul-mateship" of Wagner and Bruckner consist, a "soul-mateship" which Auer is not alone in mentioning? Occasional similarities in motives or themes and in orchestration are listed as proofs of Bruckner's "premonition" of Wagner's music. I think the exact opposite is true. Bruckner considered the elder composer his very antithesis, and it was this fact which attracted him most of all.

Orel puts it in the right way when he says: "Wagner's work finally broke the bonds. The Master Bruckner was born in this hour. It is perhaps unique in the history of music that an artist found his particular path so suddenly. One might say, complete 'mastership' made its appearance in a moment of time . . . Richard Wagner was probably the last great experience which profoundly influenced Bruckner's art." **

He was in danger of succumbing to the mighty master, but fortunately he was then about forty years old and consequently stable enough in spirit to overcome temptation and keep true to himself.

It is indeed striking that it was *Tannhaeuser* which impressed Bruckner so profoundly. Everything in this opera is so directly opposed to his nature that it must have been this contrast itself which was the great attraction. Where in Bruckner's music is there anything to show the sort of influence ascribable to the score of *Tannhaeuser*? Certain pages from the third act, Tannhaeuser's tale of his pilgrimage to Rome, in particular, may possibly have impressed Bruckner sufficiently for Louis to venture to speak of his acquaintance with Wagner's music as the "mighty impulse which dis-

* Auer, page 79.
** Orel, page 128.

closed Bruckner's hitherto latent originality as an effective power."

In the following year, Kitzler performed three more of Wagner's works: *Das Liebesmahl der Apostel* (*The Love Feast of the Apostles*), *The Flying Dutchman*, and *Lohengrin*. Presumably Bruckner attended the performances. In my opinion, *The Flying Dutchman* left more traces in Bruckner's symphonies than did *Tannhaeuser*. The beginning of the overture with the thirdless chord, Wagner's way of using the trombones, the thematic development — all must have made a deep impression on every musician of the time.

Generally speaking, one must admit that Wagner's influence on the development of music can hardly be overrated. On the other hand, one is entitled to ask: Who are the composers who show Wagner's handwriting? They are not at all so numerous as claimed by his adversaries, who predicted the decadence of music and especially of opera. I can point to only one outstanding work directly influenced by Wagner's style, and that is Humperdinck's *Haensel and Gretel*. The score bears indisputable traces of *Die Meistersinger*, especially when it is examined technically.

At the turn of the century, every composer who was not writing in the routine way was considered a Wagnerite. Since then, critical examination has led us to other conclusions. It may not be out of place to digress for a moment on Wagner's alleged influence on the later Verdi works. We have repeatedly been asked to believe that *Aida* and *Othello* display certain of Wagner's characteristics. The chromatic step in the *Aida* prelude and aria, and the harmonization in *Othello* have been pointed out as proof of this assertion. It is indeed regrettable that not one of the numerous books about Verdi was written by an outstanding musician and that none deals solely with his music. Such a book would surely reveal certain basic ideas and musical patterns which appear and reappear in altered form in various of his operas.

I have in mind, for instance, the rhythmic motive of the trombones in the death scene of *Violetta*, which we again hear in the fourth act of *Il Trovatore* along with Leonora's aria in the "Miserere" scene. The three operas *Simon Boccanegra*, *La Forza del Destino*, and *Ballo in Maschera* also exhibit features in common. It is not so much the incidental resemblance of themes as their similarity of expression that apparently induced Verdi to use them repeatedly in different places. The *Aida* theme, mentioned above, is derived from the prelude to the last act of *La Traviata*. The chromatic steps in *Aida* are irrelevant when compared with the parallel timbre of the two passages, and this timbre has no Wagner characteristic of any sort. The distinct harmonic characteristic of *Othello* is the frequent use of the chord of the third and fourth, which appeared but rarely in Verdi's earlier operas. Who would think of Wagner when listening to these inversions of the chord of the seventh? To consider Verdi influenced by Wagner's music is to follow mere legend.

CHAPTER III

THE final examination of 1861 was not the first occasion on which music lovers in Vienna could hear Bruckner play the organ. On July 24, 1858, the critic Ludwig Speidel had written an enthusiastic article on "the young and rising talent of Mr. Bruckner." Incidentally, he thought Bruckner's improvisation on the organ bore the earmarks of Mendelssohn's music. "We don't blame him for that," said Speidel. Bruckner's most fervent admirer in Linz was Bishop Rudigier. This strong-minded churchman was habitually deeply moved by Bruckner's playing. When Bruckner played "he would grow silent, completely absorbed, and listen." According to Auer, Rudigier himself is reported to have said that Bruckner's *Mass in D* moved him to such an extent he could no longer pray.

This little anecdote, mentioned by most of Bruckner's biographers as proof of his mastery of the organ, might well be the starting point for a book on music psychology. In it we see how the absorbing power of music overcomes the ingrained habit of religious practices. Mental concentration vanishes when confronted with the indefinite and indefinable sensations of tone. The emotional factor in music attains such ascendancy that we can almost understand Plato's thoughts on the moral influence of the noble art.

Bruckner, for his part, revered his bishop and considered him second only to Richard Wagner. Decsey relates an amusing story which originated in Vienna, the birthplace of so many musical anecdotes: "In his own affections, Bruckner rates Wagner between the Bishop of Linz and the Heavenly Father."

Bruckner did not meet Wagner personally until 1865. The first performance of *Tristan and Isolde* had been scheduled to take place in Munich on May 15th of that year. It had to be postponed until June 10th, however, since Isolde (Mrs.

Schnorr) fell sick. Bruckner, who had come to the Bavarian capital for the opening, decided not to leave the city as did most of the other visitors. This fortunate decision was a stroke of luck for him. He was introduced to his beloved master, who evidently took quite a liking for him. Among the other celebrities he met was Hans von Buelow, the conductor of *Tristan and Isolde*, who looked over some sections of the *First Symphony*, in C minor, on which Bruckner was working at the time. Buelow, not yet closely tied to Brahms, was evidently rather interested in the composition but he could do no more than express his interest, for it was only a few days before the first performance of *Tristan and Isolde*, an event of world-wide importance, which claimed all his attention. Later, when he severed his relations with Wagner, his feelings toward Bruckner cooled, and in 1885 he wrote the following satirical letter to the author of a book on the history of the string quartet:

"Will you please pardon my notorious frankness when I confess to you that I ordered my book binder to bind only the first 307 pages?"

Needless to say, Bruckner's new string quintet was in the section starting on page 308. Those who knew Buelow or had heard about his trenchant wit, his satirical speech, and his general culture understood why he and Bruckner had little in common. Nor could Liszt, mild and good-natured as he was, force himself into close relations with the Austrian master. Yet such relations would have benefited Bruckner greatly. The two men, with personalities so widely divergent, would have supplemented each other and Bruckner might have been stimulated to fresh incentive.

It is rather strange that Bruckner, even in later life, enjoyed no intimate, congenial friendship with his colleagues in music. There was no exchange of ideas on general or musical topics between him and other musicians of his own high standing. The musicians with whom he was in close contact were either his patrons, towards whom he was devoutly indebted, or his pupils, who were very much younger and kept themselves at a respectful distance. The reasons for this isolation are hard to determine. I think Buelow's and Liszt's indifference can be explained as follows:

Both men were accomplished linguists with a cosmopolitan background, whereas Bruckner never lost his rustic Upper Austrian dialect and manner of speaking. His vocabulary was limited and his style, so far as we know from contemporary accounts and his letters, retained a back-country flavor. A speaker's style generally discloses his level of culture. An accomplished linguist, such as Buelow or Liszt, is usually sensitive to the speech of others. Liszt, when urged to show more kindness to Bruckner, is reported to have said: "I can't bear to hear him address me as 'Your Grace, Mr. Canonicus!' "

Poor Bruckner! He was the old-fashioned, provincial type of musician, whom they considered their inferior. We should not blame them, however. All of us are tempted, consciously or unconsciously, to judge others by their ability in self-expression. Moreover, perfect control of a language means control of form, and Buelow and Liszt were masters of form. It may be that their sense of form was somehow offended by Bruckner's overly deferential and unrefined speech.

Much more friendly than his relations with these two great musicians were his dealings with Wagner. While waiting in Munich for the first performance of *Tristan and Isolde*, Bruckner was invited to show the great master his *First Symphony* but he modestly refused. "I did not dare show him this symphony," he later told his friends. In fact, he felt so deep a reverence for Wagner that he would not sit in his presence.

It has often been asked whether the performance of *Tristan and Isolde* immediately influenced Bruckner in his work on his *First Symphony*; and, if it did, to what extent. To my mind, such queries are not only futile but even misleading. The questions are wrongly put. A work such as Wagner's great love-tragedy, which initiated a new era in the history of music and which contained problems whose solution was a matter for the future, would naturally impress a sympathetic musician like Bruckner very deeply. It could even open up new paths for him to tread in the future, but it could not exert any immediate influence on work so near completion. Much more time would have been necessary.

I am borne out in my opinion by Orel, who says: "The *First Symphony* does not show that Bruckner was specifically influenced by the Tristan music. He was too much of an individualist to stand in need of any support for his ideas." *

One of the activities which contributed greatly towards Bruckner's development as a conductor, while he was living in Linz, was his work as director of the glee club "Frohsinn." He held this position for the first time in 1860 and he took it over again for a few months before he left Linz for good in 1868. He was fortunate in obtaining Wagner's permission to perform the final chorus from *Die Meistersinger* for the very first time. It was at Linz that this new and unparalleled music resounded before the world première of the opera as a whole.

Auer reports a delightful incident which occurred during rehearsal for the concert, on April 4, 1868:

"During the choral practice of Schumann's *Ritornell*, which was to be given at the same concert, the singers did not produce the triple *pianissimo* softly enough to suit the master. One day the chorus secretly decided to stop singing altogether when they came to this particular passage. Rehearsal time came around. The first two verses satisfied the choral director. Now the third verse, with the triple *pianissimo*, was about to be sung. Bruckner, his face abeam, continued to

* Page 128.

beat time while the singers faced him in silence. Finally their roars of laughter jolted the master out of his ecstasy. He had been listening to his inner harmony." *

Being leader of a glee club gave Bruckner opportunity to hear his own compositions in actual performance and furnished him with practical experience as a conductor. Both these factors were to his advantage. It was too bad the same opportunities did not present themselves later on.

A composer finds it valuable to listen to his own works from the conductor's platform. The transformation, as it were, from creator to reproducing artist gives him an unbiased attitude towards his own compositions. He becomes more conscious of the true impression his music makes on the orchestra players and choral singers. Their criticisms should not be overrated, of course, but many an orchestra player, by straight-minded thinking, has given composers precious suggestions, especially on technical matters. It is really miraculous that Bruckner, who was never closely associated with orchestras in a conducting capacity, could be so perfect in orchestrating even before he took up residence in Vienna, where he at least had opportunities for hearing Europe's best orchestra.

Bruckner never became an outstanding orchestra leader. He lacked the natural gift for the task, and, besides, there is a great difference in manual technique between leading an orchestra and conducting a chorus. The best choral conductor is not necessarily a good orchestra conductor. As an instance there is the late Siegfried Ochs, the excellent director of Berlin's Philharmonic Choir, the man to whom the musical world is indebted for the model performance of Bach's choral works. As a choir director he could not be matched. But Ochs became practically helpless when the orchestra was substituted for the piano which had been used in rehearsal.

* Page 135.

Every *ritardando* became a problem for him. The solo singers felt lost in their parts, and it often took all the skill the Philharmonic Orchestra could muster to avoid complete failure.

Other great composers besides Bruckner have proved that great creative power does not, in itself, include the gift of interpretation. Brahms was not a good conductor. He himself was well aware of the fact, as he indicated in his unpublished letters to my father, Herman Wolff. Wolff repeatedly asked him to conduct concerts when Buelow was stricken ill, but Brahms invariably refused, giving evasive excuses.

One of the worst conductors of his own operas was the late Eugen d'Albert, recognized as one of the greatest pianists of his time. The same can be said about his famous colleague Ferruccio Busoni. Nor did Richard Strauss display any outstanding qualifications as a conductor at the beginning of his career. He was not sure of his own technique and frequently asked his friends for their opinions on his conducting but during his stay in Berlin at the opera house, where he had Karl Muck and Felix von Weingartner as colleagues, he developed considerably.

One of the greatest conductors, if not the greatest of all, Arthur Nikisch, once told me Strauss' technique was singular and not to be compared with that of anyone else. With his particular technique he actually works wonders. Only a genius like Strauss, who feels his relationship with other great composers, can give the audience effects of the kind he produces when he conducts *Tristan and Isolde* or Mozart's music. If Strauss had never held a position as orchestra conductor, he would never have become the great composer he is. I believe his continuous association with orchestras has contributed greatly to the new manner of orchestration he originated in *Ariadne at Naxos*. Surrounded by the overwhelming masses of his *Elektra* orchestra, he may have felt he was reaching the climax of his long development; his knowledge of and feeling for art may have suggested the new path to be followed in the future.

Bruckner never had lasting contacts with an orchestral body. The benefit which he would have derived from such an association can hardly be overrated.

I have often wondered why so many good composers are poor or mediocre conductors. To say they lack a natural gift for conducting is not enough. I believe another psychological factor is involved: The amount of will-power necessary for leading an orchestra is foreign to many a composer's nature. He uses his psychic energy for shaping his musical inspirations. For a long time he wrestles for the most telling expression. He pours out his energies to the point of exhaustion. Then, while he is conducting, he often fails to understand why the orchestra members do not readily grasp his meaning and he lacks the will-power to impose it on them.

In this connection, Bruckner was the subject of a little story then circulating in Vienna: Bruckner, about to rehearse one of his symphonies with the orchestra, raised the baton but was hesitant in giving the opening down-beat. When the concert master, after an interval of time, urged him to start, Bruckner answered: "I wouldn't dare start before you!" Although we cannot vouch for the truth of the story, it does give us a characteristic picture of the man's odd personality.

According to Auer, Bruckner wrote more than forty compositions while he was in Linz. Among them were his first works written solely for orchestra: three orchestra movements, an overture in G minor, and, most important of all, three symphonies. The symphonies were the first, in F minor (1863), one in D minor (1864), and one in C minor (1865-1866). The first two works are not counted in the nine symphonies usually associated with the name of Bruckner. Also among these compositions were two pieces for piano, three marches for military bands, a fugue in D minor for the organ, and one composition for violin and piano. All the rest of the compositions were choral numbers, some of them with orchestra parts. The most significant of these choral works are *Psalm 146* (1860); *Ave Maria*, for seven voices (1861); *Psalm 112*, the *Germanenzug* (1863); *Mass in D Minor* (1864); *Mass in E Minor* with wind-instrument accompaniment (1866); and a *Great Mass in F Minor* (1867-1868).

Kitzler has reported that Bruckner showed no inspiration in the compositions he wrote while he was studying with him. He considered them mere school exercises. Teachers are not always wise in sitting in judgment on their pupils, as we will see later, in the analysis of Bruckner's works. Kitzler's criticisms were a bit too harsh.

When we consider that Bruckner, as an obedient pupil of Sechter, refrained, as well as he could, from composing during the years he passed as a student, we are amazed at the number of compositions he actually wrote in Linz. The three symphonies were, of course, the most important works in his growth, although none of them succeeded in becoming popular. They are generally considered "the forecourt to the sanctuary." The second of the three Masses arouses our special interest because of its individual and archaic style. The first, in D minor, has often been called the "first master work" of Bruckner.

Although Bruckner's position as organist certainly took up a good deal of his time, he had to work no harder at it than he did at St. Florian. This point should be stressed, because overwork has been ascribed as the cause of the nervous breakdown Bruckner suffered at this time. Karl Waldeck, Bruckner's successor as organist at Linz, says overexertion in counterpoint improvisation at the organ was to blame. "In spite of his stout physical condition and his healthy appetite, he showed signs of mental derangement, and he suffered greatly from melancholia and fixed ideas."

I do not believe his musical activities in Linz were solely to blame. His breakdown was most likely due to an inherited nervous weakness, since similar cases have been reported in his family. We have no information on whether sexual abstinence contributed to his breakdown or not, for we have no data on his innate sexual impulses. Surely Bruckner faced no great disappointment in those years in Linz to account for his breakdown. Some writers think Bruckner's intense religious convictions may have played an important part. Whatever the cause, poor Bruckner was torn from the most sublime of activities – creative work – and was forced to go to a sanitarium.

A letter in June, 1867, tells of his unhappy psychic condition. He had gone to Bad Kreuzen on the advice of his physician, who was, perhaps, too forthright in his prescriptions. Apologizing to his friend for not having written earlier, Bruckner wrote as follows:*

"You may think or have thought or have heard of anything whatever! – It was not laziness – it was much more! ! ! – It was complete demoralization and forlornness – complete enervation and overexcitement! ! I was in the most awful condition, I tell only you – do not tell anybody. Not much more and I am a victim – am lost – Dr. Fadinger has predicted insanity as a possible consequence. Thank God! he saved me. I have been in Bad Kreuzen since May 8 at Grein's. These last weeks I have felt a little better, am not allowed to play, to study or to work. Imagine my lot! I am a poor fellow. Herbeck returned the scores of my vocal Mass and my symphony without writing a word. Is it really as bad as that? Do try to find out. My dear friend, do write to me once in my exile, to me, poor and deserted as I am!"

The number of exclamation marks in this letter, in themselves, point to Bruckner's excitation. The tragic note has dramatic implications. Modern psychiatry would, perhaps,

* I have tried to render Bruckner's style and punctuation as faithfully and literally as possible.

regard the letter as an expression of an inferiority complex.

Actually, Bruckner was obsessed with a mania for figures, which had made itself felt some time before and was becoming more intense at that time. "He would count the leaves on a tree, the stars, the grains of sand. He was tortured by the fixed idea that he had to bail out the Danube. One day, when the patients in the sanitarium were being entertained by Gypsies, he ran away. Later he was found sitting on a tree stump, weeping. Mrs. Mayfeld, who was staying at the spa, too, could no longer wear one of her dresses, because Bruckner, whenever he met her, would begin counting the pearls which covered her dress."

In letters from this period, he described the cold-water treatments he had to undergo and tells his friend that Bad Kreuzen was, after all, just a hydropathic establishment. As Bruckner was not supposed to remain by himself, unattended, Bishop Rudigier sent a priest to serve as a guard. Bruckner is said to have disregarded the doctor's order to stop working. A few weeks after he had left the place, he asked the bishop to help him defray the expenses, which he could not meet himself.* He returned to Linz, apparently in good health.** But he was not to stay there for any length of time.

In looking back at the time Bruckner spent in Linz, one may say he certainly enjoyed many a satisfaction. The town evidently took pride in calling the famous organist "citizen," for his playing aroused admiration and enthusiasm everywhere. From the numerous reports on the impressions his art made on his listeners, a very characteristic one is: "A simple and somewhat timid man greeted the visitors and then started playing... I look at the maestro as he plays. He is no longer a timid man. With head raised and eyes alight, the artist sits

* Instead of the 225 florins he had asked for, he was given only 68.

** Auer believes Bruckner may have gone to Bad Kreuzen a second time, in 1868.

there, as though on a throne, in the midst of roaring, surging floods of sound." Organ playing must have transfigured the man, and he was carried away by his own impetus.

While Bruckner lived in Linz, his fame as an organist surpassed his renown as a composer. But that is not surprising, since the reproducing musician is always closer to the gates of glory than is the composer, especially when the latter is traveling over unusual paths. And so it was with Bruckner. Yet he had nothing to complain of in his role of composer, either. The very first performance of his *Mass in D Minor* took place on November 20, 1864. The following month the Mass was repeated. Two performances in so short a time mean a great deal in a town as small as Linz, where the number of concert-goers is naturally very limited.

A newspaper in Linz made this interesting comment about the Mass: "If Mr. Bruckner should succeed in purifying or taming his imagination and in avoiding violent cadences and sharp dissonances in his type of music, we are convinced that in the next work of this kind he will not surprise and amaze his audience but rather elevate and edify it."

The *Symphony in C Minor* was first presented on May 9, 1868, with the composer conducting. The rehearsals put both composer and orchestra on edge. The players thought several passages unplayable and asked Bruckner to modify them. He refused, and when the players did not satisfy him he cried and implored them to do better. In the end, the performance was not bad, at least musically. An item in the paper read: "Beyond the great beauties of the work, there is a noticeable attempt at exterior effect." One may study the score to try to find where an effect of this kind may be hidden, but in vain.

Generally speaking, however, the critics adopted a respectful tone towards the composer, although their attitude was no more than just friendly. Did Bruckner feel he was successful merely because he was the highly esteemed organist of the town, the organist whom everyone liked and appreciated? Could he expect the audience to understand this particular piece of music, which he himself later called a "saucy thing"? Although he was not recognized as a rising genius, he was spared the experience of being classified as a virtuoso who incidentally wrote valuable music. Other musicians have had to suffer from what they deemed the injustice of the world which admired them as instrumentalists but disbelieved in their creative efforts. There are two such instances in recent music history: the case of Anton Rubinstein and of Eugen d'Albert. Both of them struggled desperately to win recognition as composers; they even neglected their technical training in their later years. But they labored in vain. In this connection, it is interesting to learn from music magazines of the middle of the eighteenth century that the composer J. S. Bach had not yet caught up with the famous organist of the same name.

In spite of the popularity he enjoyed, Bruckner was by no means happy in Linz. Was it popularity itself which made him long for another field of activity? This question, strange as it sounds, is not asked for rhetorical effect. There is hardly an artist who does not want to acquire popularity, once he is established in a place. Sustained by popularity, he feels contented and happy. But as time goes on he faces a crucial test. He becomes acclimated. If he happens to be in a small community, such as Linz, becoming acclimated means slowing up if not standing still in his development. Consciously or unconsciously he feels that his every achievement will be approved by the people who believe in him and love him. His ambitions begin to fade. Life becomes easy, sometimes even too comfortable, and his career is in danger of never developing. The musician who is sure of his inner vocation will therefore try to change his position after a while, in order to subject himself to the criticisms of a new audience to whom he is not tied by personal friendship or obligation. He does not want to be acclaimed as the beloved Mr. X; he wants to display his art, and his art alone, regardless of personalities. A new audience stimulates his ambition, and this is why we often see great artists achieving miracles when they appear as guests of a musical institution. We musicians, as a matter of fact, cannot deny we were born in the "green car of the Gypsies." The migratory instinct is deeply ingrained in every musician. It does not make him happier but it does make his art richer.

I do not claim Bruckner felt the need of leaving Linz for the sake of developing his art. Anyway, the restlessness of the true musician had been noticeable in him comparatively early in his stay in Linz. Even while he was at St. Florian, he had asked to be made a member of the *Hofkapelle*. His tendency to depression obviously deepened his desire to change his position.

On April 30, 1866, he wrote to Herbeck: "I place my fate and my future in your hands. I ask you to save me at once – otherwise I am lost." When Sechter died in 1867, Bruckner again applied for the position as organist at the *Hofkapelle*. He even offered to come without a salary since "the title would secure him an income." And he went on to make the following remarkable suggestion in his application: "Moreover, I could be employed as secretary and teacher in the principal schools, since I have served as a teacher for fourteen years."

Those words bring us face to face with a new enigma. Notwithstanding his considerable success as an artist, would he really have bowed, once again, under the yoke of the schoolteaching profession? Again Fate decided against his wish, and for his own good.

At Easter time, 1868, through Herbeck, Bruckner was asked if he were not interested in getting the position which the late Sechter had held at the Conservatory of Vienna. What did Bruckner do? Rush to Vienna to express his happiness over the unexpected turn of events? Not at all. Instead, he hesitated. Herbeck tried in vain to persuade him to accept, and finally went to Linz to see him face to face. They took a trip to St. Florian. To press his point, Herbeck said: "You have a real vocation to teach theory." But when he felt he was not succeeding in his mission, he appealed to the Austrian in Bruckner. "If you do not accept," he said, "I shall go to Germany to get the right man." Those words, spoken two years after the war between Prussia and Austria, could not fail in effectiveness, he thought. Yet Bruckner could not make up his mind. When they arrived at St. Florian, he went to play the organ in the church. "No other musician ever brought about a decision on a vital question in this musical way."*

On the trip back to Linz, Bruckner finally gave a tentative affirmative answer. But, though urged by his friends to seize the opportunity immediately, he began to hesitate anew. Fear that he would not be able to live in Vienna on the salary offered him outweighed the satisfaction which the high standing of the new position should have given him. One day he thought he had ruined his chances by his hesitation and scruples over unimportant items in the contract. A letter to his friend Weinwurm, dated June 20, 1868, displays his utter despair: "I am terribly unhappy, cannot eat or sleep. Why did I not accept at once? . . . Imagine how honorable the position. . . Do have compassion on me because I am without hope, perhaps for ever deserted."

But the climax of the situation was reached when, on the very day he penned the above, he wrote to Hans von Buelow and asked him to help him immediately in getting a position as organist at the Royal Court in Munich. In his letter he did not hint that he had been thinking of going to Vienna. He urged Buelow to act quickly and to keep his letter secret. He said he was impatiently longing for the position in Munich. Buelow probably never answered him, but Herbeck wrote

* Decsey, page 55.

him there was no reason at all for him to be excited or unhappy. Herbeck fully understood why Bruckner was hesitating for so long a time, and he tried to encourage him. Bruckner, after all, could do no less than accept, but he kept the backdoor open – he asked the bishop to hold his position in Linz for him in order that he might be secured against any eventuality. This action was very characteristic of Bruckner's lack of determination in the most decisive situation of his life.

One might say one of the most exciting episodes in Bruckner's life had come to an end. A biographer discovers something like tension in these events. For the first time Bruckner seems to have found an incentive in life. How strong will it prove to be? How long will it last? But nothing extraordinary followed. It was just an up-beat for a slowly progressing Passion the master was to endure, another series of struggles similar to those he had experienced before. Again one waits for the stimulation life itself might give to Bruckner. Again one waits in vain.

CHAPTER IV

SIMPLE and ingenuous men are said to possess the gift of premonition to a higher degree than cultured and sophisticated persons. Looking backward from the end of Bruckner's life to the struggle just described, one is tempted to ask: Did he really have a premonition of the period of bitterness in store for him? Or was it mere fear of the metropolis where he, a smalltown man, was henceforth to live that made him so reluctant and cautious? Many of his biographers have considered his move to Vienna the most fateful step in his life. Louis reports that a friend of Bruckner's told him he thought Bruckner's move to Vienna was not a piece of good luck at all. Bruckner, in his opinion, would have developed in a freer and richer way if he had stayed in his Upper Austrian homeland. Louis disagrees and is quite right in saying precisely because of Vienna Bruckner became the artist we love and no one can tell what might have happened if he had not gone there. He concludes that Bruckner was given to the world by his move to Vienna. This conclusion is far more positive and pertinent than Goellerich's sentimental idea: "Now he went, as the cross-bearer of mankind, to the place which Destiny had decreed as his purgatory."

Herbeck, whose energy had brought this important event about, was the leading musician of Vienna at the time. He was the director of the Society of Friends of Music, a professor at the Conservatory, and musical leader of the *Hofkapelle*. In 1869 he became the conductor – and in 1870, when he was thirty-nine years old, the director – of the Imperial Opera House, for many years the leading institution of its kind in Europe. He had discovered the original score of Schubert's *Unfinished Symphony*, hidden from the world, and performed it in 1865 for the first time. He was a man of culture and broad interests, as he proved by his courageous and unprejudiced work for the advancement of music in the Austrian capital. He loved Bruckner's music and promoted it, but "of course he did not become a blind Bruckner enthusiast, though he was the first to recognize the genius of the simple organist."* Herbeck expressed his frank opinion to Bruckner, whenever he was dissatisfied with a score. Naturally, it was to his protégé's interest for him to do so.

Bruckner's *Second Symphony* evidently aroused his highest admiration. After a rehearsal of this work, he expressed himself as follows: "I have never paid you any compliments. Yet, let me tell you, if Brahms were able to write a symphony like yours, the concert hall would be demolished by applause." This remark naturally was used for a long time by Brahms' followers as the target of attack against the Bruckner party.

Later, Herbeck's son declared his father's words had been misinterpreted. Herbeck had said, he declared, "If Brahms *had written* a symphony like yours, his followers would have demolished the hall."

Whatever the truth of the matter, Herbeck's attitude towards Brahms became increasingly hostile. He made another remark, even sharper: "Brahms has nothing in common with Schumann except one failing: confusion." This criticism is rather striking. How could matters have come to such a pass that a man of his musicianship should fail to recognize consistency in Brahms' music? It is one of Brahms' main characteristics. One is puzzled by such words from a man whose critical abilities were irreproachable. We can perhaps find an explanation in the conditions which prevailed in the European music world of that time.

Richard Wagner, then at the peak of his creative work, had stirred up the musical minds of all Europe. No history of music can give us a true picture of the intensity of the battle which raged between his followers and his foes. Only the

* Louis, page 71.

personal stories of contemporary witnesses can give us an idea of the degree of emotion Wagner's music aroused. Bonds of family and of friendship were sundered by sentiment for or against the great reformer. Wagner's enemies outdid themselves in abusing him. A very interesting little book, written by a well-known musicologist, tells us how temperatures soared in musical circles at various times. It is *A Wagner Lexicon: A vocabulary of impoliteness, containing rude, scornful, hateful, and calumnious expressions used against Maestro Richard Wagner, his works, and his followers by enemies and scoffers. Collected by Wilhelm Tappert for the delight of the spirit in leisure hours.* No other book in concise form gives us so clear an insight into the struggle between pro- and anti-Wagnerites. It was published in 1877 and may have delighted Wagner himself in the last years of his life.

The anti-Wagnerites had elected Johannes Brahms as "antipope," as it were. We do not know whether or not Brahms agreed to being elevated to this position in the war of minds. To all appearances he stayed out of the war, but we know he at least tolerated it. The Brahms pictured by most of his biographers is not quite true to life. He was not a romantic idealist who cared nothing for the realities of life. He was a clever, positive man, who used his own tactics in furthering his works. He did not ask his friends for sacrifices, as Wagner did, but nevertheless he let them work for him by subtly suggesting he was granting them a favor in allowing them to be active in his behalf. He was not adored by his followers, as was Wagner, but revered. He liked the pedestal on which they had placed him. He was prudent in his attitude toward Wagner, and cautious in his utterances. The most characteristic remarks he made in this connection are:

"Don't you think that I am the musician who understands Wagner's music best of all, anyway better than any of his so-called partisans who would like to poison me? I myself told Wagner I am the foremost living Wagnerite. Do you think I am so narrow-minded that I am not enchanted by the grandeur and hilarity of *Die Meistersinger*?"

But the Brahms party was more papal than the pope himself. Every Brahmsite had to condemn *ex officio* anything in the Wagner realm. To love Brahms' and Wagner's music at one and the same time would have shown weakness of character. My father once told me that when the wonderful violin concerto by Brahms was published, he, as the editor of a music magazine, wrote a powerful invective against it. My father was an ardent Wagnerite at the time and it would have been impossible for him to approve anything by Brahms. Later he became a friend of Brahms and exchanged letters with him.

Why Herbeck was in so sharp an opposition to Brahms is perhaps quite clear now. He was a fervent admirer of Wagner, and, consequently, it was compulsory for him to fight Brahms with every means at his disposal. I know only one prominent musician who must have been torn in heart by this dissension of musicians: Peter Cornelius. He was among the followers of Wagner but he must have been greatly attracted by Brahms' lyricism. His songs leave us in no doubt on that score.

When Bruckner settled in Vienna, the climax of the struggle between the two parties had not yet been reached. However, *Tristan and Isolde* was actually in existence, and in this work professionals and laymen were given a hard problem to solve. In 1869 even Herbeck had said that Wagner "was mistaken with his *Tristan*." The battle threatened to become extremely furious, among the hot-headed Austrians in particular. Into this atmosphere tumbled the new teacher, with a heart ardent for Wagner, unconscious of the dangers lurking about him. He was no stranger to Vienna, nor Vienna to him. The Viennese press had repeatedly reported on his career. In 1865 the *Neue Freie Presse*, Austria's leading paper, had told its readers of the unusual sensation the *Mass in D Minor* had made in Linz. After the performance of the *First*

Symphony (1868), the same paper printed the following: "If our information on Bruckner's imminent employment at the Conservatory of Vienna is confirmed, the institution is to be congratulated." And, too, all Vienna had had the opportunity of hearing the *Mass in D Minor* when Herbeck conducted it in 1867.

However, it was less the composer Bruckner whom the Viennese music lovers wanted to see in the capital than the teacher who was supposed to be an asset for the Conservatory. A theory teacher who takes the practical examples for his theories out of the thesaurus of his own imagination is sure to inspire his pupils. The art of improvisation, of which Bruckner was complete master, has a didactic value hardly to be overrated. His employment on the faculty of the Conservatory was a drawing-card for this institution.

The beginning of his stay in Vienna was promising. In September, 1868, he had the satisfaction of being nominated substitute organist at the *Hofkapelle.* Although the position carried no salary, it was held in high esteem. To be on the staff of a Court institution of art was the goal of many a musician – player or singer – and actor in Austria and Germany.

Before the World War, emperors, kings, dukes, and princes were patrons of theaters and other art institutions, and, it must be admitted, they really did a great deal for the sake of art. They were free with money and at the same time took a practical interest in the development of their institutions. Some of these rulers were extremely ambitious for the success of their theaters and, at times, were personally interested in directing them. The size of the kingdom or duchy did not necessarily determine its standard of excellence. The little dukedom of Meiningen became world-famous through its actors and its famous orchestra headed by Hans von Buelow. It was there that Richard Strauss later made his debut as a conductor, directing one of his own serenades.

A post at Court not only was an honor but also offered a

measure of security, for it usually paid a pension after a number of years of service on the part of the artist. One of the most attractive features of these Court appointments was the title the artist was given – *Hofopersaenger* (Singer of the Royal Court), *Kammermusiker* (Member of the Royal Orchestra), and the like. Those titles spread a splendor over their bearers, who consequently often contented themselves with smaller salaries.

According to Goellerich, the greatest names in the history of the Viennese *Hofkapelle* are Heinrich Isaac, Caldara, Johann Josef Fux, Mozart, Gluck, and Schubert. So Bruckner must have felt proud to be *Hoforganist*. Moreover, his speculation that this title would help him get pupils may have proved quite true. His salary at the Conservatory was very small and he was, in fact, forced to look around for some way to augment his income. The Court evidently recognized the precariousness of his situation, for it granted him an "artist's stipend" of 500 florins during the first year of his employment – an unusual distinction for a newcomer to Vienna.

More encouraging prospects were in store for him. For the first time in his life he was asked to demonstrate his art as an organist in a foreign country. There was no financial profit for him in leaving Vienna for several weeks, since he received no pay from the Conservatory during his absence; but there is no musician who does not feel that his reputation is enhanced by recognition from abroad. Before the World War, America's finest musicians endeavored to get European acclaim, although the situation seems to have reversed itself since.

It was April 24, 1869, when Bruckner left Vienna, bound for Nancy. Some days earlier he had written to a friend: "Soon I will go to France – God help me!" The new organ of the Church St. Eprve was inaugurated on the 27th, and following this event an international competition for organists took place. Bruckner evidently made a conspicuous success of it, since he was invited to play in Paris. As his period of leave from Vienna was up, he had to write the Conservatory and ask for an extension of time. The letter dealing with this matter stresses his success in an impressive way: "The high nobility, Parisians, Germans, and Belgians vied in their appreciation. . . I do not know what the papers will write, nor would I understand it. . . but the verbal criticisms of the experts are in my favor."

The permit was granted and Bruckner went to Paris and played, first, in the hall of the organ manufacturers Merklin-Schuetz before a distinguished private gathering. He was immediately asked to give a recital in Notre Dame. In telling about it, he wrote: "The music magazines in Paris have said that the great organ in Notre Dame had its day of triumph when I played, and no one in Paris ever heard anything like it." He was deeply moved by the kindness and interest shown by such great musicians as Saint-Saëns, Ambrose Thomas, and César Franck. Auber and Gounod embraced and kissed him. He was invited to parties. He, the Upper Austrian schoolmaster in his rustic clothes and top-boots, trod the parquet floors of a Paris salon, surrounded by elegant cosmopolites who complimented him in an idiom which is difficult for the foreigner to understand, mainly because of its tempo. But from the charming tone of their French speech he no doubt surmised what they wanted to tell him, and, smiling and bowing to the grand seigneurs, he returned their flowering sentences. "Never again will I experience a triumph like that," were his happy words.

Yet once again he was to take pride in being a celebrity who worthily represented his homeland at an international competition. In 1871 Vienna sent him to London to give a series of concerts at Albert Hall on the occasion of the International Exhibition. For the eight recitals he was scheduled to give, an honorarium of fifty pounds was granted. Once again he was eminently successful. An invitation to play in the Crystal Palace followed. There he presumably gave four more concerts, although the total number of his concerts in London has not been definitely ascertained. "Immense applause, without end," was his message to his friend Mayfeld.

Here, as in France and his homeland, Bruckner made the deepest impression by his improvisations on the organ. He improvised on Schubert's *Serenade* and Handel's *Hallelujah Chorus*. But what can we make of the " improvisation upon the *Toccata in F* by J. S. Bach," listed on the program? Was this a practice of the times or an idea of his own? What can be added to what Bach himself wrote? Was it not characteristic of Bach to finish a composition only when he had expressed his complete idea? I do not think Bach left anything for the improviser. Unfortunately, we have no musician's report on how Bruckner handled this feature of the program. The newspaper criticisms were good although somewhat chauvinistic in that they complained about the preference shown to foreign artists to the neglect of English artists. But these same critics may have been consoled some years later when they became aware of their good fortune in having had the opportunity of hearing the world-famous genius.

Although Bruckner was satisfied with his London success, he was less happy than he had been in Paris two years previously. In London he did not meet any of the prominent musicians; he was lonely and rather lost in that metropolis. When he went home on the bus on the first night after organ practice, he did not know where to get off. By coincidence, the bus stopped in front of his hotel and the hotel barber, an Austrian like himself, recognized him through the window and called out to him. At the end of a concert, when Bruckner was asked to play an improvisation of *Die Wacht am Rhein* (The Watch on the Rhine), he could not remember the tune. One of the hotel servants, who was in the audience, helped him out by whistling the melody softly. The servant was a fellow Austrian, from Prague.

These two little episodes show Bruckner as the type of traveler who prefers the association of his fellow countrymen to that of the natives when he is abroad. Such travelers have no desire to learn the language or the habits of the foreigners they are visiting. So Bruckner, who felt strange even in Vienna, must have been far more solitary and alone in London. But, on the other hand, Auer is mistaken in his interpretation when he tells us that Bruckner, asked to study English before making a second trip to London, answered: "Tell the lady she should study German if she wants to talk to me," and goes on to say, "Here the consciousness of his own grandeur breaks through." Such consciousness on Bruckner's part would have been contrary to his very nature as it has been pictured by numerous authorities. It was nothing but rustic bluntness that made him answer as he did.

The trips to France and London were the only professional journeys Bruckner made abroad. He evidently did not like touring in foreign countries as a virtuoso or he would have persevered in his organ playing. We are told that in later years his interest in the organ steadily decreased. When he was asked about it, he answered: "What my fingers play will pass, but what they write will remain." If this is true, he had grown more conscious of self than he was when he gave his answer to the lady in London.

Bruckner's friends were completely satisfied with his successes in foreign countries. Herbeck especially was proud of his protégé who had contributed to Vienna's fame as the music center of Europe. But this lucky period of the composer's life was not to last. Shortly after he returned home, he was involved in an unpleasant and annoying situation. In order to add to his small income, he had been trying to get an additional job and in October, 1870, he had finally been appointed assistant teacher of piano, organ, and harmony at the College of St. Anna, a teacher-training institution. In the course of one of the class lessons, he called one of the girls *mein lieber Schatz* (little dear); at least, so the girl in the adjoining seat reported. Some of the parents immediately became concerned over the moral tone of the school. Anyhow, although utterly unconscious of any wrongdoing, Bruckner had to face a disciplinary trial. *Difficile est satiram non scribere.* What a paradox! Bruckner, candid and pure-minded as he was, was suspected of indecent behavior. It is rather touching to learn that he asked Hellmesberger to give him a certificate officially testifying to the perfect discipline in his classes at the Conservatory.

Shortly thereafter his innocence in the affair became evident, but he nevertheless asked to be transferred to the men's part of the institution lest "someone might appear at any moment to denounce me," as he wrote to a friend. The episode brings out two facts: first, neither pupils nor superiors recognized the true character of the man; second, there was no cause for scandal, even if he had used the "incriminating" words attributed to him. When musicians are attempting to explain something about their art, they do not weigh their words but are apt to give them an emphasis induced by enthusiasm for their topic.

The combined work at this teachers' college and his activities at the Conservatory did not bring in enough money for him to live in his customary manner. So he again was forced to give private lessons, spending time on them which would have been far better spent in composition. And he wrote an application to the University of Vienna asking to be appointed Lector of Harmony and Counterpoint. Three of his efforts in the same direction had failed, due to the opposition of Eduard Hanslick, the eminent writer on and professor of history and aesthetics of music at the institution. Hanslick insisted that harmony and counterpoint could not be considered university courses of study if they were not taught as a science, and Bruckner, it is true, was not at all familiar with the scientific basis of theory. But his fourth and last effort was successful and he was appointed Lector of Harmony and Counterpoint at the University on November 18, 1875.

The new position did not mean an increase in income for the time being but it widened the circle of those who came under his influence, a fact which seems to have given him great satisfaction. His desire to help and to share his knowledge of music with others shows a very pleasant and charming trait in the man. Not many of the great composers of the past had this attitude – it calls for altruism. But Bruckner had an inborn inclination for his noble profession. It answered the call of his communicative nature.

In his introductory lecture, Bruckner attempted to clothe his course in harmony with a scientific garment. I doubt whether he impressed his listeners. A lector at a German or Austrian university is not on the regular faculty; he is supposed to teach "abilities," language for instance, from the colloquial rather than the scientific point of view. In 1876, Bruckner asked to be appointed professor with a stipulated salary. He was refused. His disappointment is apparent in a letter written the same year: "So I've been living in Vienna since 1868 – very resentful for having moved here." In 1877 he tried to be appointed organist at the "Am Hof" Church. This application was likewise rejected. But, in 1878, his situation improved when he was made a permanent member of the *Hofkapelle* with a salary of 800 florins a year. In 1880 he became a professor at the University of Vienna and he, the greatest music teacher in the Austrian capital in the nineteenth century, was granted a salary of 800 florins a year for his work there. He was fifty-six years old before he could feel financially secure.

This security, however, he bought at a high price; he lectured twice a week at the University, taught sixteen hours a week at the Conservatory, and gave twelve private lessons a week. Since "weekends" were unknown in Germany and Austria, his work amounted to five hours a day. It is an enormous load, even for a teacher whose imagination is not so full of ideas as Bruckner's soaring musical mind must have been. All his lamentations about poor salaries, lack of recognition, and jealousy on the part of his colleagues do not move me so much as the idea of those 30 hours of teaching spent every week by an artist whose mental and physical powers should have been saved for creative work. Nothing interferes with a musician's creative abilities more than concern with music other than his own. He does not need to sit at a desk or at a piano to work; his ideas may take shape while he is taking a walk or enjoying a bit of recreation or pursuing a hobby. Richard Strauss, for instance, finds relaxation and ideas in playing cards. Even when a composer is seemingly idle, his phantasy often works quite unconsciously. He is unaware of it at the time. Bruckner once said, when he was asked how a certain beautiful melody had come to him: "It came by itself while I was eating my favorite dish." There is no doubt about it, the composer's worst foe is giving music lessons.

Was it moral heroism or was it anxiety for a dignified financial security or was it, after all, simply patient routine that made Bruckner endure this hardship? Whatever it was, his genius triumphed. He brushed obstructions aside and under the pressure of his taxing daily work and in constant friction with hostile elements he forged steadily onward and upward.

No one, not even the musicians, placed much confidence in the composer Bruckner at that time. In 1869, when Herbeck had placed the *Great Mass in F Minor* on his program, only two members of the orchestra appeared for rehearsal. Herbeck himself became discouraged and took the number off the program. He did not take it up again until 1872. Even then he must have had doubts about the success of the work, for after the last rehearsal he asked the composer to conduct it. The first performance took place in June, 1872, and met with unqualified success. Then Hellmesberger told Bruckner: "I know none but this Mass and Beethoven's *Missa Solemnis.*" Bruckner told Goellerich the story in later years. Auer claims that Herbeck himself addressed these words to Bruckner, but it is rather unlikely, since Herbeck had asked Bruckner to make certain changes in the score, saying: "Since Wagner was mistaken with his *Tristan*, why do you not admit you may be wrong with your Mass?" But the composer refused to give in.

At the time the Mass was first performed, Bruckner had almost finished the *Second Symphony*, in C minor. He had begun this work with the Finale in 1871, in London. When Mrs. Mayfeld played the symphony for him on the piano, he fell on his knees and exclaimed: "Madame, you are a goddess!" Dessoff wanted to hear the work and therefore tried it out with his orchestra. At the rehearsal he asked the composer to stand behind him and indicate the right tempi. Evidently it was difficult for a conductor, even so able a one as Dessoff, to realize Bruckner's music from a reading of the score. That is why he had the orchestra play the symphony and why he needed the composer's help and suggestions at rehearsal. After the rehearsal, Dessoff refused to perform the work in public. This experience did not discourage Bruckner in the least; he threw all his energies into work on the next symphony, in D minor. He was a good father to his "children," as he called his symphonies, and labored mightily to insure their success and general welfare.

While Bruckner was staying in Marienbad in August, 1873, he asked Wagner if there were any objections to his coming to Bayreuth. Wagner offered no encouragement. Nevertheless, before the ink on the manuscript of the *Third Symphony* was dry, Bruckner set out for Bayreuth and called at Wagner's home. He was told to return in three hours. When he re-entered the house, he heard the master playing on the piano. With the huge scores of the *Second* and *Third Symphony* under his arm, he anxiously waited in the living room. "I did not know where to tread on the carpet," he later told his friends, so elated was he at his nearness to his idol. Finally Wagner appeared on the threshold. Bruckner timidly asked him to look at the scores.

Every musician of any prominence can recall precarious situations of this sort, when an uninvited composer appears and asks for criticisms of his work. What answer shall the musician make? Should he refuse to examine the work or should he arouse false hopes? Will he find time to make a thorough study of the score or will he merely give it a superficial perusal? Bundles of manuscripts were lying about in Wagner's room. At the time, he was extremely busy supervising the building of the new Wagner theater and working on the *Nibelungen*. So he refused Bruckner rather harshly. But Bruckner was not easily deterred and kept on insisting in his modest way. Wagner finally relented and asked him to come back in three days' time. The climax of the story is a tragicomedy:

Wagner was no doubt relieved at the prospect of getting rid of an undesirable visitor, at least for the time being, while Bruckner was happy at the prospect of showing him his scores. But a new problem confronted Bruckner – three days of waiting around in Bayreuth meant expenses he could not afford.

"I told Wagner that a glance at the themes would be enough for him to form an opinion," Bruckner reported. "And the master answered: 'Well, come with me,' and we went into the music room and looked over the *Second Symphony*. 'Very good,' he said, but it seemed to be too tame for him. He picked up the *Third Symphony* and said, 'Look. . . look here. . . what's that?' With these words he went through the first section and then asked me to let him have the work to study after lunch."

Bruckner replied timidly, "Master, I have something close to my heart that I dare not mention."

"Tell me! You know how much I think of you," said Wagner.

And Bruckner asked Wagner to let him dedicate one of the symphonies to him, provided the master was satisfied with them. He would not profane Wagner's name, he said, if the master were not satisfied. And he left the score of the *Third Symphony*.

"You are invited to 'Wahnfried' for 5 P. M.," said Wagner. "You come to me there and we will talk over the D minor symphony after I have examined it."

Bruckner later often said he felt like a schoolboy whose exercises the teacher was marking. He did not know how to pass the time until the appointed hour, but walked about aimlessly. Finally he came to the Wagner theater, which was under construction. There he became so much interested in the progress of the work that he forgot the hour of the appointment until Wagner sent a servant to find him. When he entered "Wahnfried," he heard Wagner playing the trumpet theme of his symphony on the piano.

Wagner received him with shining eyes, was silent for a while, and then embraced and kissed him, saying: "My dear friend, your symphony is a masterpiece. It's all right about the dedication. You will give me great pleasure by dedicating it to me."

Wagner then discussed the state of music in Vienna with the overjoyed Bruckner and showed him his garden and his grave. Later he introduced him to Cosima and feted him with huge quantities of beer. All in all, it was one of the happiest days in Bruckner's life. But the next day was another matter: Bruckner had grotesquely forgotten which symphony he was to dedicate to Wagner. Was it the *Second* or the *Third?* He appealed to the sculptor Kietz, whom he and Wagner had visited the day before. The only thing Kietz could say was that he had heard Wagner several times refer to a symphony in D minor. Bruckner was happy and relieved, but

Wagner offering snuff to Bruckner

to make sure he wrote to Wagner on a sheet of blue paper: "Symphony D Minor, the one in which the trumpet starts the theme?" Wagner wrote underneath, "Yes, of course, cordially, Richard Wagner." So the *Third Symphony* became the *Wagner Symphony* in common parlance. The composer felt not only happy but honored by the name, never realizing that the followers of Brahms would consider him henceforth a confirmed Wagnerite.

Bruckner was very sensitive by nature and depended a good deal upon the opinion of others. Wagner's approval therefore stimulated and encouraged him in his work. What the "master of masters" had approved could not be anything but good. So he decided to introduce himself in Vienna as a symphonist and to present the *Second Symphony* (finished on July 26, 1872). The World's Fair in Vienna seemed to offer the possibility of an international audience in the concert hall of the Music Society. The members of the orchestra were rather antagonistic, but when the Prince of Liechtenstein generously offered to defray expenses, the composer could tell them at the first rehearsal: "Well, gentlemen, we can practice to our hearts' content. I found somebody to pay for it." This little story was related by Arthur Nikisch, who played the violin in the orchestra at that rehearsal.

The concert took place on October 26, 1873.* Bruckner opened the performance by playing the *Toccata in D Minor* by Bach, following it by an improvisation. The critic Helm wrote it was to be regretted that this improvisation could not be taken down by a shorthand writer. Bruckner, when asked why he did not write down his improvisations, had once answered, "One does not write as one plays."

The symphony was heartily approved by the audience as well as by the press, and Bruckner had not been entertaining false hopes. He had tried to express himself in simpler terms than he had in the *First Symphony*, in order to make his work more easily understood. He had been rather terrified by his own courage when he wrote the "*kecke Beserl,*" ** as he called his first work. "I was never again so bold and daring as I was in the *First Symphony*. I challenged the whole world," Bruckner is reported to have said.

Nowadays it is difficult to see any difference in clarity between the *First* and the *Second* symphonies. But the suc-

* Some writers give the date as October 23rd, but from Bruckner's letters it is evident that the first performance was on October 26th.

** This jargon expression taken from the Viennese students was a nickname often given to young and merry, even fresh and snappy girls. (Josef V. Woess)

cess of the *Second Symphony* then and now, I am sure, can be attributed to its fascinating thematic material. The main themes of the first three movements are so impressive and clear-cut that the listener can easily keep them in mind. No other symphony by this master of music can better acquaint the listener with the peculiar quality of Bruckner's music. Because of its frequent rests it has been called the *Symphony of Pauses*.

Herbeck had it performed a second time in 1876, although he made several criticisms of the work. This performance was not so successful as the first, but Herbeck nevertheless persisted in his belief in Bruckner's genius and placed the *Wagner Symphony* on his program. When the Philharmonic Orchestra had attempted the *Wagner Symphony* in 1875, they pronounced it "unplayable." It was David Popper, the excellent solo cellist, who pleaded for its presentation. So Bruckner subjected the work to a thorough revision in the winter of 1876-1877.

Shortly before the day scheduled for its performance, Herbeck died suddenly and Bruckner was forced to take the baton for an eager audience, impressed with the idea that Wagner had approved the music and was pleased with the dedication. In fact, when Wagner had arrived in Vienna in 1875, he had told Bruckner at the railroad station: "This symphony must be performed," and, turning to the people assembled there, had added: "There's Bruckner. He's my man." These remarks were rather unusual from Wagner, whose lack of interest in the works of his contemporaries, even those of his intimate friend Liszt, was notorious.

The symphony was heard for the first time on December 16, 1877. The performance was a complete fiasco. It was one of the darkest days in Bruckner's life. After each movement large numbers of the audience fairly ran away, and during the Finale not more than a dozen persons were left in the hall.

The person who has attended such a concert-debacle will never forget it. It is too depressing in character. I remember the first performance of several of the Strauss tone poems in Berlin, when the audience made loud and clamorous criticisms, and laughed and walked out. On one occasion, someone slammed the door noisily while the orchestra was playing *piano*, in order to prove himself a hero of his convictions. Later, in Vienna, like acts of violence occurred when Schoenberg's works were presented for the first time. Scenes of this kind sometimes have a contagious effect and induce even the unprejudiced listener into the opposing group, leaving the rest of the audience in awkward embarrassment. The situation becomes more unendurable when the composer's friends start demonstrating their loyalty with ostentatious applause.

But what happened at that Bruckner concert? The disaster had such a far-reaching effect that we may investigate it in detail. It is rather hard to determine what caused the audience to act in so pitiless a fashion. In itself the music was hardly challenging to an audience which had already heard some of Bruckner's works. Was it the length of the symphony which tired them? Was it the rather unfinished rendition, as the orchestra had not sufficiently rehearsed it? Or had the orchestra itself unconsciously contributed to the failure by spreading rumors during rehearsals? We have been told that the members of the orchestra would laugh ironically at Bruckner, to his face, and he had not mastered the difficulties of his own work as well as Herbeck had. Nothing can be worse for a première than premature criticism on the part of the co-operating elements. It communicates itself to wider circles.

Orchestra players in Vienna have always exerted a great attraction for laymen, who love to be associated with them and learn what happens "behind the scenes." On the other hand, this influence often stimulates a high interest in musical events on the part of the laymen. Yet it often creates a prejudice for or against the works of a specific composer. Generally speaking, the average orchestra member is surely not in a position to judge the merits of a new work which is still in rehearsal. He is busy studying one single part, as yet unaware of the role it is to play in the structure as a whole. As long as he is engaged in ironing out the technical difficulties of his own part, he cannot listen to what his colleagues are playing.

As to the première of Bruckner's *Third Symphony*, I almost believe so many rumors about the unusual new work and its peculiar composer had been circulating in the city that the public came to the concert with prejudiced minds. The typical Viennese gossip, born in the cafes of the lovely city, had a new victim. Not even the Wagner party was powerful enough to prevent the disaster. On the contrary, Bruckner's identification as a Wagnerite had incited Wagner's adversaries to the most virulent opposition. It is heartbreaking to read about the final scene on that night: "It was an unforgettably moving moment when Bruckner at the close of the concert, quite alone on the podium, for the musicians had escaped as quickly as possible, took his music and threw a pained glance about the empty concert hall."

When he left, some of his pupils and friends, among them young Gustav Mahler, went up to him and tried to explain how acceptable his work really was, in order to offer some slight consolation. But Bruckner exclaimed: "Let me alone! People don't care for me!" What a tragic experience after half a century of hard work, struggle, and disappointments!

But there was one bright moment that night. Among the few who came to encourage the unlucky composer after the concert was the music publisher Raettig. He expressed his confidence in Bruckner's music and offered to publish the symphony. Bruckner glared incredulously at this strange man who dared to display so much courage at such a disastrous time. Raettig, in fact, published the symphony at his own expense (3000 florins), and in 1885 he sent the composer 150 florins in royalty fees. Goellerich, to whom we are indebted for this information, compared this small amount with the 20,000 marks which Brahms received from his publisher for his first symphony. Other biographers have jealously pointed to the injustice involved in the situation. I do not understand whom they consider responsible for any "injustice." One should remember Brahms got so large a sum not for the symphony alone but for his reputation as the composer of chamber music and songs well-known to a wide circle of music lovers, who were anxiously looking forward to his first symphonic work.

CHAPTER V

BRUCKNER's finances were indeed in poor shape at that time. In 1874 he had lost his position at St. Anna College and he was therefore dependent on his income from the Conservatory and from private lessons. His applications for other positions were rejected. Bruckner used a calendar as a diary and in it he noted daily events and happenings over a period of many years – his expenses, his appointments, the names of girls who appealed to him, his pupils, his daily work and religious exercises. However, nothing in the calendar-diary is more interesting and pathetic than his numerous applications. We find there, for instance, for Thursday, September 27, 1877: "Third rejection of my Wagner Symphony No. 3. First rejected in fall, 1872. C Minor Symphony No. 2, 2nd rejection by the Philharmonic Orchestra, fall, '75. Symphony No. 3."

The document shows the inexorable severity of fate and the admirable stoicism of a man's heart. In those years of bitter experiences Bruckner was not spared humiliating remarks and advice from malicious people like the secretary of the Conservatory, Zellner, who answered his complaints with these words: "You had better throw your symphonies on a dung heap and make piano arrangements. That will mean more money for you." Fortunately, as we have mentioned earlier, Bruckner's financial troubles were greatly relieved by the income granted from the University and the *Hofkapelle*. His spirit, however, was unperturbed by outer events, since his will-power overcame all impediments and kept feeding his imagination, regardless of discouraging mishaps. His imagination worked on, spontaneously, and proved him a genius.

At the time of the first performance of the *Third Symphony*, the *Fourth* and the *Fifth* were already finished. The *Fourth* was written in 1874; the *Fifth* took much longer, for it was begun in 1875 and finished in 1877. He gave the *Fourth Symphony* the subtitle *Romantic Symphony*. His reasons for doing so have never been definitely ascertained. As a matter of fact, it was conceived without this subtitle, which he did not add until 1876. Bruckner himself explained the beginning of the *Romantic* as follows: "A citadel of the Middle Ages. Daybreak. Reveille is sounded from the tower. The gates open. Knights on proud chargers leap forth. The magic of nature surrounds them." Decsey is right in saying this explanation is not to be taken literally. "His music was stronger than his pictures." Bruckner, when asked what he had in mind as he was writing the Finale, answered: "I do not know myself what I had in mind." It sounds as though he wanted to make sport of his overzealous interpreters.

The *Romantic Symphony* was not performed until seven years had elapsed. This time the famous Hans Richter was conducting. He held a prominent position in Vienna as opera and concert director, and he did a great deal for Bruckner although he was not among his closest friends. The composer often complained that Richter did not do enough for him. But when this authority actually conducted the work, Bruckner happily demonstrated an extreme degree of devotion for him during the rehearsals. When the conductor once asked him, "What note is this?" Bruckner answered, "Any you choose. Quite as you like." After a rehearsal Bruckner gave Richter a thaler as an earnest of his gratitude.

"The thaler is the memento of a day when I wept," said Richter. "For the first time I conducted a Bruckner symphony, at rehearsal. Bruckner was an old man then. His works were performed hardly anywhere. When the symphony was over, Bruckner came to me. He was radiant with enthusiasm and happiness. I felt him put something in my hand. 'Take it, and drink a mug of beer to my health.' It was a thaler (three-mark piece)." Richter did not want to hurt the naive old soul, and so he fixed the thaler to his watch chain.

The symphony met with unusual success both with the audience and in the press. The *Fifth Symphony*, which he considered his contrapuntal masterpiece, starts the row of Bruckner's giant works, with the exception of the *Sixth*. It has characteristics we do not meet in any of the others. The first performance of the *Fifth* was given in 1894 by Franz Schalk, the young conductor of the opera house in Graz. Bruckner was then a sick man and he could not attend the concert. He died two years later without ever having heard this most significant of his works. Goellerich called it "The Tragic Symphony," while Auer felt it expressed "the will to life." Bruckner spoke of it as his "Fantastic Symphony." These very divergent interpretations of the meaning of this music, interesting though they are, have one significant factor in common: The very essence of music is not to be defined in words; it causes everyone to use his own particular form of speech in talking about it. People may not understand one another but they are drawn together by their common love for Bruckner's music.

* * * * *

The year 1879 brought a surprise for everyone: Bruckner wrote a string quintet. It is the only chamber music he ever created and it is praised by many critics who think it continued the style of Beethoven's last string quartets. I do not think it has a relationship to those quartets by Beethoven and I am more concerned with the fact that Bruckner, according to Auer, did not get acquainted with those Beethoven works until after he had written the quintet. Is it possible that during all of his years of study none of his teachers drew his attention to these compositions? If they did not, why did he not study them by himself? The quintet was not accepted in the repertory of chamber-music performers until a relatively late date, but now it is greatly admired by European concert-goers. Its first performance took place in Vienna on November 17, 1881, and met with unqualified success, even in the part of the press which was usually in opposition to Bruckner's music.

When Hellmesberger performed it in 1885, he told the composer the work was a "revelation" to him. From the letter in which Bruckner told this story, we learn that the *Quintet* and the *Third Symphony* were the only compositions published at the time. "Oh, might I find a publisher!" Bruckner laments. "I am now writing my Eighth Symphony." Some years earlier he had not even had the money to have his manuscripts copied. It is pure heroism in an artist not to give way to despair but to follow the command of his inner voice, which tells him: Go on creating!

The *Sixth Symphony* was composed in the years between 1879 and 1881. The director of the opera house, Wilhelm Jahn, who was also the conductor of the Philharmonic Concerts for a short period, performed the Second and Third Movements on February 11, 1883, for the first time. He told Bruckner that he, himself, was one of his most fervent admirers and certainly thought he was acting for the composer's good in presenting at least these two fragments. To give selections from a symphony was not so strange in those days as it is nowadays, when it is only occasionally done in programs on the air. Even strict Hans von Buelow performed single movements time and again, and Mahler presented his *Second Symphony* for the first time in Berlin without the Choir Finale. What was so regrettable in the concert directed by Jahn was the fact that he did not perform the First Movement, which we customarily consider as determining the character of the whole work. The Second Movement in the sonata scheme, we feel, follows the law of contrast. When the First Movement is omitted, the Second has no reference to anything and means the opening. But it has no opening character; it tells us nothing about its origin nor about the part it plays within the framework of the composition as a whole and it leaves the listener at a loss. A brief review of the most popular symphonies by Beethoven and Brahms shows that the slow movements do not disclose in any way the character of the composition as a whole, regardless of their beauty or value.

Arthur Nikisch considered the Second Movement of Bruckner's *Sixth Symphony* one of the most beautiful of his creations, and he was not mistaken. Bruckner never heard the whole symphony, unless he heard it in rehearsal before Jahn decided to present only the two middle movements.

"On the noteworthy Sunday of the concert, Bruckner, accompanied by his pupil Lamberg, entered the concert hall, which was, of course, empty at that early hour of 9 o'clock in the morning. He wore shoes that did not match, and, what was more startling, one of them had a patent-leather tip. The pupil, however, refrained from mentioning the fact to his nervous master. In a restaurant near by, he received his orders, the most important of which was to watch the dreaded critic Hanslick." The pitiful and humorous little scene tells us more about Bruckner's true being than many a page of conjectures in the biographies.

The concert was not a complete success and the hostile part of the press was more vociferous in its opposition than it had been before. The symphony, which, incidentally, is unique in character compared with Bruckner's other compositions, never received as much applause as the same audience gave to his other works. Right or wrong, the stigma attending the first performance has persisted, even to the present day.

While writing the First Movement, Bruckner had taken his first pleasure trip abroad. Did he take the score with him or did he interrupt his work for the time? We are tempted to ask these questions because we are anxious to learn what impression the sight of the majestic Alps made on his fertile imagination. It was in the summer of 1880 that he started on his trip to Switzerland. He stopped in Oberammergau to attend the Passion Play and immediately fell in love with a seventeen-year-old peasant girl who was in the cast. He wanted to marry her. He gave her a prayer book and started a correspondence with her which lasted a long time.

The suddenness with which Bruckner used to fall in love has been documented by Goellerich, who wrote about his first meeting with Bruckner when the composer visited his home town. On that occasion, everybody in the town had been transported by Bruckner's wonderful organ playing, but he startled the inhabitants far more by his audacity the next morning when he asked for the hand of a beautiful girl, the daughter of a well-known family, whom he had seen for the first time in church the day before.

From Oberammergau Bruckner went to Zurich and Geneva, and sojourned for some days at one of the most wonderful places on earth, Chamonix. The view from the valley to the soaring, icy summits of Mount Blanc can never be forgotten, once one has seen it. Bruckner's calendar-diary records no impression made by the overwhelming grandeur of nature, and we are led to believe in Friedrich Klose's observation that Bruckner lacked the sense for beauty in nature to an extent such "as we do not find in any other artist." On his way home, Bruckner played the organ in the cathedral at Bern and aroused the greatest admiration.

Whatever the impressions may have been which he brought home, they are not noticeable in his later works, especially not in the *Sixth Symphony*, on which he was working. In the Third Movement one might sense the atmosphere of nature, but certainly not that of the lofty Alps. The diary shows a remarkably long list of names of girls who had appealed to the traveler. His interest in a woman lasted only as long as he thought her honest and worthy of becoming his wife. Then he would try to get information about her character, family, and dowry. Time and again he would ask a friend to investigate these pertinent items. He wanted her to have enough money to guarantee dignity in marriage, and he quite practically took into consideration the fact that if he died, he would have nothing to leave her. Women of light natures were symbols of sin and hell to him until his later years.

In 1890, in company with Hans Richter and some other friends, he went to a restaurant where the service was done by waitresses instead of waiters. Those restaurants did not always enjoy a good reputation in Germany and Austria. His friends gradually departed and he was finally left alone with the waitress. According to pre-arranged agreement with his friends, she perched herself on his knee. Horrified, he rose and shouted: "*Apage Satana!*" His fear of sin had been stronger than his sense of humor.

As I report these odd little stories, I am fully aware of the fact that there may be many an admirer of Bruckner's genius who deems them too unimportant for repetition. Again let me say, I have told them specifically for one purpose: To stress as much as possible the divergency between the man himself and the creative artist – the "Problem Bruckner." The man virtually never changed, but the artist in him rose higher and higher despite all the obstacles life put in his path. And there were plenty of obstacles up to the last years of his career, when the world finally began to alleviate his hardships by financial support, when well-known societies made him an honorary member, when the emperor gave him an audience, when publishers became interested in his works, and when, last but not least, some of his symphonies started their march of triumph through Austria and Germany. He was an old man then, not so much in years as in physique, and thus it happened that when he heard a Viennese audience enthusiastically applauding one of his compositions, he uttered the melancholy words: "Too late, all too late."

Bruckner's life, as I mentioned at the beginning, is no drama or romance, but it is replete with moments which make it a tragedy of soul. Its hero was no figure of Classic grandeur nor of Shakespearean dimensions. He was only a poor schoolmaster who suffered and sacrificed himself for the sake of music, who expressed belief in his mission in the naive words: "When God finally calls me and asks, what have you done with the talent I gave you, my lad, I will show Him my scores and I hope He will judge me mercifully."

When Bruckner came back from Switzerland, the series of disappointments in store for him had not yet come to an end. He applied for the position of Assistant Conductor of the Viennese Male Glee Club, a chorus of high rank and reputation. He was refused. The little incident would have no importance in itself if it did not signify the low esteem in which he was still held. Even admitting he was not a first-rate conductor, was his reputation as a composer not good enough to be the pride of any glee club? But Fate had something better in store for him. It did not bother about his temporary needs but put him in the mood to create the work that bestowed immortal glory on him, for the following year, 1881, he began his *Seventh Symphony*, and with this composition he laid the cornerstone of his world-wide fame. He finished it on September 5, 1883.

The symphony has gained special renown through the Adagio, which was partly conceived as funeral music on the death of Richard Wagner. Bruckner wrote Mottl about its origin: "Once I came home and felt very sad. I did not think the master would live much longer. Then I conceived the Adagio in C sharp minor." This happened three weeks before Wagner passed away. According to Goellerich, he had just written the general *fortissimo* in C major when he was notified of Wagner's death. Deeply moved, he added the last thirty-five measures, which are funereal in mood mainly because of the soft tone of the four tubas. Bruckner felt Wagner's death as a personal misfortune. "*He* passed from me," he said.

The *Seventh Symphony* was presented on December 30, 1884, and by its success the Bruckner Battle was definitely won. Arthur Nikisch conducted the first performance in the Municipal Theater in Leipzig, since the famous *Gewandhaus* had refused to present it. This young conductor held a prominent position in Leipzig before he was called to Boston to be the leader of the symphonic orchestra there. He effectively propagandized the new work by playing the score on the piano for the music critics and he wrote Bruckner every time he won one of them over.

Nikisch's foremost gift was intuition. His wonderful achievements were not so much the result of his persistent study and practice as of his perception and divination of the inner sense of a score. I once saw him conduct a novelty at a rehearsal – the pages of the score had not yet been cut. Nobody would have noticed he was sight-reading if he had not had to take out a penknife to open the score, an action which aroused the hilarity of the whole orchestra. He was a fine psychologist and he knew how effective in performing music is the element of surprise. He once told me that surprise meant a great deal not only to the audience but to the orchestra as well.

"If you try out all the effects of a score at rehearsal, the orchestra will not play with the highest tension at night," he said. "That is why I do not try out every detail to its fullest extent but leave something to be performed at the concert. Then the players, subjected to my surprising suggestion, a suggestion they have not experienced before, will carry out certain passages with a degree of tension that guarantees the highest effectiveness."

The success of this unique manner of rehearsing was

proved by the unanimous enthusiasm of the orchestra members. They became no less excited than the audience. They would say they had played half-consciously, carried along in a spell, the nature of which they could not explain to themselves. As a conductor, Nikisch was the antithesis of his colleague in Leipzig, Gustav Mahler, who never considered a rehearsal finished until he was thoroughly convinced that the orchestra would play its part in full accordance with his most minute directions. He did not leave anything to the orchestra.

Nikisch had another wonderful gift: he could feel what a composition needed beyond what was indicated in the printed score. Bruckner's compositions do not have nearly so many indications as other modern scores, such as those of Strauss or Gustav Mahler. In many respects they need the attentive love of their interpreter. Nikisch gave them that, and so he was the ideal conductor for Bruckner's symphonies. He practically took care of them like a tutor to whom children are entrusted by their father. He proved his deep knowledge of the score when he wrote to the composer on December 21, 1884: "You will have to change some passages in the orchestration because they are not practical and do not sound tuneful."

Soon after its success in Leipzig, Herman Levy presented the work in Munich, on March 10, 1885. Its success was possibly still greater than it had been in Leipzig, and the fact is remarkable, for the program was so long that one would think the audience would have tired. Here it is:

I.	Overture	Mehul
II.	Violin Concerto	Viotti
III.	Lieder	Schumann
IV.	Violin Solos	———
V.	Symphony No. 7	Bruckner

At the party after the concert, Levy in his toast to Bruckner said the symphony was the most significant work since the death of Beethoven. After the performance of *Die Walkuere* the next night, Bruckner asked Levy to have the Adagio of the *Seventh Symphony* played in commemoration of Wagner. Bruckner wept bitterly. The audience had already left. "I cannot describe the scene in that dark Royal Theater," he wrote a friend.

Levy became one of Bruckner's greatest admirers and most efficient propagandists later on, and he made strenuous efforts to collect the money needed for publishing some of Bruckner's compositions. He himself gave a considerable amount of money for the project. Up to the last years of Bruckner's life, no publisher would risk producing his works without some financial underwriting. In 1892, Emperor Franz Joseph contributed 1500 florins for the publication of the *Eighth Symphony*. The same year the firm Eberle & Company acquired exclusive rights to the *First*, *Second*, *Fifth*, and *Sixth* symphonies, and to some of the choral works, assuring Bruckner a yearly income of 300 florins. Bruckner was dead when the first royalty payments fell due.

* * * * *

A particular feature in many of the Bruckner biographies is the complaint that although his symphonies have world-wide significance the city of Vienna did not recognize his genius earlier than other music centers. Austria should have headed the list of admirers of her greatest musician. The fact that she did not has been rated as her mistake, her fault and a piece of negligence. Whenever the first performance of a Bruckner symphony took place outside Vienna, the capital was blamed for its lack of interest. And when a Bruckner work was given first in Vienna and did not meet with the desired success, the audience and the press were censured for their stupidity, and the malevolence of the prejudiced opposition was stressed. I perhaps would have shared this opinion had I been a contemporary follower of Bruckner, but looking at the sequence of events from a present-day point of view, as the writers do, I cannot share it, for historical evolution can no more be blamed than nature itself.

Some writers consider it a shame that the *Seventh Symphony*, and other works too, were not presented first in Vienna. After his experiences in the capital, Bruckner had avoided any occasion for criticism and had asked the Philharmonic Society on October 13, 1885, to drop the planned performance of the *Seventh Symphony* "for reasons which arise from the sad local situation, referring to the criticisms of authorities which come my way and may damage my recent successes in Germany." The performance in Vienna on March 22, 1886, proved him right in his attitude. The leading critics showed "open hatred." At their head was Eduard Hanslick, music critic on the *Neue Freie Presse*. In his criticism he said, among other things, "Part of the audience ran away after the Second Movement of this symphonic anaconda . . . In a letter to me, a distinguished German musician calls Bruckner's symphony the confused dream of an orchestra player who became hysterical because of twenty rehearsals of *Tristan*."

It cannot be denied that Hanslick, the author of the famous book *The Beautiful in Music* and a highly educated musician, was the first to attempt to explain music through musical concepts and terms, eliminating as far as possible the customary circumlocutions which do not explain the essence of music. This method of his gave lasting value to his books. Although he headed the Brahms party, he could not be considered an outspoken adversary of Bruckner when the latter moved to Vienna. He even displayed a certain interest in Bruckner's talent as a composer and an organist. His opposition to Bruckner's application for a lectorship at the

University of Vienna had a real foundation and was certainly not dictated by jealousy. When Bruckner finally did become lector at that institution, it was Hanslick who supported his effort to get remuneration for his services. The reason for his growing enmity towards Bruckner was Bruckner's attachment to Wagner, whom Hanslick was fighting with all the means at his disposal. Bruckner's dedication of his *Third Symphony* to the Master of Bayreuth caused the first open break.

Wagner was Hanslick's *idée fixe* and anyone connected with Wagner or his friends was the target of his hatred. His books, mainly collections of criticisms on current musical events, are those of a very fine stylist who has mastered his mother tongue with extraordinary skill. From a purely linguistic angle, Wagner's librettos offered him excellent opportunities for attack. It may be that the librettos were the starting point for his opposition. Yet he hated the music too. When he played the Prelude of *Die Meistersinger* on the piano, he said: "In the noise of the Wolf's Glen in Nuernberg, every concept of music disappears."

I never thought I would meet, forty years after Wagner's death, an anti-Wagnerian whose feelings matched those of Hanslick. Yet the great Ferruccio Busoni proved to be one. After one of my symphony concerts in Hamburg, one of the last in which he played, he told me about his deeply ingrained antipathy to Wagner.

"You are telling me this," I asked him, "because you disagree with Wagner in principle? I am familiar with your principles through your writings."

"Not at all," he replied harshly. "I dislike the music itself to the same extent."

A year later I called on him to discuss some questions concerning his opera *Arlecchino*, which I was to conduct in Hamburg. He was ill in bed. Death had marked him for his own. I made occasional mention of Wagner in the course of our conversation. A terrible transformation took place before my eyes. He rose up in bed with great difficulty and screamed: "No Wagner! No Wagner! I don't want to hear his name." Exhausted he fell back on his pillows. I had seen him for the last time.

This experience has enabled me to imagine the intensity of the feeling centering about Wagner when his works were presented for the first time. It followed as a natural consequence that so great an enemy of his as Hanslick would extend his hatred to Bruckner, who was the new idol of the Wagner party. "It is ridiculous to doubt Hanslick's sincerity; rarely has a critic explained the reasons for his opposition in so clear and open a way," Decsey wrote. Nevertheless, Hanslick became the target for the heaviest and most furious attacks of the Brucknerites. I personally can find no one to blame for a situation that looks as natural as this one. Moreover, by his attitude towards Bruckner, Hanslick served the cause of Brahms. This has been his unquestioned and permanent merit.

In this connection, it may be pertinent to point to Hugo Wolf's criticism of Brahms' symphonic works. It does not differ greatly in general tone from Hanslick's articles on Bruckner. Wolf, a musician of towering ability, a man able to appreciate the true value of Brahms' symphonies, poured out sarcasm and scorn on the German composer in so harsh a manner that one would expect Brahms to have remonstrated against them. He did not. Self-conscious and self-confident as he was, he went on his way never complaining about his enemies but rather relying on his friends and followers.

* * * * *

Brahms' attitude towards Bruckner has not been explained to this day. Some of his remarks which have been handed down seem to prove he was in open opposition to Bruckner. The most interesting of them is, at the same time, a description of the origin of the two hostile parties in Vienna. I quote: "As to Bruckner, his works do not matter, but the whole affair is a swindle that will be over and forgotten in two or three years . . . Bruckner owes his fame exclusively to me . . . but it all happened against my will. Nietzsche once said that I became famous only by coincidence: The anti-Wagnerian party needed me as an anti-pope. That is nonsense, but it is right for Bruckner. After the death of Wagner his followers were at a loss for a pope and they could find no better one than Bruckner . . . Bruckner's works immortal? It makes me laugh."

I do not believe these often-quoted words are historically true. Brahms' criticisms were never blunt nor rude, as far as I have been able to learn from his friends, but rather enveloped in a light satirical veil. His speech was sometimes malicious but never hateful. To be hateful in speech, he would have had to climb down from the pedestal on which his partisans had placed him. Remarks were passed on both sides which hurt both. Buelow spoke of Brahms' *First Symphony* as "The Tenth," thus putting him in the closest proximity to Beethoven. Wagner, on the other hand, is said to have remarked: "There is only one whose ideas approach Beethoven's and he is Bruckner." As a matter of fact, we have reason to assume Brahms and Bruckner were aware of each other's genius, to a certain extent, but would not express their beliefs for fear of disappointing their ardent followers, who, for their part, often intensified their antagonism for the sake of their own positions within their party, which might have weakened if animosity were allowed to fade.

The true situation is even more difficult for us to understand when we learn that Brahms warned the famous conductor Hans Richter not to introduce Bruckner's symphonies during his projected stay in England and, on the other hand, is reported to have said: "And yet Bruckner is a great genius." Bruckner, for his part, told his friends: "He is Dr. Brahms, and my respects to him, but I am Bruckner and I like my works better." Once, when Brahms told him he had not understood one of his symphonies, he answered: "You know, the very same thing happened to me with your music." He was not given to satire in speaking.

Friends on both sides tried to relieve the tension and so they made arrangements for the two composers to meet in a restaurant. Bruckner arrived first. After a while Brahms appeared and sat down in silence at the opposite end of the long table. Nobody said a word. The atmosphere grew tense. After he had finished studying the menu, Brahms ordered a dish which was also a favorite of Bruckner's. "You see, Doctor," Bruckner said, "on this point we understand each other." The hilarity which followed this remark set the party in an agreeable mood. However, the two men never established cordial relations, for they were too different by nature and felt no attraction for each other. Goellerich, in his appraisal of the Brahms-Bruckner relationship, quite rightly said: "In Brahms and Bruckner the eternal contrast is evident between North and South, between Protestantism and Catholicism."

With all this evidence in mind, I must make the following statement: By its relentless, sharp opposition the Brahms party contributed its share to the tardiness with which Bruckner's genius was recognized. But it was not too late, after all. If the Wagner party, on the other hand, had succeeded in their fight against Brahms, his compositions might have been heard really too late and they would then have hardly gained the recognition they won at the time. And so we had better not censure anybody at all but rather be glad the world was given both of these great composers.

There is another fact to prove it was not the opposition of a prejudiced group alone which had brought about the failure of the *Seventh Symphony* in Vienna. The performance of the *Te Deum* in the capital was so great a success for the composer that he did not have to wait so long for its publication. This work, written between September, 1883 and March, 1884, belongs to those Bruckner compositions which aroused audience enthusiasm from the very first performance and have never yet failed. It was first given on May 2, 1885, at a semi-private concert of the Academic Wagner Association. Two pianos substituted for the orchestra. Hans Richter then presented the work at one of his great concerts, on January 10, 1886. The *Te Deum* is one of Bruckner's mightiest compositions, comparable in power of expression with Bach's cantata *Nun ist das Heil.* If any of Bruckner's works can be called popular, this is it.

Richard Wagner evidently enjoyed seeing Bruckner, who could not conceal his deep reverence for the master.

Bruckner had met Wagner for the last time in Bayreuth on the occasion of the first performance of *Parsifal* in 1882.

Wagner had assured him of lasting interest in his work and had given him his benediction, as it were. "He took my hand," Bruckner wrote to a friend, "and said, 'Depend upon me. I shall perform the symphony and all your works.'" Wagner's son, Siegfried, at a later period remarked that his father could not have been speaking seriously, in his opinion. Wagner is said to have addressed Bruckner, occasionally, in a patronizing tone but Bruckner always regarded Wagner with the deepest devotion, sometimes expressed in a peculiar manner. For instance, Wagner's servant told Auer that Bruckner often stood for hours in front of "Wahnfried," staring at the windows. He always carried a black tailcoat over his arm in order to be ready to exchange it for his everyday coat at a moment's notice, should he meet Wagner. When Wagner asked: "Have you seen *Parsifal?*", Bruckner fell on his knees, kissed Wagner's hands, and exclaimed: "Oh, master, I worship you!" Wagner replied: "Do calm yourself, Bruckner. Good night!" "These were the last words the master said to me," Bruckner reported.

The very idea of Bayreuth must have excited Bruckner, for he was always nervous before he even arrived at the station. In 1882 he did not so much as notice a thief at the station who picked 300 florins out of his overcoat. When he came back in 1886, he forgot to wait for the porter to whom he had given his baggage. Greatly alarmed, because his manuscripts were in the bags, he set off in search of the man, who in the meantime had deposited his effects at the police station.

During this visit Cosima Wagner asked Bruckner to play the organ at the funeral services for her father, Franz Liszt, in the Catholic church at Bayreuth. Liszt had displayed a greater interest in the *Seventh Symphony* than in any other of Bruckner's works, although "he never really understood Bruckner's music," according to Auer. Liszt's idealism and altruism are unparalleled in the history of music. When his oratorio *Christus* had been placed on the program for a music festival, he asked that it be omitted in order to give Bruckner a chance to have one of his works performed in its place. Bruckner's *Quintet* and the First and Third Movements of the *Romantic Symphony* consequently had a hearing, before an élite audience composed of musicians and music critics.

Another great satisfaction came Bruckner's way when the Emperor Franz Joseph gave him a decoration on July 9, 1886. In addition, the sovereign promised him a grant of 300 florins a year besides his regular salary. On September 23rd of the same year he enjoyed the highest honor a loyal Austrian citizen could experience when he was given the opportunity of thanking his monarch in person in a private audience. He reiterated his gratitude in 1890 by dedicating the *Eighth Symphony* to His Imperial and Royal Apostolic Majesty.

A very characteristic anecdote has been related in connection with this audience. When the emperor, at the close of the reception, asked Bruckner what special favor he might show him, Bruckner replied: "Would Your Majesty be kind enough to tell Mr. Hanslick not to write such bad criticisms of my work?" Aside from the unrivalled naïveté of this request there is a tragic undercurrent, for these words came from a tortured heart. Hanslick was the Demon in Bruckner's eyes. The composer felt persecuted and was convinced the critic exercised pernicious power over his career. Hanslick was the topic of all his complaints to friends, to pupils, and even to Kathi, his housekeeper. He was actually afraid Hanslick might "annihilate" him.

The reaction of famous musicians to criticisms would be worth a special study as a contribution to the psychology of the artist. Criticisms are, of course, more important to the reproducing artist, the performer, than they are to the creative artist. The latter's supreme judge is time, which survives him and his critics. The reproducing artist, on the other hand, depends on the estimation of his own day, as it were.

Within both groups of musicians are those whose egos are usually hurt by adverse criticism and those whose self-confidence becomes fairly staggering. From personal experience, I know that Max Reger belongs in the latter class. He used to study the articles written about his compositions with meticulous care and then write long letters to his friends, explaining how mistaken the critic was in disliking this or that passage in his works. Time and again he forgot the recipient was not a professional musician and could not follow his arguments in defending a modulation or an instrumental effect. He really did not take it personally but he did use the strongest expressions in attacking his "aggressors," who, of course, never became aware of his defense. It was the people who were unconcerned to whom he tried to prove himself right.

Bruckner, on the other hand, felt that unfavorable criticisms were hurting his career. But he offered no defense. After his many years of concentrated study, he had become so self-confident that he deemed defending his compositions unnecessary. He studied the criticisms as closely as did Reger but drew no conclusions from them. These words of his are very characteristic: "They want me to write in a different way. I could, but I must not. Out of thousands I was given this talent by God, only I. Sometime I will have to give an account of myself. How would the Father in Heaven judge me if I followed others and not Him?"

Whether newspaper criticism is at all necessary has often been questioned. Public criticism, in essence, is only the natural and spontaneous reaction of the audience to the performance offered by the artist. It is democratic in principle. To suppress it, as the totalitarian countries have attempted to do, deprives the public of its natural right of free speech. And suppression is incompatible with the development of art. If we call criticism a reaction, then "Des Helden Widersacher," the second section of Richard Strauss' *Ein Heldenleben*, is a reaction to a reaction. It tells us clearly that the hero cannot escape criticism as an experience in life. Only the fresh and daring spirit of a young genius such as Strauss could express the composer's own belief in this fashion.

* * * * *

Bruckner did not aim only for applause from the public and from the press. He wanted recognition in a more visible form and so he applied to Cambridge University in England for a doctor's degree in music. When this attempt failed, he wrote to the University of Pennsylvania in Philadelphia, saying: "I again venture to request the University of Pennsylvania graciously to accept the dedication of my *Romantic Symphony* . . . and to confer on me the degree of Doctor of Music."

He was then advised to send his application to Cincinnati University, and his hopeless attempt was furthered by a swindler who took advantage of Bruckner's naïveté and drew financial profit from the affair. He did not win the recognition he desired until 1891 and it was the University of Vienna that honored itself by naming him *Doctor Honoris Causa.* On this occasion, the head of the University spoke these memorable words: "I, the Rector Magnificus of the University of Vienna, bow before the former elementary school teacher of Windhaag."

Bruckner felt highly honored by this title and wanted everybody to show it a like respect. Even Kathi, his housekeeper, was to use it in speaking to him about everyday matters. The publisher of the male choruses "O koennt ich Dich begluecken" and "Der Abendhimmel" (1860) gratified his fondest wish by printing on the scores "by Dr. Anton Bruckner." Bruckner expressed his gratitude to the University by dedicating the *First Symphony* to it. In 1890 and 1891 he had thoroughly revised the score, although Levy had written him: "The *First Symphony* is wonderful. It must be printed and played. But I ask you not to change too much, everything is all right as it is, the orchestration too." Revising earlier compositions had become a habit with this indefatigable composer. The second edition of the *Third Symphony* was made in 1876-1877; the third edition in 1888-1889. The *Fourth Symphony* was revised in 1877-1880 and in 1888-1890.

CHAPTER VI

WITH the approach of the last decade of his life, Bruckner was working on his *Eighth Symphony*. Auer called this period "Years of Mastership and the End," in the index of his Bruckner biography. When Bruckner was sixty years old, he was given the title "Master" by one of the most ardent followers and students of his life and works. Auer certainly had no intention of implying, by this statement, that Bruckner's earlier works bore the stamp of immaturity or imperfection. Rather, he was pointing out how slow Bruckner's development was, as we indeed have had occasion to remark. Late in life he finished his studies, and late he started his series of symphonies. He was an old man when he finally began to win the recognition due his genius.

One observer made the perspicacious comment that, generally speaking, we always think of Bruckner as the "old" master. This is as strange as it is true. We know the portraits of Verdi, Wagner, Brahms, and Liszt drawn at the climax of their careers, when they were in the full bloom of their creative years. But the young or middle-aged Bruckner never seems to arouse a real interest. This, again, is peculiar to Bruckner. The Bruckner in his sixties and seventies is the one who impressed the world and is so remembered.

If we want to catch a perfect glimpse of him, we should halt temporarily in our description of his life and watch him in his daily habits and his ways of working – at home, at the Conservatory, and in the University.

Although he was living in a metropolis, he remained aloof and lonesome, for he was a stranger by origin, habits, and spirit. He had come to the capital when he was too old to acclimatize himself to a new environment. Vienna, for her part, felt he was a newcomer with peculiar provincial habits rather than a citizen of her own. He won a popularity of a special kind. His private life, his activities at the Conservatory, his habits, all became the subjects for conversation, disputes, and numerous anecdotes, some of which were only partly true inasmuch as typical Viennese wit and humor had given them shape.

Whenever Bruckner walked the streets of the lovely capital, people would turn around and smile at the peculiar man. He did not notice them. Absorbed in thought, with lifted head, he would walk on, occasionally stopping to take out his notebook and jot down the result of his thought. Yet he seemed no more odd to the Viennese than he had seemed to the residents of the villages where he had spent his earlier years. According to Auer, "he was of good, average size and towered above his contemporaries in art – Wagner, Brahms, and Hugo Wolf. His powerful chest and upright, almost noble, carriage made an imposing impression. His head, with its mighty nose, beardless face, and short-cut blond hair which later turned gray, gave him the look of a Roman emperor."

A member of the glee club in Linz said Bruckner might possibly have looked like a Caesar in the later years of his life but at the time he knew him Bruckner had no such expression at all in his dear, good face. He wore his hair cut so short that many people remembered him as bald. In fact, this habit was very peculiar, for the identifying mark of the musician in those days was his long mane. I remember his haircut impressed me strongly when I met him. Some writers claim he was actually beardless, but in reality he wore a very short moustache, which was almost invisible. These differences in description are very interesting, for they are part of the general uncertainty surrounding his whole personality.

The great painter Fritz von Uhde was deeply impressed by Bruckner's appearance but he could not get the composer to come to his studio to sit for a portrait. He wanted to paint Bruckner as one of Christ's disciples in his picture of The Last Supper. He had to resort to a photograph and paint from that. When Bruckner later saw himself in the picture, he looked at his portrait for a long time and was deeply moved.

At any rate, Bruckner did not look like other musicians of his day. "Only the loose-bound braid on his collar displayed the artist," says Auer. In general, his clothes aroused general curiosity because of their indefinable cut. Was it a peasant's Sunday suit? The short jacket and enormously wide trousers seemed to hint that such was the case. Until his death he had his clothing made by a tailor from St. Florian.

As Bruckner walked along, with the edge of a colored handkerchief hanging out of his pocket, he would fan himself, as he always suffered from the heat, even on chilly days. Holding his hat in his hand, he used to walk so fast that even his young pupils could hardly keep pace with him. He really made a peculiarly rustic appearance in the fashionable city of Vienna.

Bruckner had a two-room apartment on the fourth floor of a typically Viennese house, more spacious than comfortable. After 1877 he paid practically no rent, for his landlord, Oelzelt, was one of his fervent admirers and felt honored in having Anton Bruckner among his tenants. Bruckner's sister Anna kept house for him until her death in 1870. Her successor was Kathi Kachelmayer, who won a certain fame with Bruckner's friends besides the confidence of her employer himself.

The relations between an elderly bachelor and his housekeeper are usually quite amusing if both are rather original characters, as were Bruckner and Kathi. When they clashed over some domestic matter, she would pack up and leave — but she would return the next morning and tell him he ought to be happy she came back, since he would not easily find another woman to put up with his peculiar habits. He loved to take his meals in restaurants with friends or pupils, one of whom was always delegated to see him home at night. Kathi had strict orders as to which visitors to admit and which to keep out. But it often happened that Bruckner would hear the name of a visitor who was refused admittance and would come out of his room and give Kathi the lie direct.

August Stradal, in his *Erinnerungen an Anton Bruckner*, has given us a clear description of the composer's home. It should be better known. He says: "At the beginning of January, 1883, I went up to Bruckner's apartment and became his pupil. He was living in two rooms on the top floor of Number 7, Hessgasse. In the middle of the first room there was a very old Boesendorfer grand piano, and its white keys could scarcely be distinguished from its black keys as a consequence of dust and snuff. Against one wall was an American cottage organ – a pedal harmonium with two manuals. Against another wall there was a bed with a large crucifix hanging above it; and in front of the window stood a little table which was used for writing and, in later years, for dining too. Next to the door and hardly visible was a small washstand. There was nothing in the room except the bare necessities for daily living. The furniture in the apartment was a lesson in renunciation.

"Pieces of music were piled on the piano. I was impressed by the many scores by Bach, Beethoven, Schubert, and Wagner. Bruckner had only two books at that time – the Bible and a biography of Napoleon. The master often studied both of these and he was so well versed in the Scriptures that he was a match for any theologian, as far as knowledge of the Bible was concerned. The master shared Beethoven's enthusiasm for Napoleon, and Beethoven, as is known, had a great admiration for Bonaparte before he became emperor.

"The second room was completely bare of furniture and was not used. But in one corner bundles of criticisms, papers, and letters were lying in a heap. Manuscripts of his symphonies and Masses lay mixed up with newspaper articles and letters from Levy, Nikisch, Richter, and others. Bruckner once asked me to help him find his *Quintet* in the mass of papers.

On this occasion I discovered the manuscript of the only piano composition the master ever wrote. Its name: *Erinnerung* (Souvenir). He gave me the little work when I asked him for it. Unfortunately, he could not remember when he had written it."

Other eye-witnesses have mentioned an ante-chamber with a bathtub and a bust of Bruckner. He sometimes stroked the bust with his hand and said, "Good old fellow." All agree that his room was in terrific disorder. His former teacher Kitzler was actually alarmed when he called. In this respect, at least, Bruckner was something of a Bohemian.

Friedrich Klose, who became Bruckner's pupil in 1886, gives us a similar description of the composer's home. He says clothes as well as music were strewn over the piano. When he used to call on Bruckner at night, the room would be lighted by only two tall candles. The reason for this strictly observed custom was Bruckner's fear of fire. He had seen the terrible conflagration of the Ringtheater in 1881, when hundreds of persons perished in the flames. He had hurried home that evening when he heard the news of the fire, with only one idea in mind – to save his scores, his manuscripts, his only treasures. His home was across the street from the burning building. He became so overwrought he would not stay alone the following night. He had been about to go to the performance on the night of the fire, but had decided not to go when the scheduled program was changed. This was certainly a stroke of good luck for Bruckner, much like that on another occasion when, as he was returning from England, he missed the boat. The ship went down and many passengers were drowned.

The day after the catastrophic fire in Vienna, he went to the mortuary and viewed the charred remains of the victims. This action was in keeping with his strange inclination towards the sensational. He is said to have attended murder trials and to have displayed high tension when the day of the execution of the guilty criminal approached. When the body of the unlucky Maximilian, the murdered emperor of Mexico, was shipped to Vienna, he wrote to Weinwurm from Linz, on January 16, 1868: "I must see the corpse of Maximilian at any cost... please find out if Maximilian's body will be on view in an open coffin or through glass or if the coffin will be closed. Telegraph me the information, lest I arrive too late." When Beethoven's body was removed from the cemetery in Waehring to the Central Cemetery in 1887, Bruckner was present at the gloomy scene and passed his hands over the skull.

Klose mentions four books Bruckner read during the years he visited the composer's home. The first was a history of the Mexican War; the second, an account of a polar expedition; the third, a little illustrated volume of biographies of Haydn, Mozart, and Beethoven; and the fourth, a treatise called *The Miraculous Marie of Lourdes.*

Poor Kathi had reason to despair of Bruckner's disorder, for she was not allowed to touch a thing on his desk or piano. In contrast to these Bohemian traits were Bruckner's parsimony and lack of pretension. In his calendar-diary he meticulously noted down all his expenses. This reminds me of Verdi's housekeeping accounts, which I saw in his home, Sant' Agatha. Up to the last days of his life Verdi put down his expenses and his income with a degree of care that does not fit into the picture of the grand seigneur.

Certainly Kathi enjoyed Bruckner's full confidence and decent respect. He never appeared partially clothed in the morning, even when he was an old man. What a delightful scene it must have been when he came into the kitchen for his morning cup of coffee! He would sit down and talk to Kathi about the happenings of the day before and complain about the malignity of his enemies. Sometimes he would tell her about his harmless little adventures in love. He might, on occasion, ask her to help him in making an appointment with a girl or in getting a gift for a sweetheart.

As we know, all Bruckner's little romances met the same fate: His proposal was refused and he seemed to be the unhappiest man on earth. But soon he would fall in love with another "beauty," who was flattered by the famous composer's attachment. But the "beauty" never returned his affections. "Only once in my life," he told Kathi, "when I was young, did I ever kiss a girl. I have repented it deeply as a sin." The chronicler of this unique story adds nothing further.

Sometimes Kathi would be given a foretaste of the role she would play in stories about Bruckner's life, when he told her: "You will become a historical personage through me." We have not been told how she reacted to such remarks or whether she really was happy in performing her tasks. She was a faithful soul, and she served and nursed the sick composer for many years, up to the time of his death. He bequeathed her a small sum, which the heirs promptly increased. And, after all, she actually did become a historical figure.

At that time Vienna offered most interesting attractions to anyone concerned with cultural matters. There were the imperial theaters, museums, delightful surroundings which had enchanted Beethoven and Schubert, the imperial library, and the opportunity of association with outstanding men of science and art. Bruckner, however, made no use of these opportunities. "Why do you frequent the Burgtheater," he asked Klose, "do you want to become a poet?" Bruckner is said to have attended only one performance at the Burgtheater. It was a Shakespearean drama, and it bored him to death. Anyway, he never went a second time.

In face of these facts, it is surprising to read the following in Kurth's book on Bruckner: "We know he was very much attached to German literature and esteemed the art of acting." Bruckner's chosen texts for his secular vocal compositions do not bear Kurth out. But the composer did attend the performances in the Opera House frequently. And he was seen in the concert halls, in the standing section "while

Brahms sat in his box in the first circles," as jealous writers have emphasized. Bruckner did not mind; he was not associated with the "élite" in Vienna.

He preferred the companionship of his friends and pupils in a modest inn, where *Gemuetlichkeit* was the mood and where polite behavior and fashionable dress were of no consequence. There, at his *Stammtisch** he was lord and king, whom nobody dared oppose. There his sense of humor came into play, sometimes at the expense of his enemies. There he felt carefree and young, and enjoyed life, forgetting trouble, sickness, and even the doctor's diet prescribed when his ailment grew worse. It was extremely hard for him to follow the diet, for he was very fond of Austrian food, good but rather heavy.

One must have lived in Vienna to appreciate what a cozy restaurant means to bachelors. The customer enjoys special privileges; both the host and the waiter vie with each other to satisfy the guest in his individual desires. When Bruckner entered his favorite place, he would tell the waiter: "Bring me three portions of smoked meat with dumplings." And he was sure of getting his favorite dish in ample quantities.

Bruckner always enjoyed good food and plenty of it, as we know from an amusing story of his earlier days: In St. Florian he once played the organ so strangely during the service that the prelate called him at once and asked him, rather resentfully, for an explanation. Bruckner explained that at dinner, since he sat at the foot of the table, he got only the remnants of meat which the others had left. With so little food he could not play better. The prelate promised improvement, and we hear of no further complaints on that score. Bruckner's thirst was as keen as his appetite. He liked Pilsener beer and sometimes drank as many as thirteen mugs at a sitting. He never got drunk, but many observers believe too

* Regular table, habitually reserved for him.

much beer precipitated the attack of his illness. When the doctors forbade all these harmless little pleasures, he complained bitterly. These were the only joys in life the modest fellow had left.

He always had been a lively and good dancer. In his home town he had gone to gatherings and joined in the country dances, maybe to the tunes of Schubert and Beethoven. In Vienna the waltzes of Johann Strauss may have inspired him. He loved this Viennese composer's music as much as did Brahms; and, vice versa, Strauss gave him full recognition as a composer and wired him after the first performance of the *Seventh Symphony*: "I am deeply moved; it was one of the strongest impressions in my life." Bruckner, for his part, is reported to have said: "I like a waltz by Johann Strauss better than a symphony by Brahms."

Bruckner had an original way of speaking in his quaint Upper Austrian dialect. In the German biographies of the composer, his remarks are related in this patois. Wagner, as is well-known, spoke Saxon dialect; Brahms could not conceal the accents of North Germany. But their remarks are not quoted in their own particular idioms. With Bruckner it is different. Transposed into High German, his speech loses the characteristic Bruckner flavor. His steadfast nature, firmly rooted in his homeland, made him use his native dialect to the end of his days.

As a rule, a musician is a good linguist. His sensitivity to phonetics makes him adopt the accent of his environment rather readily. But Bruckner evidently listened only to the voice from within; he did not consciously hear differences in accent or speech. His adherence to his native dialect is to be interpreted as a consequence of the total absorption of his inner ear in music.

Bruckner's style of speaking was straight and simple; he was not given to *bons mots* or remarks sparkling with wit. When he addressed persons in influential positions he spoke with a humility quite incompatible with his rank as musician. He was profuse with "Your Honor," "Your Grace," and the like. He did not realize that Wagner was embarrassed when he told him: "Master, I worship you!" Bruckner used forms of address and expressions of devotion which did not always apply to the person addressed. For instance, he called Brahms "Mr. President." Once, when he met Brahms in a restaurant, he served him with beer, perhaps remembering that Wagner had done the same for him at "Wahnfried." These little traits of character and manners are reminiscent of the time when the young chorister kissed the hands of the canons in St. Florian and when the school teacher addressed his superiors. Official formalism within the hierarchy of the Church and within the monarchy had left inextinguishable traces.

Bruckner meets his dreaded enemy Eduard Hanslick

On the other hand, his naïveté occasionally led him to the other extreme, as evidenced by the following little story: At a party he was introduced to a princess, a member of the German imperial family. He shook her hand vigorously and said,

"I am delighted to meet you. I have heard such nice things about you." Anyone acquainted with the ceremonious formality of a German court can realize what *éclat* this little passage added to the party.

Occasionally he would speak quite differently. He was a "school assistant and a Caesar in one person," as Stradal has expressed it. To a publisher who asked him why his works were not more popular, he answered: "It was the same with Beethoven. Those oxen did not understand him either."

In spite of Bruckner's lack of ready self-expression in speech, he must have cast a spell on his entourage. Bruno Walter has said: "I explain this power of attraction as due to the radiance of his lofty, godly soul, to the splendor of his musical genius, glimmering through his unpretending homeliness. If his presence could hardly be felt as interesting, it was heart-warming, yes, uplifting."

Bruckner's odd way of speaking isolated him, but he had close and rather patriarchic relationships with young people and with his pupils. They constituted a group of equal-minded and equal-ranking men who worked on the prejudiced public and held high the banner of musical progress. Bruckner himself once remarked: "I owe my success to my students. They go around and tell other people about my music."

The picture of Bruckner's relations with his pupils is of heart-stirring character. His pupils repaid him for many things he could not enjoy as did his contemporaries. They are the most immediate sources of information about the man. Their reports are far more reliable than later conjectures and artificial or arbitrary constructions erected by many a wishful thinker.

Bruckner's lectures at the University were somewhat popular in character, since he thought it impossible to teach harmony in one semester. They were well attended, partly by students who were impressed by his prominence and partly by persons who wanted to demonstrate their fealty to the Wagner party. His extreme, even humorous, figures of speech and analogies, with the help of which he illustrated the secrets of chord relationships, were very appealing although quite unusual in the auditorium of a university. Sometimes Bruckner referred to personal matters, such as the attacks he had to endure from Hanslick, and he demonstrated on the piano how right he was and how wrong his opponent. Another time the "Gaudeamus," as he called his students, were the first audience in Vienna to enjoy the music he had been writing when he left his desk for the lecture hall. He played a portion of it for them. Though the atmosphere of the class was sometimes rather too animated, the magic of the genial musician and his good nature soon established the desired mood.

Bruckner's fundamental thesis was "First the rule, then free creation." He started the first lesson by writing one note on the blackboard, saying: "First God made Adam." Then he added the fifth and went on: "He soon gave him Eve, and the two did not remain alone." With that he put down the third. The second was "a poor devil, since nothing is left for him." In order to explain the liberties of single tones which build the dominant seventh, he called the fundamental "the house father, to whom is given the greatest liberty." The seventh was "his wife"; the third, "the little daughter"; and the fifth "Mr. Son, who has more liberty of motion." The diminished chord was characterized as "a poor thing, because of its tight nature." The seventh, if not prepared, became "the aunt, since she drops in unexpectedly!"

As amusing as they sound, these explanations have a certain amount of didactic usefulness. Yet more significant were the characteristics which he ascribed to the different keys and degrees. The tonic chord was called "joyful," the second degree "sad," the third "lyric." The dominant was the "generalissimo." The earmark of F minor was "melancholy," of

F sharp minor "yearning," D minor "solemnity," A minor "smoothness," E minor "lyricism." He also called the tonic chord the Trinity.

These comments on keys, coming from the mouth of a genius, are of course interesting. But their validity, in general, is limited. All minor keys have the same structure, and all major keys have the same structure. There is a difference only in pitch. And this difference is not perceived by the average ear; only the person with absolute pitch will get a definite sensation from a given key. The succession of keys discloses the difference in their characters only by contrast. E major following C major may be sensed as brighter, but it has no different nature in itself. Were this not so, we would have to transpose Bach's music in order to get the sensations corresponding to his own, since, as a matter of fact, the pitch was lower at the time he wrote his compositions than it is now. Certain externals contribute to our alleged feeling for key. D minor seems solemn to us because we think of Beethoven's *Ninth*; A major is sensed as joyful and radiant because of our recollection of Beethoven's *Sixth* and Wagner's *Lohengrin.* But the average listener, *not informed* of the key in which a composition is going to be played, will not feel changed tonality.

At the Conservatory Bruckner's methods met with opposition from his colleagues. Such opposition to progressive musicians was typical of the conservatories and music schools at the time. Their practice was the observance of "tradition." The royal *Hochschule fuer Musik* in Berlin, headed by Joseph Joachim, was steadfast in its opposition to the growing influence of Wagner and Liszt as long as the celebrated violin virtuoso and friend of Brahms was alive. My violin teacher, one of Joachim's pupils and an excellent member of the Philharmonic Orchestra, pursued his master's way. His influence prevented me from getting acquainted with Wagner's works as long as I studied with him.

Bruckner taught the rules of harmony as axioms, without explaining their origin or foundation. He thought three years of study necessary for this course alone. In fact, a pupil not familiar with the foundations of harmonic principles, will need a longer time of training than the student who knows something about their origin and purpose. Bruckner's critical remarks on great composers showed that he placed Bach far above Handel. This is understandable, for Bach's music may be more inspiring for a creative musician, from the point of view of development, than Handel's melodic splendor. Beethoven was his idol as a symphonist and as the composer of the last string quartets and sonatas. He did not know Chopin. And how significant was his remark that the slow movements in Schumann's music do not really have the character of the Adagio.

Observers have reported Bruckner's instruction as more inspiring than useful in practice. But all music instruction is like that. The pupil must add from his own resources that which cannot be taught by anyone.

Bruckner demanded respect and conscientious application from his pupils. Occasionally he spoke to them bluntly and even roughly, but his lovable nature prevented anyone from feeling hurt, with perhaps one or two exceptions. He once noticed a girl among his students. "Are ladies interested in counterpoint now?" he asked. He repeated the question at the following lessons until the girl stayed away. His students remonstrated. On another occasion, when he entered the classroom he noticed a Jewish boy sitting in the front row. He looked at him for a while, put his hand on the boy's head, and asked, almost with compassion: "My dear boy, don't you really believe that the Messiah has already come to earth?"

Though Bruckner's instruction at the Conservatory was thorough, it was his private pupils who felt its full weight. Anyone who wanted to take private lessons had to take a sort of examination. If he passed, Bruckner would suggest he start his study of harmony from the very beginning anyway and advance slowly. His method was based on Sechter's meticulous and casuistic theory. For him Sechter's system was "the expression of the highest logic, consistency, and law, not only of Nature but also of all ethical Being and divine righteousness." A good many years had elapsed since Bruckner had studied with Sechter, years in which the world had become acquainted with Wagner and Liszt, whose compositions were revolutionary, especially in the realm of harmony. Unlimited possibilities seemed to have been disclosed; tonality, modulation, and dissonance had changed their meanings. But in his teaching Bruckner consciously ignored this evolution. He could not even understand how some of his pupils could be devoted to Liszt and to himself at the same time. He demanded full surrender from his students. Those who did surrender were rewarded with his paternal confidence and care. But even so, he remained unyielding in instruction. He followed Sechter's example in asking them not to compose while they were studying with him.

Klose reported he had to make 180 elaborations on one *cantus firmus* and write 300 canons while he was studying with Bruckner. Here is what that eminent musician wrote: "As I very well remember, this method of teaching, which seemingly had nothing to do with music, made me thoughtful at times. It needed all my belief in Bruckner and in his mastery, which had originated in that school, to keep down my rising doubts. It is inconceivable to me that an artist such as he was never thought of criticising the results, which often were questionable." But Klose came to realize that Bruckner considered these strict studies mere preparatory work. "If, later, somebody would come and show me something similar to what we made in school, I would throw him out," he told Klose in his frank, rustic way.

It is interesting to learn from Klose that Bruckner did not practice ear training with his pupils. Nor do we hear of any instruction in rhythms. In this connection his individual conception of "periods" in music deserves our special attention. Bruckner's symphony manuscripts show a characteristic which is unique in the history of music: He wrote the number of bars which were supposed to constitute a period beneath the lowest scored instruments, generally at the bottom of the page. His plan evidently was to form symmetric periods of four or eight measures each. These figures offer a striking, almost puzzling, problem. Why did he subject his imagination to the only coercive stricture of the Classic period which may be considered obsolete? Who had taught him that symmetry is the ideal of the musical period? Kitzler might have made suggestions of this kind, we are told. According to Goellerich, as late as 1877 Bruckner examined the periodic structures of Beethoven's *Third* and *Ninth*.

Did period and symmetry mean the same thing to him? I cannot answer the question. It is difficult to explain because he had had a great deal of experience as a composer of vocal music when he began to write his symphonies. The vocal compositions do not have any reference to symmetrical structure in periods, as do the instrumental pieces. Incidentally, in spite of the efforts of Berlioz, of occasional attempts by Schumann, and of the onslaughts of the younger Stravinsky, music creation is not yet rid of the hampering chains of symmetry.

Klose, although he is mistaken in making German composers alone responsible, is virtually right in his following remark: "Figuring the bars from 1 to 4 proves the German is still in leading-strings as far as his feeling for rhythm is concerned." He points to the theories of Jaques-Dalcroze, who was a pupil of Bruckner too, to indicate the way to freedom.

Bruckner left no visible traces of his teaching in the work of his pupils who became composers. Hugo Wolf traveled his own gifted path; Friedrich Klose displays very few

Bruckner features, and those in slight degree only. Gustav Mahler, often referred to as a Bruckner pupil, never studied with him and can more correctly be called his disciple. But the general influence of Bruckner's personality on the musical development of his numerous pupils can hardly be overrated. Among them, besides those mentioned above, are the outstanding conductors Felix Mottl, late leader of the Munich Opera; Joseph Schalk, who played a great part in progressive musical circles in Vienna; his brother Franz Schalk, for many years conductor of the Imperial Opera House in Vienna and leader of the German productions at the Metropolitan in New York in 1899; and Ferdinand Loewe, the Bruckner conductor *par excellence.* Goellerich, Decsey, Guido Adler, Louis and August Stradal, all of them pupils of Bruckner, enjoyed enviable reputations as musicologists and writers on music.

Although it is true, as Decsey and others have stressed, that the financial necessity of teaching laid a heavy and oppressive burden on Bruckner as a composer, teaching nevertheless gave him great satisfaction. The longer he had to wait for recognition of his works, the more he enjoyed the immediate response of his pupils. Here there was no opposition; here he did not need to fight. Here he sensed the joy of unqualified success.

CHAPTER VII

No PORTRAIT of Bruckner can be drawn without contemplating both the composer and the teacher. If at the beginning of this book I stressed the fact that there was no culminating point in his career, I did not mean that there was no intensification. But this intensification developed inwardly and was not observed by his contemporaries. He himself was not conscious of the realm into which his genius was leading him. His works prove the point better than his peculiar personality. An increasing conciseness and an intensification of expression became noticeable in his creations. How could anyone say Bruckner wrote only one symphony in nine versions? Yet this remark was actually made. No work is better proof to the contrary than the *Eighth Symphony*, which he started writing at the threshold of his old age, in 1885. It would be a mistake to attribute superiority to any of the last three symphonies, which hold a special rank among all Bruckner's works. But as far as its structural perfection is concerned, all of the critics have agreed the *Eighth* is a surprising achievement. Also, the dark timbre at the beginning was quite new for him and differs greatly from the brighter colors in the corresponding movement of the *Seventh*.

We are rather surprised to learn that Bruckner conceived the *Eighth* from images and inner pictures which were anything but somber in character. Listen to the heavy-breathing theme of the Adagio over the dull D flat in the bass. It is unequivocal in the earnestness of its expression. Every conductor of the symphony whom I have heard directs the opening of the Adagio in this manner. Now, many years after I first heard the symphony, I learn that Bruckner told his friends in connection with this deeply moving theme: "There I looked too deeply into the eyes of a girl." Have I been so mistaken all my life? And what about the beginning of the Finale, where the very forces of Nature seem to shake themselves loose? Of this part of the work, Bruckner wrote to Weingartner: "Finale – our emperor had the czar as a visitor at the time, in Olmuetz. Hence, the strings: the Cossacks on horseback. Brass instruments: military music. Trumpets: a flourish when Their Majesties meet." The analyst is completely disarmed!

As strange as Bruckner's interpretations may seem at a glance, they are really easily understood. Everyone who was ever associated with him has testified that his musical concepts never had their origin in poetic ideas, actual facts, or experiences. Descriptive music was foreign to his genius. But the public was in favor of descriptive music, as he knew, and so he tried to fall in line with the trend of the times. Consequently he made programmatic remarks about many of his works. He probably did not take them any too seriously, for he showed no consistency in attributing inspiration both to "the eyes of a girl" and to the "Siegfried theme" in the Adagio of the *Eighth*.

In this connection, there is another Bruckner remark of "explanatory character." It deals with the lyric melody in the Finale of the *Third Symphony*. The wind instruments play a chorale-like theme of serious nature while the violins execute a moving counterpoint of lighter character, called a "polka" by Goellerich. Goellerich tells us that as he and Bruckner were going home one night they heard dance music coming from one of the houses on their way. In the building next door lay the body of a well-known architect. Bruckner turned to him and said: "You see, here in this house they dance, and next door lies a body upon its bier. This is life, what I tried to describe in the last movement of my *Third Symphony*."

Descriptive music is not supposed to set up a riddle. We are not expected to guess what its composer was endeavoring to express. It serves its purpose if, after having read the program, we feel it attains in musical expression the aims set forth in the explanatory notes. But in Bruckner's symphonies we would certainly be confused, were we to take his explanations literally. What we do not feel in music, we do not believe; mere words are not effective. Bruckner's symphonies are "absolute music," if such exists.

Then there is the composer's explanation of the Scherzo in the *Eighth Symphony* as another point in evidence. He called the theme the "German Michael," whom Pitts Sanborn characterized as the "plain, honest, much-enduring (but slow) German." This definition is not complete. "German Michael" in folklore is also loutish and ungainly. Some of these characteristics are in fact noticeable in the Scherzo. Bruckner was so fond of the picture of German Michael that the figure almost attained physical reality in his imagination. One night, after he had left his apartment, he ran back and climbed the three flights of stairs to cover the page on which he had put down the theme of German Michael with a blank piece of paper.

"I must cover Michael," he said, "lest he catch cold. Sleep well, Michael." He made other remarks about his Michael, too, such as "Here Michael wants to sleep but they won't let him alone. . . There he is, taking up the fight against his adversaries and beating them. . . His situation is bad but at the end he will be on top. . . In the Trio Michael looks dreamily over the country." In the Coda of the Finale, where the theme of the Scherzo reappears in the augmentation, German Michael is transformed into the Archangel Michael.

In strange contrast to Bruckner's own explanations are the program notes written by his friend Joseph Schalk for the first performance. Schalk heard the *Prometheus* of Aeschylus in the First Movement, the "Loving Father of All Mankind" in the Adagio, and "Heroism Serving the Godly" in the Finale.

Here, again, we have contradictory explanations, tending to prove that absolute music is subject to widely divergent interpretations. They certainly offer violence to the art but it manages to endure and survive all attacks through the strength of its very nature.

The *Eighth Symphony* is undoubtedly the clearest of all Bruckner symphonies, as far as structure is concerned, and perhaps that is why Brahms gave it his unqualified approval. He had become friendlier towards Bruckner and is reported to have said: "Bruckner is still the greatest living symphonist!"

The score of the *Eighth* was subjected to thorough revision during the years 1888-1890. Surprisingly enough, Herman Levy, the gifted interpreter of the *Seventh Symphony*, could not fully understand the new work. When Bruckner asked him to conduct the first performance, in 1887, he wrote to Joseph Schalk in great embarrassment: "I cannot find my way into the *Eighth* and I do not have enough courage to present it. Give me your help. I myself am helpless." He then recommended the work to the young conductor in Mannheim, Felix von Weingartner, who hesitatingly began to prepare the performance. But a call to the opera house in Berlin ended his preparations, to the benefit of the symphony. Although Mannheim was a music-loving town, it did not have the necessary dignity for so important an event as the première of a Bruckner symphony.

The first performance took place in Vienna on December 12, 1892, with Hans Richter conducting. It was a great success for the composer although it met with the usual opposition from the Brahms party. The hostile critics, however, seem to have been less vehement in tone than in earlier years. They no longer indulged in personal invective, such as "Bruckner composes like a drunkard" and "Bruckner composes only high treason, riots, and the murder of tyrants." Yet Hanslick could not refrain from attacking the conductor, and he wrote: "We doubt whether Hans Richter pleased the audience when he devoted the whole Philharmonic Concert to the Bruckner symphony."

Bruckner had the great satisfaction of seeing the work published, through the financial support of the emperor, at about the time of its first performance. He was very ill then and he had difficulty in obtaining his doctor's permission to attend the concert. He had been suffering from dropsy for several years and the disease was steadily growing worse. His letters during these years are full of complaints about the ailment and especially about the strict diet ordered by the physician.

Failing health forced Bruckner to resign his position at the Conservatory but from 1891 on he received a pension from the institution. Friends raised an additional annual stipend, and the Upper Austrian parliament granted him 400 florins a year. His position at the *Hofkapelle* had never taken much of his time, for his organ playing lacked appeal in the opinion of his superiors, who claimed he did not perform his part in suitable style but dragged in accompaniments instead. He was not allowed to play for the High Mass but largely restricted to service for the Benediction.

A few years before Bruckner had to resign his public activities, he made one of his remarkable applications for a new position. This time it was his last and it was for the position of musical director at the Burgtheater. At this prominent old house, it was a traditional custom for a small orchestral group to present musical selections during intermissions. The performances were naturally of little importance and hardly attractive to a well-known musician. The director of the Burgtheater made inquiries of Bruckner's friends and fortunately was told not to consider hiring a man of the composer's rank.

Why Bruckner applied for the position is impossible to understand, for his financial affairs were not in a poor state at the time. Perhaps the answer to the riddle is that a man who has been poor all his life never feels secure when he is old, even though his situation has improved. Probably this was the case with Bruckner, who had always indiscriminately competed for every vacant position he heard of. The little episode is therefore psychologically significant. Maybe he was thinking less of himself than of his heirs when he tried to secure new sources of income. His will proves he was dissatisfied with the sum he was able to bequeath. The third paragraph of this document contains a moving passage, stating the hope that his brother and sister might be paid better royalties in the future than he had received in the past. "I, myself, during my lifetime, drew hardly any material profit from my works," he wrote.

On the other hand, there were many events during the last years of his life which were surely satisfying for Bruckner. Towns and cities in which he had lived and worked made him an honorary citizen. Societies honored themselves by electing him to membership. His works were being performed with increasing frequency at home and abroad. The *Te Deum* was played in Berlin in 1891 under the direction of Siegfried Ochs. It was a triumphant success. Even Hans von Buelow was pleased with the work. Ochs was the right man for conducting the *Te Deum*, for in some sections it requires theatrical direction. Ochs was one of the most forcibly fervent conductors I ever saw and a past master in producing contrasting effects. He was only faithfully following the score when he insisted on the triple *piano* in a certain passage. Proudly he demonstrated the result of his effort to Bruckner, who was present at the rehearsal. Bruckner seemed to be highly delighted with the rendition but asked to have the passage played just a little louder. Astonished, Ochs complied. "Still a little louder," Bruckner kept saying. He was not satisfied until the passage was finally played *fortissimo*.

Ochs himself told me the story, and, aside from its oddity, it proves that a composer does not always cling to his indications on the score. The actual sound of his music in the hall taught him something different from what he had written at his desk. It was, of course, the most natural thing in the world and should lead those who consider a composer's given directions sacrosanct to revise their opinion. This question will be dealt with later on, when the different editions of Bruckner's works are discussed.

The success of the *Te Deum* brought about a second performance in Berlin, in January, 1894. Karl Muck had presented the *Seventh Symphony* a few days before in the Royal Opera House. Bruckner, enveloped in a woolen cloak, had arrived at the northern capital to receive new, enthusiastic acclaim on the part of the audience. Ochs told a delightful little story about the old master's gratitude, which was so heartfelt that he said he would give every woman in the choir a kiss. He posted himself next to the stairway by which the ladies left the platform and started kissing them, one after the other. After he had demonstrated his thanks eight or nine times, he was approached by a girl whose charms had long since withered. She was making straight for Bruckner to receive her reward when he turned abruptly and loudly proclaimed: "No, this one doesn't appeal to me!" The same evening he proffered Ochs a 20-mark gold piece. When the conductor refused it, he was told to give it to the tympanist.

The occasion at the Royal Opera House was equal to that at the Philharmonic Concert, and Bruckner must have been completely happy in Berlin, when the trumpets and kettledrums played a flourish at his appearance on the platform, from which he looked down at a jubilantly applauding audience. There was another reason for him to like Berlin: While he was staying there in 1891, the chambermaid at his hotel had given him a little love letter telling him she wanted to marry him. At least, that was his version of the affair. One is tempted to assume some overtures on his part. Anyway, he took a great liking to her and had himself introduced to her parents. In January, 1894, his engagement to Ida Buhz was actually celebrated in the Buhz home. He was seventy years old and he would have married the young woman had she acceded to his wishes and become a Catholic convert. He could not buy worldly happiness for himself at the price of "sin." Perhaps we had better say his faith in the Catholic Church saved him from disappointment. Later, in his bitterness, he referred to her as "the Prussian girl." It is rather surprising to learn from Goellerich that Ida was not the last of his flames; yet he remained celibate to the end of his life.

* * * * *

The *Te Deum* was not Bruckner's final choral work. Although he was busy with symphonies, he found time in 1892 to compose several pieces for liturgical service, the last of them being an *a cappella* composition called "Vexilla Regis." In the same year he wrote the ecstatic *Psalm 150* for soprano solo, chorus, and orchestra. The fire and temperament of this work are reminiscent of Verdi's later operas. In 1893 came *Helgoland* for male chorus and orchestra. These compositions were all produced when he was starting the *Ninth Symphony*. He approached this work hesitatingly. "I do not like to begin the *Ninth*," he said. "Beethoven ended his life with his ninth." He felt the same might happen to himself. Gustav Mahler, too, was hesitant about writing his ninth symphony, and for the same reason. He called the work he completed after his eighth symphony *Das Lied von der Erde*. He survived his ninth symphony, which he composed sometime later, only for a short while.

According to Goellerich, the first sketches for Bruckner's *Ninth* date back to 1887. Auer, however, places the initial work on the composition in the year 1891. In that year Bruckner wrote Herman Levy he was going to work on the *Ninth*, in D minor, "most of the themes of which I have already written down." This brief remark is interesting aside from its historical significance, for it tells us how Bruckner set about his work. His starting point was collected thematic material, which he then developed creatively and technically.

In this connection we call to mind what Egon Wellesz, a prominent musician, wrote in *The Musical Quarterly*, Volume 24. He said: "Some composers visualize the architecture of a piece conceived in a moment of creative power and then gradually become aware of the component parts and turn their attention to details. Other composers first of all conceive a theme and then exhaust all the possibilities which the development of the theme suggests." Bruckner belonged to the latter group, says Wellesz, and he is quite right.

The *Ninth Symphony* is the third Bruckner wrote in D minor. "It grieves me," he later told Goellerich, "that I conceived the theme of the *Ninth* in D minor. People will say, 'Obviously Bruckner's Ninth *must* be in the same key as Beethoven's Ninth.' But I cannot discard nor transpose the theme because it appeals to me just the way it is and it looks well in D minor."

These simple words of Bruckner's belie all possible far-fetched explanations of his choice of key. The manuscript sketches show how he gradually gave the main theme the shape in which we know it. The fundamental idea had taken possession of him in D minor from the very outset. He had no ulterior reasons for choosing this particular key, for it was there from the beginning. Once he had accustomed himself to think of the theme in that way, he could no longer change to another. He considered it an integral part of the work. All this, of course, is not to say that he might not have conceived the theme in a different key.

The *Ninth* has been called Bruckner's swan song, as have so many other last works. But the *Ninth*, in truth, deserves the name. It is not the melancholy presentiment of an early death, so clearly expressed by Tschaikowsky in his *Pathetique*, that gives the work this identification. It is something above and beyond that. If the Apocalypse were to be set to music, the First Movement of the *Ninth* could illustrate the austere tale. The Adagio stands for the transfiguration. The earth is left behind, the soul soars toward heaven.* Bruckner himself was deeply moved while he was writing the Coda of the Adagio. He felt what was to come, and he had only one wish in his heart – to complete the Finale. He often prayed God to let him live long enough to finish the work. "If He does not," Bruckner remarked, "then He must take the responsibility for its incompleteness." But he was not granted grace and he did not live to finish the work.

I must confess I am rather glad the symphony suffered this fate, for there is no art expression more sublime than the Adagio. Bruckner repeatedly expressed the wish that the *Te Deum* be substituted for the Finale, should he be disappointed in his hope of finishing the work. I do not think his wish should be respected in this instance. I did respect it for one performance and I later regretted my action.

After Bruckner had given up his activities at the University in 1894, because of ill health, he increasingly lost contact with the world. He would sit at home composing. He did most of his work in the daytime, but occasionally he would get up at night, light two candles, and write down what he had in mind. To Kathi, who remonstrated with him for working at night when his health was so poor, he said: "One must compose when the right idea comes." He was surrounded by quiet, so much so that at times he longed for company. In particular he missed his admirer and pupil Hugo Wolf. It was not an intimate friendship which drew the two geniuses together. The great difference in their ages made intimacy impossible. But Bruckner loved young Wolf and held his music in high esteem. Wolf respectfully reciprocated these feelings. He had written a sensational article on Bruckner, saying, "Bruckner? Who is he? Where does he live? What can he do? You may hear such questions in Vienna, asked by

* This is not to be considered an explanation of the Adagio. The reader who is not familiar with the background of the work need not feel the same way at all.

people who regularly attend the Philharmonic Concerts. . . It is worth your while to pay more attention in the future to this gifted rebel composer. . . It is thoroughly depressing to see this notable man banned from the concert halls! !" At the time, Bruckner was some sixty years old. When Robert Schumann had written his well-known proclamation for Brahms, Brahms was a young man.

Hugo Wolf could not always follow his teacher, as is evidenced by a letter he wrote to a friend in December, 1891, in which he said: "Last Sunday the Philharmonic Orchestra played Bruckner's *First* (revised) *Symphony*. . . except for the Scherzo and some sections of the First Movement I understood not a thing." On the other hand, Bruckner himself wrote Goellerich the same year: "The new (that is, the revised) symphony in D minor is now dear to my heart. Hugo Wolf embraced me after the concert, weeping copiously, and thereby made me and a third artist do the same."

Hugo Wolf, who applied in *Lieder* Wagner's principle of declamation and consonance between word accent and musical stress, might have become an excellent adviser to Bruckner in selecting the texts for his secular vocal compositions. Unfortunately, Bruckner evidently never asked Wolf for suggestions and he himself was totally unable to discriminate between distinguished and ordinary poetry for his vocal compositions.

We do not know whether Bruckner ever talked to Wolf about the opera he was planning to write. Whether his ideas materialized to the point of an actual project is not known. Maybe he would never have thought of opera at all, had it not been for a librettist who asked him to set a text to music. In 1893 Bruckner received a letter from a certain G. Bolle-Hellmund, who was presumably a writer. The name turned out to be a pseudonym for Elizabeth Bolle, who wrote him that the ordinary listener could not understand his symphonies completely, so rich were they in ideas. "Even the well-educated person finds great mystery in them," she continued. "You may say you are not a composer of opera, yet you have the gift for it as surely as Handel, Mozart, Beethoven, and Richard Wagner. In your symphonies there are abundant motives for opera . . . I could give you a text which, in my opinion, would suit you. It is religious in character."

Good old Bruckner answered: "Your magnificent letter shows me you have great genius . . . I would like to do a dramatic work á là *Lohengrin* – romantic, religious, mysterious, and above all, free from all impurities."

Aside from the question as to what is impure in itself, there is hardly a subject which art, especially music, cannot ennoble. First of all, music has a peculiar "veiling" quality which can transform a subject. One need not point to an extreme example, such as the opera *Salome*, which was first rejected because of its "indecent" libretto. Even the opening scene of *Don Juan* might be considered shocking from a moralist's point of view. Yet who could possibly feel shocked when he hears the words wrapped in Mozart's music? Bruckner, however, never entertained such thoughts as these when he considered the question of purity. Impurity to him meant anything that might offend the religious feeling of devout Catholics. The Roman Church has good reasons, indeed, to be proud of this son of hers.

It was Bruckner's good luck that the negotiations with Miss Bolle came to nothing. He was spared the fate of many a composer who is attracted to opera as though drawn by a magnet, be this realm of music ever so foreign to him. Bruckner had an infallible instinct in everything pertaining to his art.

* * * * *

One of the satisfactions which came Bruckner's way during the last years of his life was his joy over any news about performances of his works in the United States. Goellerich stressed this fact in his biography of Bruckner whenever the opportunity presented itself. Performances were certainly rare. The *Fourth Symphony* was the first work performed in America. It was presented by Walter Damrosch at a concert of the New York Symphony Society on December 5, 1885. A performance of the *Third Symphony* took place shortly after in the Metropolitan Opera House in New York under the direction of Anton Seidl. When Bruckner read the criticism in the *New York Tribune*, he said: "America approves of me. I am delighted." The *Seventh* was given in Chicago in 1886, soon after its success in Europe. The *Romantic* followed in 1887 in New York; and Chicago, again alternating with New York, was the scene of the first American performance of the gigantic *Eighth* in 1896. The *Te Deum* was first heard in Cincinnati in 1892 under the baton of Theodore Thomas, 800 singers and 120 orchestra players taking part in it. In a letter, Bruckner emphasized the fact that three orders for the printed scores had arrived from America.

Auer, in mentioning the great success of the *Te Deum*, made the following obtuse remark: "Seven thousand prosaic Americans were transported by the music." This is the way musical life and the love of music in America were reported to us on the Continent. When Bruckner celebrated his seventieth birthday, he was delighted to receive newspaper clippings from his friends in the United States. "I like Americans so much," he once told autograph collectors who had asked him for his signature.

After Bruckner's death, the *Fifth Symphony* had its first American performance in Boston, in 1901. The *Second* was first played in Philadelphia (1902), the *Ninth* in Cincinnati (1904), the *Sixth* in New York (1912), and the *First* in Brooklyn (1938). The *Quintet* was first performed in Chicago (1899), where the *Mass in D Minor* also had its première (1900). The *Mass in E Minor* had its initial presentation in New York in 1900, and the third Mass was played the same year in Cincinnati.

* * * * *

The old master's forces, both physical and mental, were fast fading, yet he continued his work in astonishing fashion. He was relieved of all financial worries during the last year of his life by the Austrian emperor, who furnished him with an apartment in Belvedere Palace. Bruckner moved into it in the summer of 1895. He no longer had to climb three flights of stairs when he came home. He could get outdoors and enjoy the warmth of the sun without taxing his failing strength. With the fading of his mental forces, his religious fervor grew to a religious obsession. He prayed for hours on end and asked his visitors to join him in his prayers.

On New Year's Day, 1896, Bruckner attended a performance of his *Romantic Symphony*, Richter conducting, and on January 18th he witnessed the great success of his *Te Deum*. The last public performance he was able to attend was *The Love Feast of the Apostles* by his beloved master, Richard Wagner. He spent most of his time in an armchair, occasionally rising to try out a chord on the piano and then writing it down with a trembling hand. All his thoughts were on the Finale of the *Ninth*. He started to work on a transition from the Adagio to the *Te Deum* when he felt that the Finale might possibly remain unfinished because of his weakening condition. However, he gave some attention to the last rites which would be performed for him: He asked to have his body embalmed after his death and placed in a coffin with a glass lid over the face. He was given assurance of burial in St. Florian.

A short time before Bruckner's death, Hugo Wolf came to see him but the old master was no longer in full possession of his faculties. Tiptoeing to the half-open door, Wolf watched him for a second. "What he saw there was as peculiar as it was heart-rending. Lying in bed, with face pale and emaciated, gazing at the ceiling with a rapt look, a smile of transfiguration on his face, Bruckner was beating time on the bedspread with his index finger for music which he alone could hear." * Was a rhythm from the Finale pulsing in his mind?

Anton Bruckner arrives in Heaven. Liszt, Wagner and Franz Schubert hurry to cheer the newcomer. Robert Schumann and Weber, though interested in his arrival, seem undecided. Mozart turns back to explain the importance of the event to Beethoven and Haydn. Handel, standing on the organ gallery, holds out his arms as Bach plays a powerful prelude on the organo pieno.

* Konrad Huschke in *Die Allgemeine Musikzeitung*, 1931.

On October 11th, while a chill autumn breeze was blowing, Bruckner passed away.

*   *   *   *   *

The beautiful church in which the funeral services were held was crowded. Wolf was not admitted, for he did not belong to the societies which were taking charge. Brahms waited outside the church for the funeral procession. When asked to enter, he mumbled: "Go ahead – soon it will be my coffin." And so it happened that neither of the two men, kindred in spirit to Bruckner, could pay him their last respects.

Lonely Bruckner had been in life, and in loneliness he left Vienna to rest in his lonely tomb under the organ of the church in St. Florian.

für Kirche und Concerte.
Von den eigentlichen Studien
componirte ich eine Messe
ein Requiem (aus Dankbar-
keit für den + Beamten "Franz
Seiler", der mir im Testamen-
te seinen herrlichen Bösendor-
fer Flügel widmete;)
Männerquartette, Psalmen
etc, Cantaten u.s.w.
Um Hochdeßhalben Gewogen-
heit bittend verharre
ich Euer Hochwohlgeboren
dankschuldigster
A. Bruckner.

Facsimile of signature page from one of Anton Bruckner's letters.

PART II

BRUCKNER IN THE LIGHT OF HIS BIOGRAPHERS

CHAPTER VIII

FORTY-FIVE years have passed since Bruckner died. He had in fact become very old, years before the end of his life. The fading of his mental and physical forces had been a long Coda, though not so sonorous and jubilant as those in his symphonies. This was a dark period for music, with Buelow, Anton Rubinstein, Tschaikowsky, Bruckner, and Brahms dying within one lustrum. Bruckner's death was felt least of all by the world in general. "Only Vienna," says Decsey, "missed the rustic king . . . the figure that had enriched the pageant of the city."

Life had not been kind to him. He had labored hard until death came to give him peace. But there was no peace in the music world around him even then. It was a daring undertaking for great conductors – Nikisch, Loewe, Karl Muck, Franz Schalk, and others – to put a Bruckner symphony on their programs at the time of his death. Their performance meant a risk for the concert management. His friends certainly had as much reason as ever to be preoccupied with the future of his works. His death did not make their task easier. It was not at all sure whether his works would gain a firm foothold in the concert world or continue to be rarities. There were various reasons for this uncertainty. First, to the more conservative concert-goers, Brahms' works were the culmination of symphonic music. Second, new trends in the development of music seemed unfavorable to the popularity of the new absolute music. Richard Strauss' and Debussy's tone-poems pleased the taste of the musical public apparently more than Bruckner's works. And, too, there was Gustav Mahler, whose compositions are more explanatory in character than Bruckner's. The music-minded public was becoming accustomed to program music to an increasing degree.

Mahler's position in this type of music is rather ambiguous. According to his friends, he often wrote program notes on his scores which he cancelled before the music was published. He has sometimes been called "the bashful composer of program music." There was a time when his compositions seemed to be rated higher in public estimation than Bruckner's, but time, the most reliable means of recognizing the true value of new art, has brought about what the most fervent enthusiast could not achieve. It has reconciled the antagonistic contrasts – program music and absolute music. In the end, both were given an equal distinction, and the great masters in each gained higher esteem. Bruckner ranks high among them. Many think him the successor of Beethoven, and some place him above Beethoven as a symphonist.

Almost nothing was known of Bruckner's personality when he passed away. Those who wanted to get information about him had to ask his friends in Vienna, where innumerable anecdotes were circulating. Vienna cannot be let off without censure for having neglected a serious study of Bruckner's personality at the time, for information could have been easily obtained from the persons who were close to him. Strangely enough, the composer's works, which stirred the musical life of Vienna so greatly, did not arouse very much interest in his personality within musical-minded literary circles. As a matter of fact, there was no biography nor any real book on Bruckner when he died. The year before his death Franz Brunner had published a sketch of his life, *Dr. Anton Bruckner, Ein Lebensbild*, which acquaints us with a number of items, valuable because they rest on the contemporary accounts of the author. It was not until 1905 that the first biography was written. This was by Bruckner's former pupil Rudolf Louis. Although the book does not cover all the data in the composer's life, it is distinguished for its unprejudiced and sincere spirit.

Then again there was a long silence, like the frequent general pauses in the symphonies. A few monographs dealing with selected details appeared and Max Morold wrote a biography. In 1919 Ernst Decsey finally wrote his book on Bruckner, in which he depicted the composer in the most individual manner. Although this work is attractive in many respects, it initiated the series of biographies which spell certain dangers for a true understanding of Bruckner's nature. The author was not always in command of his subject but came under its domination time and again. Decsey's personality makes itself felt no less than that of Bruckner, and it raises the book, which deals with art, into the realm of art itself. Max Auer's book seems to me the most reliable of all the biographies, while August Goellerich furnishes the most complete collection of data.

Goellerich holds a particular position in the roster of Bruckner biographers. This unselfish, idealistic man, who dedicated decades to the work he was expected to write, certainly arouses our sympathy. In a letter dated 1885, Bruckner himself addressed him as "My dear biographer," and in 1891 he wrote: "It is a matter of course that you are my duly qualified and authorized biographer." Conscious of the great responsibility, Goellerich started collecting material, made pertinent trips in search of information, possibly from eyewitnesses, and never neglected the seemingly unimportant details which might later serve a purpose. This faithful follower was still busy with research work many, many years after Bruckner was dead. The biography was anxiously awaited, yet Goellerich could not seem to get beyond the stage of "going to write." He was helped by his friend Max Auer, who was also preparing a book on Bruckner. Finally Goellerich died in 1923, leaving bundles and piles of notes but only a very small amount of manuscript actually completed. Out of the nine volumes that comprise the biography, Goellerich actually wrote only the first. But an almost unique friendship and idealistic altruism saved the work. Auer had been waiting for years to publish his own biography of Bruckner, holding off in order not to anticipate his friend's production. He now finished Goellerich's book, regardless of the competition he was creating for his own work. Loyalty to the dead Bruckner inspired him to sacrifice his own interests for the sake of the higher goal. Goellerich's labor had not been in vain, thanks to Auer's magnanimity.

The extent to which both of these writers succumbed to the spell of Bruckner's personality is amazing. Their emotional responses to unfortunate events in his life often strongly affected their writing. They treated him as tenderly as a child in their discussions of his naïveté and helplessness in the face of life; in fact, they apparently tried to make up for all the hardships he had had to endure. Time and again they considered him the innocent victim and they wrote as though their master were able to take note of their defense of him. But one cannot tell with whom they were quarreling. Everyone who regarded Bruckner with a discriminating eye and did not join in their paean became the target of attack and an object for sarcasm or even contempt. Their purposes seem to have been to make us believe Bruckner's personality developed along with his art.

As has been stated several times in this book, one of Bruckner's most distinguishing characteristics was the lack of change in his personality – the man remained as he had always been to the day of his death. Unevenness in an individual's rate of development in personality and in art is frequently found in the history of music, but usually in an order the reverse of that of Bruckner. The general development of personality usually precedes the development of the individual's art. The consciousness of an unattainable goal then creates a tragic situation for the artist. His artistic intellect points at an ideal which his creative power cannot as yet reach.

Bruckner was spared this fate. His musical impulse was never hampered by scruples or doubts on the part of his intellectual powers. He did not formulate principles to observe; he aimed at no goal when he was creating. He listened to the "voice from within." An infallible instinct, which he believed to be God Himself, guided him on his way. Timid and frightened in the face of life, he was resolute, uncoercible, and unyielding in his music. Not even the pitiful first performance of the *Third Symphony* in Vienna disconcerted him. It was less self-consciousness than irresistible urge that pushed him along in a straight line. He wrote his music because he felt the inner need to do so. This is characteristic of the creative genius.

Auer and Goellerich tried to explain Bruckner's music as having its origin in his personal experiences. They tell us his misfortunes in love caused him to write occasional elegiac songs, and his reactions to the sorrows of life found their expression in the melancholy sections of his Masses because he believed these sorrows to be heavenly dispensations. Likewise, happy events were expressed by jubilant melodies in his compositions, they claim. In his explanation of the Adagio of the *Fifth Symphony*, Goellerich goes so far as to say: "What sufferings the creator of the sequences of the skipping seventh must have endured to find this expression!"

I think the matter is somewhat more intricate than the biographers would have us believe. Experiences in life and their reaction through creative imagination do not follow the law of cause and effect in the logical sense. We rather imagine that a composer's reactions to unpleasant experiences are ruled by his resolutions to overcome his depression and to free himself of entangling emotions merely through the power of music. It is time to discard the methods of pseudo-psychological research. They are remnants of the Romantic period and have lost their validity. Music is autochthonous art; it is not bound to render the realities of life.

Ernst Kurth, the well-known musicologist, has given Bruckner's picture the most concentrated colors. He ignores the discrepancy between the composer's personality and work, and sums up all Bruckner's characteristics as "mystic." Kurth claims the Mystic merely sees the outer sphere of intellectual matters and things of the senses. He does not work and live in and with them, but within himself.

I do not agree with Kurth because I do not see how mysticism can be applied to music nowadays. It has turned into a mere religious conception of historical significance. The term can no longer be used to explain the artist's nature. Kurth apparently concludes that Bruckner's intuition was stronger than his intellect. He spreads a dim light about the composer, a light which darkens the open frankness of his nature. Kurth's voluminous book is replete with profound ideas, which deserve special study, but, after all, the Bruckner he portrays is quite different in character from the Bruckner we are familiar with from other sources.

In fact, it is surprising to see that the older the sources the simpler does Bruckner's character appear to be. The reports of the composer's friends and pupils make the following conclusion evident: His music at first seemed to be problematic; only gradually did it become understandable. On the other hand, his character at first seemed to be simple and frank; in the course of time it turned into a problem. What later biographers have made of the man is amazing. They surrounded him with philosophic systems and declared him saint, redeemer, and saviour.

What ecstasy must have gripped Oscar Loerke to make him say: "I have kept silent when I felt nothing but resistance to Bruckner, because I did not want that *transfigured* and *invulnerable* soul to be hurt." * Yet in the same book he admits, "Those who wrote about him were not always the most clear-minded – or they had lost their clarity."

* Oscar Loerke, *Anton Bruckner*, 1938.

PART III

PSYCHIC FORCES BACK OF BRUCKNER'S CREATIVE IMAGINATION

CHAPTER IX

THE true genius has no earthly ancestry. The genealogist may be interested in tracing the ancestry of a great musician, but what does it profit us to read long arguments about whether Bruckner's ancestors originally came from Upper or Lower Austria, whether they had been peasants a longer or a shorter time? The only important fact for us in studying his character is that his grandfather had risen from the peasantry to the position of school teacher. This fact helps us in determining that some of Bruckner's characteristics were family traits. Since we have heard of no musicians in the Bruckner clan, we may say the composer was not directly indebted to his forefathers for his genius.

The Bruckner family can be traced back to the year 1400. The family lineage has been considered estimable enough by a man of Robert Haas's prominence for him to argue as follows: "It is important that Bruckner's pedigree was rooted in one of the most hidden regions of Austria, where the population, German to the backbone, kept itself free from any infusion of foreign blood." Whether any section of the former Austrian Empire, with its common mingling of races and creeds, was kept free from "foreign blood," especially the Slavic, is, of course, open to question. If it was, it is of no moment. Bruckner was certainly a genuine Austrian. He never left his homeland during the first forty years of his life and later only occasionally for short times. He did not go abroad because he did not feel the spell of foreign countries and because even Vienna seemed too large for him, who had spent forty years in the little towns of his provincial homeland. But from his letters we see he entertained the idea of leaving for Mexico or Russia when he thought his fatherland did not care for him. Since none of these projects materialized, he remained in Austria and lived close to his Austrian countrymen. No wonder he remained a typical Austrian and became a "landmark of Vienna," as he was once called.

In the face of these very plain facts, it is rather astonishing to see outstanding writers give his origin as the deciding factor in his compositions. Alfred Einstein in *Das Neue Musiklexikon* says: "As a composer, Bruckner can only be understood as an exponent of his homeland, Upper Austria (as Schubert can be understood only as a Lower Austrian), and from the fact that he was a Catholic." As to the first part of this sentence, I must confess I cannot hear any dialect in Bruckner's music. I rather think one should be amazed that Bruckner, "pure" Upper Austrian, did not write music of local or national character. The only exception to this sweeping statement is in the *Laendler* in some of his Scherzi and Trios. He conceived them, no doubt, in reminiscence of the times when he listened to tunes for the village dances or played them himself on the violin. But whenever they appear in his symphonies, they are striking in character just because they bring in an element foreign to the piece.

We are told that the main theme of the First Movement of the *Sixth Symphony* is similar to an Austrian military theme. Right or wrong, we do not recognize this characteristic. If there is any music we can call "Austrian," it is Schubert's and Johann Strauss' rather than Bruckner's.

When we come to Bruckner's religiousness, it is a different matter. In fact, Kurt Singer says: "Religiosity was the center of his heart. He was seeking God in his music. God Himself was his goal. God meant purification of grief, liberation from chains." These words explain the very meaning of religiousness as expressed in music. We have recognized Bruckner's religious spirit in earlier pages of this book; it was one of his main traits. As he grew up at St. Florian, he was under strong clerical influence. He kept faith with this place beyond death. He liked the company of the canons, and he thought at one time of becoming a priest. He strictly observed all the commandments of his church. Although he was exempted from fasting by his bishop, he rarely made use of the dispensation. When the church chimes rang out for vespers, he used to stop teaching and let his pupils wait while he said his prayers. When he played the organ for special occasions, he first knelt and prayed. *Omnia ad majorem Dei gloriam.* Every composition he wrote was in praise of God, and he dedicated the *Ninth Symphony* to the "good Lord," adding timidly, "if He will accept it." Did the man who had taken so many examinations during his lifetime feel the need of a certificate for admission to Heaven?

Though he was pious, Bruckner never became a pietist. His Catholicism had no asceticism in it. It was, rather, assertive. It did not restrict him. He enjoyed the blessings of the Catholic Church; they made him indulgent. His strong bent toward religion was genuine and naive as that of a child. He did not have the "priestly gesture of Liszt." He never had any scruples or doubts about the commandments of his church nor did he need to explain its doctrines to himself. Haas's assumption that Catholicism left no traces in Bruckner since it was overpowered by his Germanism is hard to understand.

Einstein is more clearly correct when he says that Bruckner was "the greatest and the only true Catholic composer of the nineteenth century." He does not tell us what he means by a "Catholic" composer. The composer of sacred music need not necessarily be a religious man, and even if he is, his music need not necessarily display his feeling. The *Missa da Requiem* by Verdi is not considered in Italy a truly religious composition. Nor is Berlioz's *Requiem.* Neither composition convinces us of a true devoutness on the part of the composer.

The difference between Catholic and Protestant composers becomes evident by a comparison between Bruckner's sacred music and Bach's. The Protestant is in closer communion with the Bible than is the Catholic, who depends upon the priest as intermediary in the interpretation of the Scriptures. The Protestant approaches his subject as a free partner in the association of God and mankind. There is one example which will explain my idea: The duet "Et in unum Deum" in the *Mass in B Minor* is supposed to proclaim, by the canon in unison, the Homoousian doctrine of the perfect likeness of God and Jesus Christ as to their substance. It would be futile to look into Bruckner's Masses for any musical illustration of doctrine, for the Catholic believes without any additions or interpretations on his part.

However, the point of our question is this: How did Bruckner express his deep religious feeling in absolute music, that is, in the symphonies? What feature of religiousness do we hear in these works? What emotion did his religious feeling and his music have in common? Many of the chorales in the symphonies are merely significant on the exterior. But there is no Bruckner symphony which does not have several passages that move us deeply and make us forget all human suffering and woe. Such music has a liberating, redeeming character. We feel transported into "heavenly spaces."* This music could not have been written by a man whose soul had not reached the stage of inner peace and security through the consolation of religion. We never leave a Bruckner symphony excited or oppressed but, rather, alleviated and edified. The Codas in his Finales do not mean "victory," as we have been told again and again, but security and confidence. The audience becomes a congregation. The final cadence works on us like the "Ita missa est" of the priest.

* See Olin Downes in *Musical Masterpieces*, N. Y., 1935.

Only the greatest spirits are accorded so high a power of creative expression.

Was this religiousness of Bruckner's an inborn inclination or was it the result of his great loneliness, a loneliness which made him long for association with God? He was indeed a lonely man. He wanted to be so, because he felt he must be so. In this connection Franz Schalk said: "An immense cleavage separated him from his environment." This isolation was, of course, only psychological. He did not retire from the world in later years because he was embittered but because he was of a retiring nature. His latent genius in his earlier years had estranged him from the world around him. The peasants in the villages had shrugged their shoulders at the foolish man, and even in Vienna the orchestra had laughed when the peculiar composer appeared on the podium for rehearsal. Nowhere did he fit in, nowhere and never. "Bruckner faced the world helplessly – a man born too late." He might just as well have lived his whole life in the first half of the nineteenth century. It sometimes seems unimaginable that he lived almost to the threshold of the twentieth century. And, according to Richard Wetz, he did not display any desire to be in tune with his time.

If this is true, it is even more strange that the works of a man who was "born too late" came too early to light and had to wait so long a time for proper appreciation. Here again we see the discrepancy between the man and his work. After all, it helps explain why he was so solitary. We have a clue to why all his harmless little love affairs ended with the rejection of his proposal. Though Bruckner in his disappointment used to say, "No one likes me," his dejected mood never lasted very long. His love would find a new object. It is doubtful whether he ever really experienced the actual pain of love, which transcends every other feeling, and, more important, whether he ever really came under the influence of a woman. But both of these questions are rather unimportant when compared with the greater question: Why did all these girls refuse him? Why did none of them return his love, and why did none accept him as a husband?

Although Bruckner was not exactly seductive in appearance, his friends considered him quite imposing during the best years of his life. He made enough money to support a modest and economical couple. He would have been a good-natured, faithful husband for the girl lucky enough to be his bride. Why did all the girls he approached refuse him? Women instinctively feel the part they are to play in matrimony. Bruckner was evidently unable to conceal his inner exclusiveness and quite clearly did not long for companionship. Only a high-minded, self-sacrificing woman will share the lot of a man who dedicates every waking hour to his work. We hear of no such woman in Bruckner's life. The girls he loved were simple, primitive souls; they felt the difference in inclination, education, and general interests between themselves and him and were afraid of being tied down to a man who lived on a level foreign to their own. They rejected him because they knew him better than he knew himself.

The man who has no contact with the world forgets its habits, ways, and dress. And so Bruckner turned into the peculiar individual we have described. Still another feature in his portrait can be explained from this point of view – his old-fashioned, unrefined, and devout manner of speech. An individual style of speech and a wide vocabulary are usually the result of association with other people. They develop with daily experience and practice. The man who lacks free association is apt to fall back on fixed phrases and formal figures of speech. They are his bridge to an understanding of the world. The more removed from the world Bruckner felt himself to be, the more he was bound to use those odd turns of speech which sounded so ridiculous when spoken in rustic dialect.

Just as Bruckner kept himself aloof from people, so did he

remain indifferent to all intellectual matters except music. In Wagner's *Gesammtkunstwerk* he heard only the music, a practice which Wagner disapproved of, as he did not like to be considered from this angle alone. Robert Haas has pointed to a striking example of Bruckner's exclusive preoccupation with the musical part of Wagner's works. At the end of a performance of *Die Walkuere*, Bruckner asked: "Why did they burn Brunhild?"

According to report, Bruckner liked to get information on medical subjects from the physicians he met at evening gatherings in the restaurant. This habit has been interpreted as an indication of interest in scientific subjects. Occasional amateurish questions seem to me to show a lack of serious concern for scientific matters. Bruckner's absorption in his own work was so complete that he once refused to listen when his friend Mayfeld played works of other composers on the piano. He was afraid these compositions might divert him from his own work. In fact, his psychic isolation surpassed belief. "He never went to parties; he had no circle of friends like Schubert, no world-shaking projects like Beethoven, no royal friend like Wagner, and no family like Bach." His compelling desire to be alone extended beyond the grave, for, shrinking from the idea of being buried close to others, he asked that his coffin stand isolated. St. Florian respected his wish.

Perhaps Bruckner sometimes suffered from the loneliness he desired and needed, but his music did not. The melodies which move us so deeply are precisely those of the loneliness which never complains but stands by itself and for itself. We feel strongly attracted to the man who was so aloof in his lifetime. Neither religious feeling nor spiritual remoteness, features inherent in Bruckner's character, could have served any specific purpose if it had not been transformed into a psychic force, a resource for his creative power. His immense amount of artistic energy was the factor which brought about the transformation. Helpless he was in facing the realities of life, but towards art he displayed the highest degree of will-power. Nature does not seem to have singled him out in preference to the average musician. He himself did not feel music was his destiny until late in his career. There were junctures in Bruckner's life which arouse apprehension on the part of the observer as to his seeming somnambulism. Nor does the slowness of his development ease the tension until we see him definitely dedicated to music alone.

Bruckner's slowness in development was an ominous factor in his career. First, he had an unusually long row of teachers whose influence might have killed his originality. He asked every one for a certificate. He took more examinations than were required because, uncertain of his own abilities, he wanted them acknowledged by the authorities – and who was not an authority in the eyes of the modest young man? As a mature musician he assumed the yoke of Sechter's instruction, and only after having been "absolved" by Kitzler did he consider himself free for that type of music which was to become his own particular domain. Then at about forty years of age, he felt he must make up for his overlong period of preparation. He wasted no time but rushed straight into work on the symphonies.

Franz Schalk has described Bruckner's development in this way: "Talent bewilders the masses; genius satiates the soul. Talent, so to say, is there from the beginning and it manifests itself. Genius develops slowly and finally overtakes talent, and sucks it up. There has perhaps never been a genius with so little talent as Bruckner."

In fact, as we have remarked earlier, Bruckner's genius did not break forth spontaneously. Without his tenacious and unswerving efforts it would never have come to the surface. The schoolmaster's nature, supposedly hampering to the composer, was a blessing in Bruckner's case. Again we are made aware of the fact that any conclusions we might be entitled to draw from our own experiences prove false when applied to Bruckner. As simple as his character appears to be, just so puzzling is it when examined closely. He had to take the step from sacred music to the symphony if his genius was to become evident. He certainly took it quite unaware of its consequences, following only the power of divination, a gift peculiar to great spirits.

When Bruckner decided to study with Sechter, he had already written a rather large number of vocal compositions, most of them liturgical in character. They show inventive imagination and notable skill. Having grown up as an organist and being experienced in choir work, he mastered this type of music well enough to leave further achievement to natural development and further experience. But his creative impulses imperiously demanded a new way of self-expression. He felt a need to free himself from the limitations imposed by sacred styles. No elements originating outside absolute music, such as texts for Masses or songs, were henceforth to hinder the flow of his ideas. His compositions were to become self-evolving; his imagination, self-kindling.

In our consciousness of Bruckner's precocious and conscientious habits, as far as his art was concerned, we expect to see him gradually passing into the new field of absolute music. In reviewing the list of compositions up to that time in his life, we see no sonatas or other chamber music. This lack is unique in a composer's catalogue of works. If we recall how hesitantly, in spite of his long experience in the sonata form, Brahms approached the symphony, we must admit that Bruckner's step seems to have been an adventurous experiment, an experiment made by courageous resolve. How could he master the difficulties and the problems he would encounter?

In certain respects the composer is the freest of all creative artists. Painting and sculpture have a more or less close reference to Nature or to things actually in existence, even when the creator has not conceived a work of imitation or close fidelity. Mimesis is never the highest type of art. The substance of poetry and literature is the idea which somehow answers logical concepts. The idea gets its shape in language. Elevated speech is a form of expression, and expression requires an object which is to be expressed. The process in music creation is quite different. Beyond the artistic emotion there is no idea which comes into existence sooner than its form. All musical thinking, as soon as it has left the sphere of unconscious inspiration, develops through forms only.* Any melody is certainly a musical idea, but at the same time it is the form of the idea. Music has no substance to be shaped because musical substance and form are not two different things but, rather, two aspects of one essence. The idea of a piece of sculpture is disclosed even in a torso, but take one tone from a musical theme and you will feel that not only the form but the idea itself has been completely altered. Form and content in music should not be so sharply distinguished from each other as they usually are.

A discriminating examination of Bruckner's compositions before and after his lessons with Sechter shows that these technical studies brought about a change in his creative imagination. His mastery of art began to stand for a new type of inventive power. His relentless work on the form of his expression resulted in a general transformation of inspiration. As a further proof of iron will-power are the elaborations of work he had finished years, even decades, earlier, work which he, self-critical as he was, considered in need of revision. It

* See the author's article "Zur Formfrage der Brucknerschen Symphonie" in *Musikblaetter des Anbruch,* November, 1920. In reference to this question I wrote: "The metaphor of musical thinking is the tone. When we think in tones, we are already thinking in a given form. . . Both concepts – content and form – have a considerable field in common, within which they have the same characteristics."

takes firm resolve on the part of a composer to transfer himself back to a period which he has left behind not only from a technical point of view but, most important, from a psychic state. Bruckner revealed true grandeur of soul in deciding to rearrange the score of his *First Symphony*, in C minor, when he had started work on the *Ninth*.

When Wagner changed and enlarged the score of his Bacchanal in *Tannhaeuser* for Paris, he consciously revealed the fact that he was no longer the composer he had been when he wrote the opera in its original form. We feel it in the first measure of the new portion of the score. His ideas on orchestration and harmony had changed. He saw new features in his vision of music. The new manner of using the trumpet and strings had not been familiar to the composer of the original *Tannhaeuser*. The most convincing proof, however, is the chord of the major seventh and ninth, which had entered the mind of the composer of the *Ring* and which substituted for the diminished seventh, profusely used in the original score of *Tannhaeuser*.

When Bruckner revised his partituras, he denied his own development, at least as far as psychic factors are concerned. He kept faith with each one of his "children" when he reshaped them. J. S. Bach once said: "I have had to work hard in my lifetime"; modestly adding, "if a man works as hard as I did, he will accomplish as much." I think Bruckner perhaps worked as hard as the great cantor of Leipzig.

PART IV

BRUCKNER'S WORKS

CHAPTER X

In approaching the section in which I shall explain the main features of the individual compositions, I feel how eloquent the mute baton of the conductor is in comparison with the inadequate resources of musical terminology. Music is the youngest of the sister arts; words are too definite and incisive in dealing with this tender child. Furthermore, there is no book which gives us authoritative criteria for judging music. We have no volume like Lessing's *Laokoon* to point out the border lines between music and the other arts. And so, whenever we talk about music, we are restricted to metaphors, comparisons, figures, and concepts borrowed from other realms.

This paucity of terms should, of course, not serve as a pretext for the use of cheap, hackneyed circumlocutions which are rather apt to efface the true picture. Some writers have given pseudopsychological explanations the air of scientific methods and have elevated the metaphor to the rank of actual definition in the attempt to explain expression in music. One of the analysts of Bruckner's *Te Deum* has tried to make us believe that ascending scales mean "hope, struggle, and yearning"; descending scales, "fear, resentment, and resignation"; the organ point, "courage and perseverance."

Things are especially bad in the symphonic field, where the fiction of a "hero" eternally recurs. This idea, introduced into music by Beethoven's *Eroica*, seems to have fixed itself firmly in analysts' minds. Sometimes the composer himself becomes the hero. He is then credited with drawing a portrait of himself in his symphony. Again and again Beethoven has been depicted as a Titan who did nothing but strive and labor all his life. His symphonies have been regarded as the expression of superhuman combat, and the Mozartean grace in many of his compositions has not even been taken into account.

Bruckner's symphonies have also been subjected to such analyses as "The hero is going to war, battling his foes with supernatural force but in danger of succumbing to a hostile fate, praying for victory, and in the end awarded the final triumph." Bruckner was no hero. His labors were directed towards music, which was not at all inimical to him.

It is worth mentioning that the analysts of *all* nationalities did not insinuate the same amount of bellicose spirit into the symphonies. Some flatter themselves by attributing Bruckner's "heroism" to his race.

I believe it is time definitely to abandon these ways of thinking and modes of criticism. Starting with the work and examining its value according to the norms of music-aesthetics has not brought us any nearer the solution of questions involved in music analysis. After Hanslick published his essay *The Beautiful in Music* we might have expected positive results from aesthetics. Our hope has not been realized. This branch of science has come to a deadlock. All the more does music psychology, so greatly neglected, deserve to be developed. It deals with the effect of music on the listener and investigates the causes. This is mainly the way in which I have gone about examining and explaining Bruckner's works. My experience as a conductor has provided me with a great amount of pertinent material.

THE SYMPHONIES

Bruckner has remained as solitary a figure in the history of music as he was in life. The passing of time has not helped us to assign him a place in the evolution of symphonic music. He had no colleagues, no predecessors nor successors. There are no lines of communication leading to him such as those from Haydn to Beethoven or those from Berlioz to Liszt and Richard Strauss. He started and closed his own era. His art remains unique.

It is more than unique, however. It is eloquent, persuasive, and finally convincing. It is easy to offer criticisms and objections while reading the scores of his symphonies, but as soon as his music is heard in actual sound the picture changes radically. Music is an art to be perceived by the senses, not alone by the one sense of hearing. Bruckner's music is aimless, even thoughtless, but abundant in ideas. It does not tell a story but it speaks to us with a voice and an accent which is his own particular idiom. We not only hear his music, we feel it because it has a heartbeat which affects us. In the end, our objections are silenced.

The structure of Bruckner's symphonies springs from the Classical sonata form. At least, this scheme is carefully observed. The features which are peculiar to Bruckner are the following: first, the heaviest emphasis on the contrast within a movement; second, the introduction of a third theme, which considerably enlarges the dimensions of the work; third, numerous caesuras.

The subsidiary theme derives its inner origin from contrast. Music without contrast is plain in its working; contrast gives it plastic shape. As an organist Bruckner well knew this means of creating an effect. Whether it can be transferred to the symphony to the extent in which he used it will be examined later.

The introduction of an additional secondary theme to the usual single secondary theme contributed to making the movements not only larger but also polymorphic. This item was not absolutely new with Bruckner. Some writers have pointed out that the First Movement of Beethoven's *Third*

Symphony has three themes too. I do not agree with them. The question arises, What is a "theme"? It has often been assumed that the development section proves what is a "theme" in the exposition and what is not a "theme." But in the Classical sonata we can even see episodes recapitulated and developed. So this assumption cannot be the true criterion.

To answer the question one should rid himself of formal concepts and examine the expressiveness of the various factors which build the structural material of a movement. Following this method, it is easy to see that there are some melody-like turns which cannot be brought into a ratio of expression with the main theme. In this instance, there is no theme but merely a melodic continuation and no more. From such a point of view, the First Movement of the *Eroica* offers quite a different aspect as to the number of themes, and this may consequently be one of the reasons why Beethoven succeeded in giving the movement its incomparable concentration and cohesion.

Bruckner spared us any doubts about what is to be considered a theme and what an incidental element.* The caesuras in his symphonies give a clear answer to the question. In most instances it is the general rest which quite definitely tells us when to expect a new theme. These pauses had been employed very rarely in symphonic music prior to Bruckner. They are highly effective and have been widely used for dramatic purposes by opera composers. Recall Wotan's words: "*Weisst Du was Wotan will?*" (Hear thou, what Wotan wills), and you will feel no music can impress you more than the ensuing silence at this point.

The general pause may also be part of a rhythm. In this

* Philip Hale, however, has noted the fact that analysts of Bruckner's *Eighth Symphony* have not been in unanimous agreement on this question. See *Boston Symphony Programme Notes, 1936*, by Philip Hale.

instance it works in us like inaudible music because we feel the rhythm pulsing on, and the sensation deceives us in regard to the actual acoustical silence. Bruckner certainly had no insight into these differences when he naively remarked that Beethoven's *Fifth* began with a general rest. He used the pauses as dividing elements as well as a means of surprise. His explanation to Nikisch, "You must take a new breath when you intend to say something important," proves how unconscious he was of the effect of his own music. His explanation conceals more than it reveals.

What is actually new in Bruckner's symphonies is the amplification of the exposition, wherein the two subsidiary themes are given their own development to such an extent that one would better speak of two *subsidiary sections* within the exposition. Sometimes one or the other of these subsidiary sections is of longer duration than the first portion. Then, perhaps, the listener's recollection of the first theme may begin to fade, especially when the secondary theme is very expressive. One is consequently tempted to assume that Bruckner intended to co-ordinate the three themes in the degree of their significance and meaning. As a result, the movement gains in weight and requires the utmost concentration on the part of the members of the audience if they are to be properly oriented.

For the conductor the question arises whether to help the listeners along by differentiating between the expressive powers of the various themes or to follow the composer's indications strictly, even if these do not reveal the slightest hint of variety in expression.

Nikisch was undoubtedly the most imaginative of all Bruckner interpreters. Under his baton the compositions seemed to be re-born and not reproduced. But Muck was the most faithful. His renditions of the scores were always full of life. He accomplished this, in my opinion, by his unyielding attitude towards any sentimentality. He wasted no time, although he never hurried the tempi. The general rests seemed shorter than they customarily were. His productions of Bruckner's symphonies were the most clear-cut I ever heard.

THE FIRST MOVEMENT

There is an inexhaustible variety of expression in the main themes of Bruckner's symphonies. Writers on musical subjects have studied and probed them and arrived at widely differing explanations. Some of the themes have been called "Nature" themes, and in support of this assertion the intervals of the fifth and the eighth, which are their constituent elements, have been pointed out. I have no argument to oppose this idea, for somehow it suits our feelings, but I do not see how the term helps us to a better understanding. As a matter of fact, the opening theme of the *Romantic* justifies the appellation. But the first theme of the *Third* does not warrant it, in spite of the fifth and the octave at its beginning, because of the structure of its ending. Intervals determine the nature of a theme to a far smaller extent than does the rhythm, which becomes the "motor" factor in its evolution.

Examining the form of a theme is more important in understanding the architectonics of a movement than is any classification of its nature. Two types of themes are discernible in Bruckner's symphonies: first, the themes sharply marked in shape. They are four, eight, or more measures long and end with a cadence. Such are the themes of the *Third*, *Fifth*, *Seventh*, and *Ninth*. Second are the themes which are more like motives in meaning, not only because they are of shorter length but also because they are not ended in shape. To this type belong the themes of the *First* (C Minor), *Second*, *Fourth*, *Sixth*, and *Eighth*. They are not finished by a cadence and need immediate continuation.

Consequently they are the very nucleus for further development and prove to be useful at least for the continuity of the exposition. Each cadence signifies an ending after which a new start is to follow. In the case of Bruckner, this often means a caesura or general pause, which is avoided in those themes which require a continuation in the melodic flow.

As a rule, the first of the subsidiary themes is lyric in character. Here the well-known "Bruckner rhythm" often makes its appearance, a rhythm built up by two fourths and a triplet of quarter notes, or *vice versa*. You find it in the *Third*, *Seventh*, *Eighth*, *Ninth*. The second subsidiary theme is merely rhythmic in meaning and it is in contrast to the foregoing. It serves the purpose of re-establishing the original motion, which was gradually decreasing in the second section.

For the development of the theme in the following part, Bruckner employed, in the main, augmentation, diminution, inversion, stretto, and combinations of the different themes.

Most remarkable is the fact that the themes almost never undergo essential alterations of their nature and substance. New counterpoints added to the theme leave it virtually unchanged. For this reason Bruckner's ways of developing a theme differ fundamentally from those of Beethoven. Bruckner loved his melodies and kept faith with them – a very Brucknerian feature. Consequently he could not bring himself to deprive them of their true nature and original form.

The recapitulation in a Bruckner symphony is an almost literal repetition of the first section with transpositions into the pertinent keys. At first, the development does not seem to have gained any inner result. The gathered forces reappear separately. The Coda, which is extended at length as a rule, develops upon an organ point or a *basso ostinato*. The Coda's unmistakable origin is the Coda of the First Movement of Beethoven's *Ninth*. Bruckner was not the only composer to make that idea of Beethoven's his own.

Anton Bruckner

The Adagio

The Adagio is the very core of Bruckner's symphonies. He was often called the "Adagio Composer" *par excellence* and he was proud of the title. He was conscious of the fact that few of his fellow composers were able to write a slow movement such as his. The idea of "difficulty" in writing a true Adagio is traditional. It has been given substantial support by the assertion that melodic invention unfolds itself more clearly in a slow movement than in an Allegro, where motion, rhythm, and other factors can be substituted for sheer melody. A singing melody has always been the lodestar for musicians, and Bruckner was its ideal composer.

Three structural ideas are noticeable in the Adagios: first, the well-known scheme ABA; second, the recapitulation form; and third, the variation. The last two forms appear united in some of the slow movements. As a rule, the variation does not affect the substance of the theme nor its outlines for reasons mentioned in the discussion of the development section. The counterparts, by the changing treatment they undergo, throw varying lights on the theme. This action is the very purpose of counterpoint. The well-maintained shape of the theme in a Bruckner Adagio admits the application of the term "variation" to about the same extent as it is used in a Chaconne.

The name "Adagio Composer" was given to Bruckner in a more extended sense than one at first realizes. There is, in fact, some justification for applying the name to Bruckner. But it is questionable whether it is the tempi which actually bring about an effect of slowness on the listener. Generally speaking, one might say it is the beat which decides whether a theme is slow or fast in its nature. Yet, besides the tempo, there is another factor of importance and that is *motion*. The motion occasionally exceeds the tempo so much that it makes the listener forget the fundamental tempo of the movement in question. This phenomenon is easily explained by the psychological fact that the last impression prevails over the preceding impression, especially in a temporal art such as music. This reaction becomes evident in the variations of an Adagio at the very moment when the motion increases so strongly that the slow nature of the music is changed although the tempo keeps on. There are many examples of this phenomenon in Classical Adagios.

Vice versa, a Bruckner Allegro may have a fairly fast beat while the inherent motion often gives the theme a slow expression. The First Movement of the *Fifth* and the Fourth Movement of the *Sixth* and the *Seventh* are outspokenly Allegro in character. Bruckner must have felt an Adagio following an Allegro of the above-mentioned nature insufficiently contrasting in tempo, and this feeling was evidently the reason why he placed the Scherzo right after the First Movement, and the Adagio in the third place in the *Eighth* and *Ninth Symphonies.*

The Scherzo

A Bruckner Scherzo is the easiest of the four movements for the average listener to understand. The themes are based on a clear-cut rhythm, their form is concise, the orchestration fascinating. The conception of dance-form is left behind. The spiritual birthplace is the Scherzo from Beethoven's *Ninth.* One may say that in the Scherzi Beethoven found his peer in Bruckner. Nor is it an exaggeration to speak of an evolution in the sense of development to a higher organism in connection with the Bruckner Scherzo. The chief characteristic is irresistible impetus. Here the composer appears in a new light. There is no longer a gathering of forces, as needed for the development; there is concentrated force from the outset. As soon as it is let loose, it gains quickly in volume and power. Contrast is put back for the sake of mere dynamic development. The steady re-exhibition of the same thematic idea serves the purpose of attaining the summit of expression by a gigantic crescendo. The continuing re-inforcement of the tone volume affects the listener almost physically. The last and lasting impression is that of an immense and threatening increase.

The abused expression "titanic strength" is not out of place here. Even the picture of "rushing centaurs" to illustrate the Scherzo of the *Ninth* somehow fits the nature of this movement. But it is a tendential alteration of the master's portrait to consider his archforce, as some recent biographers have, "Teutonic paganism overpowering his Catholicism." Hanslick's invectives could not have hurt Bruckner so much as these far-fetched contemplations.

The Scherzo of the *Sixth Symphony* diverges from the regular type in its expression, while the Scherzo of the *Eighth* differs in tempo only.

The contrasting element within the Scherzo is the Trio with the cheerful *Laendler*. The harmlessness of the melody is time and again even too sharply contrasting to the weight of the Scherzo.

THE FINALE

The Bruckner Finale has often been the topic of arguments, explanations, and attacks even on the part of those who numbered themselves among Bruckner's followers. "After having said all that can be said, the ineffable is to be uttered. A closing movement is supposed to summarize the contents of the preceding movements and, in addition, to surpass them." Since the first Bruckner biographer, Rudolf Louis, wrote these illuminating words at the beginning of the century, much has been written about the problem "The

Finale in Bruckner's Symphonies." The dimension of the Finale is not the point at issue but, rather, its difference from the traditional final movement. With the opening of the Finale, a new symphony seems to begin within the frame of the larger symphony. It has its own existence. It brings about a new tension, new questioning, and new efforts before the assertive and bright Coda appears.

Stress on the last part of a symphony is a trait of Romanticism. It is not noticeable in Mozart's symphonies nor in Beethoven's first four. In them, reference to the foregoing movements is made by an expression which has the conclusion as its goal. Both themes and tempo contribute to this purpose. The Coda is merely formal in nature. No attempt is made to move "the center of gravity" to the Finale. Those works come to an obvious close as soon as everything the composer wished to express has been uttered – no sooner and no later. In Romantic music the composer's need for individual self-expression prevails over established norms set for form. The composer of the Romantic period, Bruckner in particular, seemed to resent parting with his work. When he started the Finale, he discovered ideas and feelings he had left unexpressed. His self-abandonment then protracted the end. An increased store of expression is saved for the Coda, which is not placed at the natural end but, rather, at the zenith of a climactic curve.

The autonomous spirit of the Finale is typical of Bruckner's works. In some of the symphonies he attempted to bring the Fourth Movement into close relationship with the preceding movements by recapitulating their main themes. We do not feel their reappearance was always motivated from within. Moreover, this thematic review usually takes place too late to give the Finale as a whole the characteristic "ending" touch.

In spite of his many peculiarities, Bruckner retained the fundamental Classical conception of form. The last question to come to mind in this connection, "How did it happen that Bruckner did not create a specific form, a form which would be adequate for what he wanted to express?" can be answered by the very nature of his character, as we have described it. He would never have ventured to break with traditions hallowed by his predecessors. Incidentally, he thereby gave the lie to his venerated Richard Wagner, who had said the symphony no longer had a right to existence after Beethoven's *Ninth.*

THE ORCHESTRATION

Bruckner's orchestra technique, as displayed in his symphonies, is very peculiar. First, it must be emphasized that the scores show no mark of the virtuoso. There is hardly any movement which owes its effectiveness to crafty elaboration, exterior *élan*, or virtuoso passages. The lines in a Bruckner partitura, as they offer themselves to the eye of the reader, are straight and form a picture of somewhat archaic charm. But our ears hear something different from what our eyes see. The orchestration is so nearly perfect that only natural intuition could have brought it about. It could not have been learned. Bruckner did not orchestrate his ideas; they emerged from the spirit of the instruments which make them known. This characteristic distinguishes him from those composers who, so to say, conceive the bare idea and dress it later in fitting garments. It has often been said that Schumann's orchestra scores are "orchestrated piano music," and not even Brahms' symphonies have fully escaped similar criticism. The instrumental mode of expression in Bruckner's music is always adequate for his inspiration. No other instrument can express the particular idea so well as the one which actually plays it.

Bruckner introduced a new feature in the symphony when

he made use of the four Wagner tubas in his last three symphonies. New, too, was his frequent employment of the soft tremolo in the opening bars of the First Movement. Its birthplace was the beginning of Beethoven's *Ninth*, from where Wagner's tremolo also derived.

Bruckner's scores, as far as the orchestra players are concerned, are of average technical difficulty. Technical difficulties could not have been the reason why the players declared the symphonies "unplayable," as they did with some of the first. But his work took and still takes players who are musically well-trained and who have a stock of divination sufficient to enable them to perform what they cannot be told.

Bruckner's Harmony

As a result of Sechter's method and his own experience in sacred music, Bruckner had the cadence as a main factor in his harmonic endowment. The cadence rules the succession of degrees with unsurpassed clarity and consistency. The most daring modulations develop upon the cadence as their fundamental. In addition, the cadence is a sort of link between two sections or a transition to the Coda. Then it appears unveiled, working through the mere splendor of solemn harmonies. These cadences are sometimes mistaken for chorales, a novelty introduced into instrumental music by Bruckner. In these chorales he seems to be looking back at the shores he left behind. Their impressive power is so immediate that, were the words not missing, the audience would sing them.

Chains of harmonic sequences are another Bruckner characteristic. They sometimes extend over long stretches and show peculiar tone colors, especially when they are played by the woodwinds in the low registers. The somewhat sweet, free suspended tones on the heavy beats are of rare occurrence, whereas the regular suspension is fully in accord with the Bruckner style. The diminished seventh in its authentic form and the augmented chords which Wagner and Liszt used abundantly are rare in a Bruckner work.

Very remarkable and certainly striking in effect when they first appeared are the modulating main themes, which seem to lead us far from the starting point but soon find their way back to the tonic or related keys.

The organ point is very important in Bruckner's harmony. It also serves structural purposes and in that capacity it occasionally affects the natural action of the work by its retaining force. There are pedal points, on the other hand, which heighten a growing tension and create an overpowering impression. The potentialities of the holding notes in the upper and inner parts have not been fully evaluated.

Oddly enough, the master of cadences no longer laid stress on them once the Coda was reached. After a long organ point on the tonic, the listener anxiously waits for the last reconfirming cadence. But it does not reappear or it passes quickly and is not noticed, leaving the listener surprised by the end of the movement, which, after all, is quite unexpected.

BRUCKNER'S COUNTERPOINT

"The counterpoint must always sound well," Bruckner told his pupils, according to Mr. Gallico, now a resident of New York City. Bruckner's counterpoint is the kind which we usually call "harmonic counterpoint." Features of Palestrina's style in church modes are also rare. Strong harmonic feeling does not leave simultaneous sounds to the coincidence of melodically progressing parts. The vertical idea prevails in Bruckner's symphonies. A few exceptions can be found; for instance, at the end of the *Fifth*, where the chorale is played for the very last time and the horizontal lines "cross" each other.

Bruckner completely mastered every technical means of contrapuntal development – augmentation, diminution, stretto and inversion. He used them largely. The last, unfinished movement of the *Ninth* was planned as a fugue. Its subject, as displayed in the sketches, was one of his most wonderful inspirations.

Bruckner's Polyphony

Bruckner's polyphony was not the result of combinations assiduously ferreted out. It was, rather, inherent in his nature. The effect of polyphony is the veritable mystery of music. We cannot imagine music exerting its spell without polyphony. On the other hand, there is no reason to overrate it or to minimize homophony, as is often done. Academicians have tried to persuade us that polyphony ranks higher in music, but the final criterion of any art is its ability to express itself in convincing terms by its own specific means. Polyphony is merely one of these means. Some writers have considered polyphony as representing "ethics" in music. From their point of view, Berlioz, Verdi, and others are to be ranked lower in esteem because they preferred the homophonic style. To answer fairly the question which arises at this point, one must take into consideration the relationship between means and result. In the operas of his middle period, Verdi wrote melodies which owe their overwhelming expression exactly to their simplicity, a simplicity so utter as to be almost poor. But the least "arrangements" of these scores would immediately deprive the melodies of the magic of primitiveness.

On the other hand, it spells "misproportion" to muster strong forces and then fail to reach the expected high, soaring flight. Bruckner's powerful climaxes demonstrate this danger *ad oculos*. Though they bring in the culmination, this point is abandoned so quickly that the time of preparation (climax) and the duration of the reached stage (culmination) are not always in proportion. This gives rise to a slight disappointment on the part of the listener. But he is soon repaid by a new inspiration from the overflowing imagination of this genius.

CHAPTER XI

FIRST STEPS IN THE SYMPHONIC FIELD

Symphony in F Minor

When Bruckner ventured to compose his very first symphony in F minor, he had already had some experience in writing orchestral music. Several of his sacred works have orchestra accompaniments, and in 1862 he had written *Drei Orchester Saetze* (Three Movements for Orchestra), following it up with his *Overture in G Minor* in 1863. Certain passages in this last-named composition make the connoisseur prick up his ears. Nobody but Bruckner could have written them. In the same year, 1863, while still studying with Kitzler, he composed the *Symphony in F Minor*. This is the work to which Kitzler did not attribute any "special inspiration." He even told the composer that the key of F minor was not very appropriate for orchestra. The reasons for this assertion remain an impenetrable secret, to my way of thinking.

The orchestra score of the *Symphony in F Minor* has not been published, but the piano arrangement as found in Goellerich's biography displays more interesting features than one would expect after reading Kitzler's statement. There is one item which is remarkable: The symmetry of periods is not yet developed to the extent shown in the later works. Was it opposition to Kitzler that made Bruckner disregard his advice in this respect? Summarizing the general tone of the symphony, one may say it is eclectic in character. The Finale has the freshness and some of the rhythm of Schumann's early compositions.

ANTON BRUCKNER

SYMPHONY NO. O

The next in the series of Bruckner's symphonic works is a unique item perhaps no less interesting to the musicologist than to the music lover. It must be catalogued as No. O. Bruckner himself wanted it so. It seems that he had forgotten this work when, by a mere coincidence, it came to light in 1895. During the packing-up preparatory to moving to Belvedere, the manuscript was found in a bundle of old dusty music. Apparently Bruckner was not very happy over the discovery, for he hastened to write on the first page: "Symphony No. O not at all valid (only an attempt)." Surely these words mean that Bruckner wished this work to be disregarded because he could no longer revise it as he had revised other symphonies. He was absorbed at the time with work on his *Ninth*, and so he tried to suppress this symphony by labeling it "No. O."

The discussion as to its date of composition is not yet closed. Auer sets 1863 as the date and I am inclined to agree with him. Josef V. Woess, its first editor, assumes it was 1869, a date which would place it after the *Symphony in C Minor*. A study of the score, it seems to me, would help decide the date better than any amount of research work. The score, at least in part, is not up to the level of the *First* in C minor. Although it is interesting aside from historical reasons, it bears the stamp "not finished." The very beginning is peculiar and surprising to anyone familiar with Bruckner's music. A *basso ostinato* is the foundation upon which the violins bring a moving figure of introductory character. It sounds like a counterpart to a theme, a counterpart such as Bruckner used in other symphonies. But the theme never appears. Bruckner without a main theme? Utterly unlikely – but it is so. I mention this detail in order to show the improvisatory character of the beginning, which is not devoid of great originality. The extended cadences which interrupt the movement are a significant premonition of this genuine Brucknerian characteristic. They are found in the later works.

The second theme is unusual for its syncopated rhythm, a rarity in a Bruckner creation. A second subsidiary theme in embryo is not so important here as it is in corresponding places in later works. The Bruckner power is already evident but the proportions are smaller than they are later on.

The Andante is somewhat Classical in fragrance and conciseness. The abandonment in the melody, chanted by the violins, is remarkable. The Scherzo is full of Bruckner life and strength, and it leaves only a little for later development. The Finale starts *moderato* (andante) and, like the last movement of the *Fifth*, it does not begin with the main tempo. Its principal theme has a typical Bruckner trait: the large interval skip. Here it is the diminished tenth, taken from the chord of the Neapolitan Sixth, and it gives the theme a resolute ending. The composer loved this harmonic progression and used it abundantly in his works.

It is interesting to encounter a number of motives which are only intimated in this symphony and are again taken up and clearly stated in the later symphonies. The work was presented for the very first time in Vienna in 1924.

CHAPTER XII

THE NINE SYMPHONIES

First Symphony, in C Minor

This work has one characteristic for which we must love it: marked youthful freshness. Who could object to a few unrefined passages in orchestration and odd harmonic progressions in a work that shows such a wealth of creative imagination and genuine temperament as this symphony shows? The number of structural ideas is amazing, ideas which nevermore left the mind of their creator but, rather, became musical assets of a sort, usable and actually used in his later creations. Starting with the *First Symphony*, some of these ideas run like directing lines throughout all the other symphonies. Here appears for the first time, although in embryo, the second subsidiary theme and certain rhythmical concepts which we meet again later. Here we already find the leap of the octave, its enlargement to the ninth and the tenth (the former receiving its last consecration in the Adagio of the *Ninth*). We meet here, too, the numerous caesuras and general rests, the solemnly starting Coda in the Finale. And here we receive a premonition of the task which will later be assigned to the trumpets and the low woodwinds. In fact, Bruckner's imagination was replete with creative ideas when he resolved to release them through symphonies.

I. Allegro molto moderato

The youthful nature of the *First Symphony* is especially in evidence in the First Movement. Only gradually does the composer yield to the customary sonata scheme and then only after he has expressed in a very unconventional manner what was close to his heart. The greatly admired improviser at the organ is revived in the exposition of the movement.

The initial theme belongs to that group of themes which are "not ended in shape." (See page 166.)

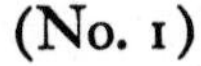
(No. 1)

It develops upon a steady and equal motion of 4/4, which gives the beginning the character of a march. It is the sort of motion we meet later in Gustav Mahler's symphonies. The dotted rhythm of the theme is to play a prominent part in most of the other eight symphonies. Here, in the *First*, the dot is replaced by a sixteenth rest. The passing notes and free suspensions bring about peculiar frictions, especially when the tone of resolution is heard at the same time in another part. On the other hand, they give rise to daring and unusual harmonic associations.

At the end of the first short climax, the leap of the octave appears in the strings, followed by boisterous sextuplets.

(No. 2)

Woodwinds perform the transition to the lyric melody in the related key of E flat major.

(No. 3)

We meet the fundamental idea of this theme again in the First Movement of the *Ninth*.

The "rhythmical motive" makes its first appearance in Bruckner's symphonic works in the flutes, oboes, and clarinets.

(No. 4)

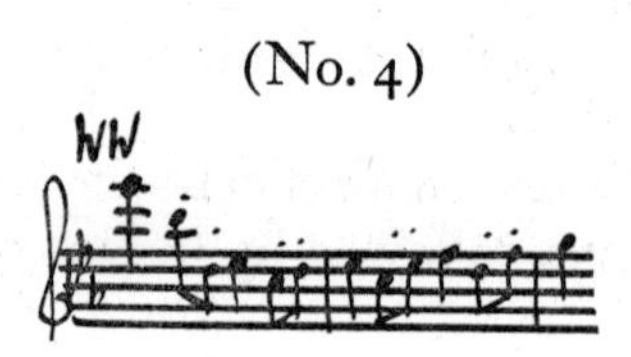

The counterpoint in the horns has an incidental meaning. Thereupon, instead of the expected episode, a new theme follows in the trumpets and trombones, surrounded by roaring thirty-seconds in the violins and violas.

(No. 5)

Here our self-orientation temporarily deserts us; we are in No Man's Land. But we are not alone. Life is around us. The working-out section parts hesitatingly from this realm of the composer's self-abandonment. First the main theme is drawn together with the sextuplet rhythm, the latter gradually prevailing. The development ends *pianissimo* on a tympani roll which has the actual significance of a general standstill.

The recapitulation receives its distinguishing characteristic from the weight of the trumpets and the trombones especially. The last version of the score at some junctures exhibits the hand of the master who was to write the *Ninth*. The crowning part of this section is interrupted by a long hold in the trumpets alone. After two soft phrases performed by flutes and violoncelli there is a new stop. Then the violins and woodwinds take up the main rhythm, but after the first phrase of the principal theme there is a third caesura. Finally the orchestra rushes, in one breath, to the agitated end.

II. *Adagio*

At the beginning of this movement the composer of the famous Adagio melodies does not yet show himself. Rather, he starts with a climax marked by dark tints and strange progressions. Here, once more, the improviser is at work. He is in a creative mood and therefore he creates first the atmosphere in which his melodic structures are later to live. He is confident his imaginative power will not desert him when he needs it.

Here is what we have in place of a Bruckner melody:

(No. 6)

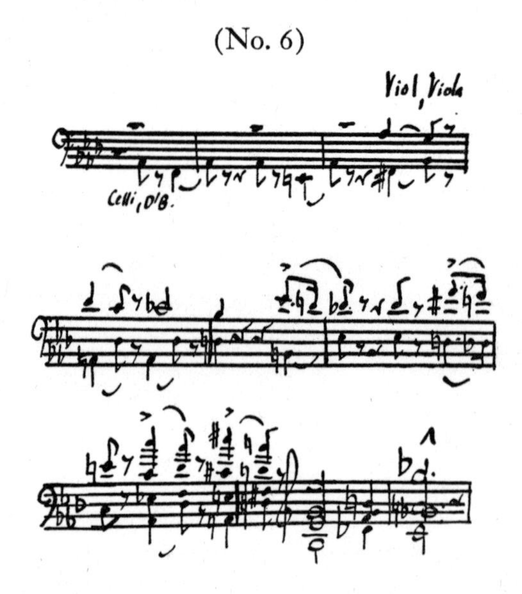

The second ascent brings in the subdominant of A flat. The following cadence is the definite statement of A flat. Woodwinds lead to the long-expected melody:

(No. 7)

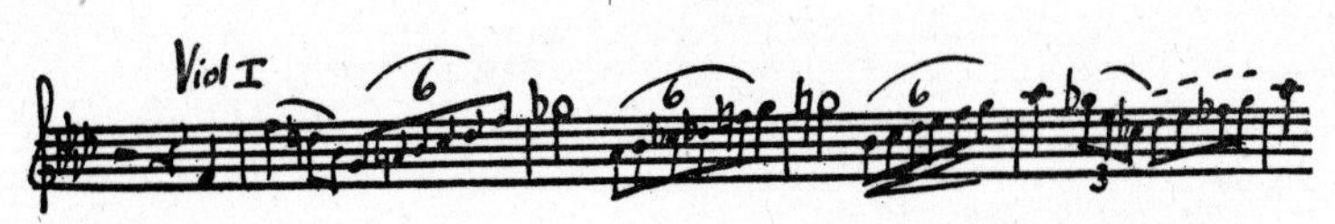

It is a long chant in the violins. With the change of tempo and time (3/4) something of Classical grace becomes noticeable in the string melody.

(No. 8)

The sixteenth motion becomes permanent and also accompanies the recurring initial phrase (No. 6). The cadence above, which introduced the tonic, is taken up first by the horns and serves as a transition to the reprise of the melody (No. 7). The Coda, with its crystal-clear open harmonies, displays the master of orchestration.

III. Scherzo

Vivace

The beginning of the Third Movement is related to that of the Adagio insofar as the theme itself is not encountered at the very opening. Lively motion in the strings and heavy beats in the wind instruments do not leave any doubt about the drastic character of the Scherzo. The main theme, a rustic dance melody, reconfirms it.

(No. 9)

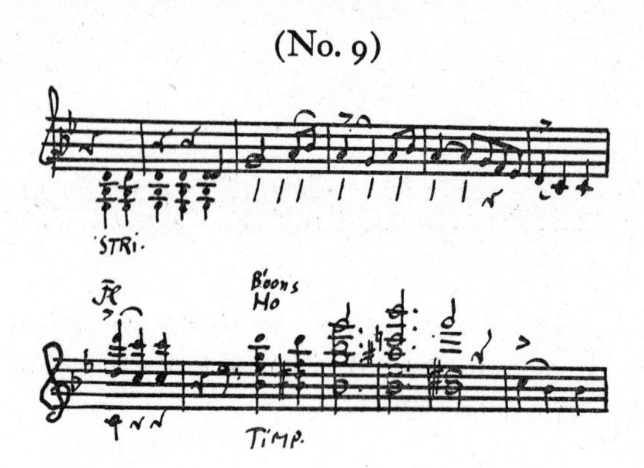

It is a theme of 12 measures. Its phrases differ in length. The echoing repetition of the first phrase in the flute subdivides the melody into 7 plus 5 measures, a very unusual departure from the "symmetry" to which Bruckner was deeply devoted.

With the increasing weight of the orchestral complement, the dance character of the theme is overpowered, especially in the prolonged Coda of the Scherzo.

Trio

The Trio has a short motive related to the theme of the Scherzo:

(No. 10)

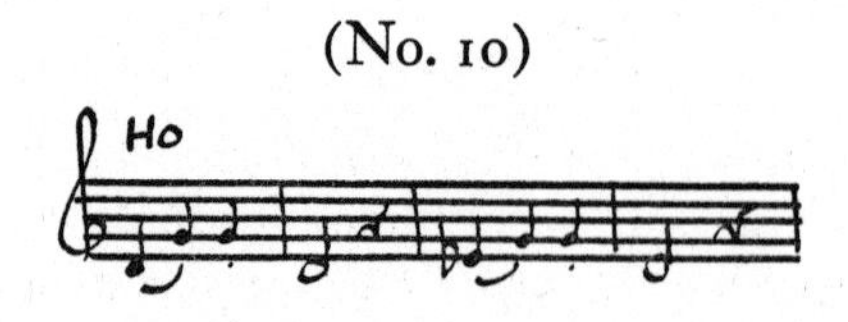

Staccato violin figures give it a graceful air.

IV. Finale

Allegro con fuoco

The Fourth Movement is characterized by youthful impetus, as is evidenced by the fresh starting theme:

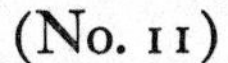

Conceiving this theme cannot have caused Bruckner to rack his brains. In face of its unmistakable character, it is rather amazing to read in some analyses about the "fateful meaning, gigantic wrestling, and victory" announced by this movement.

The secondary theme

(No. 12)

has, at first, only a temporary meaning. A new outburst suppresses it completely. But this outburst itself breaks off suddenly. No third theme is presented. After a general rest and a short episode, the working-out section re-introduces the dotted main rhythm, transformed into soft, smooth phrases. In the following *forte*, where this rhythm undergoes diminution, there are a few measures of long-held notes in the woodwinds which stand there as though forgotten by the improving hand of the master in the final edition. The second measure of the subsidiary theme becomes more important than is in keeping with its harmless nature. The picture, filled with trills, looks strange to the reader of a Bruckner score. Unusual, too, is the *fugato*, which has some academic fragrance.

In the recapitulation, a few newly added counterpoints do not noticeably alter the score. The Coda is typically Bruckner! It starts once more *tranquillo* and in one long breath includes a climax and the majestic end. Just before the very close, the trumpet intones a final hymn which sounds like a thanksgiving.

SECOND SYMPHONY, IN C MINOR

It is an open question whether Bruckner, while writing the *Second Symphony*, really made any attempt to yield to those persons who had criticized the "revolutionary spirit" of his *First*. His own remarks have not contributed much in explaining questionable items in his works. I even doubt whether he could have followed any advice from others, since his creative impulses kept him from feeling any influence from the outside. And did he really believe the *Second* "tamer" than his "*kecke Beserl*"? Anyhow, his remarks relating to these questions have induced some writers to attribute an "inferior power and emotional appeal" to this work. To my way of thinking, the symphony must have represented quite a new type of inventive imagination when it was first performed.

I. Moderato

At the beginning of the *Second Symphony*, there is no more than a thematic nucleus two measures long. Its self-evolution begins at once. The horns try three times to keep back the increasing motion. After they give up, the melody moves swiftly. There is no pause between the following phrases, which rush into a sharply rugged violin-rhythm, radically transforming the elegiac mood of the beginning.

(No. 1)

The listener remains at a loss over the meaning of this climax. Is it a continuation of the main theme? The stressing cadence seems to admit such a conclusion. Or is it an episode? Its extent points to this assumption. Whatever it is, carried out by the violins, which plunge from the high positions into the lowest register, it is utterly exciting in effect.

After a general rest the violoncelli intone a long-extended melody accompanied by an *ostinato* rhythm in the second violins.

(No. 2)

Immediately upon the close of this theme, the rhythmical motive

(No. 3)

follows. It proves to be a "motor" factor of importance. It challenges other conflicting counterpoints, but at times it appears alone, always keeping up the motion.

There is a short episode before the development section starts.

(No. 4)

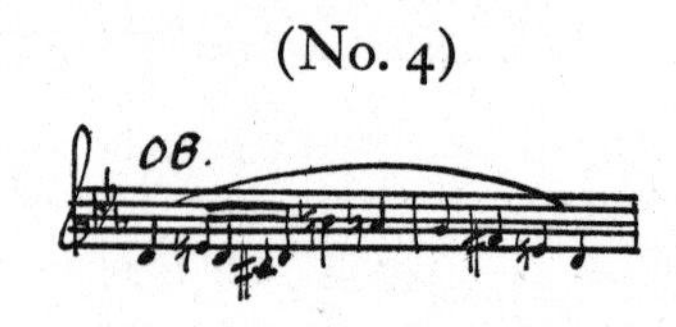

Its characteristic is the turn, that is, the type of melodic grace which Wagner and Liszt used abundantly and which Brahms employed parsimoniously. In Brahms' compositions it does not have the somewhat "sweetish" Romantic effect, but rather a Classical one. It is considered out of fashion now, but there is hardly a composer who could do without it.

The development takes us to a climax, in which the first motive appears in stretto. The rhythmical motive undergoes varying treatment. The oboes and horns play it in augmented form. Shortly before the recapitulation the contrabasses alone take it up. The reprise brings in no new characteristics. The Coda, based on an *ostinato*, is marked by two general rests which interfere with its tendency towards the end. It is like a review of past events and a hesitancy in the face of a definite close.

II. Andante

Solenne poco mosso

With the initial melody in the strings, Bruckner presented the world with his first symphonic *cantilena*. It cannot have failed to contribute to the great success of the first performance of the work.

(No. 5)

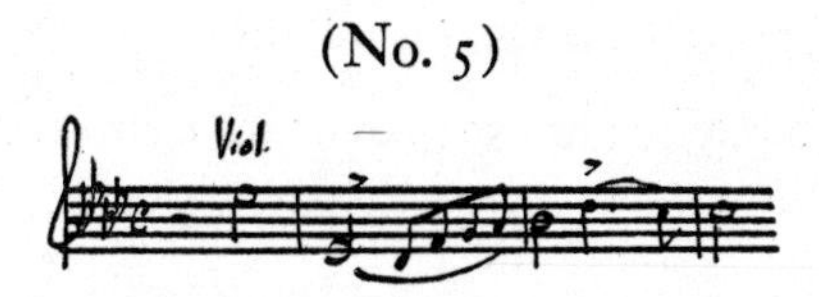

This theme with its sequel is a self-abandonment to sheer euphony on the part of the composer.

The second theme has two contrasting motives. The strings perform a pizzicato rhythm while the first horn sets forth a *dolce* legato phrase.

(No. 6)

This type of two-voiced theme is a Brucknerian feature of his own. The *contrast* emphasized throughout his works penetrates even into the themes themselves. The further development of this movement displays the composer's vision of *variation*, as described on page 168. The increasing motion of the secondary parts leaves the outlines of the main theme intact but brings about the climax of the movement.

In the Andante of this symphony the usual polyphony has been partly given up in order to make the pure melody prominent. This is exceptional for Bruckner. The violin phrase which introduces the Coda has a human eloquence. It is a song without words. The leap of the descending octave taken from the principal theme leads to the close.

III. Scherzo

Allegro moderato

The first theme is almost provocative in character.

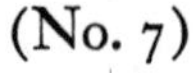

The division of the first beat into two eighths brings this effect about. At the very moment when the rhythm appears *piano* and *legato* in the flute and clarinet, it changes the mood and assumes the charm of Weber's grace.

The Trio is built on a genuine Austrian *Laendler* with an Alpine yodel at the end of the melody.

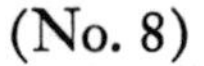

IV. Finale

The Finale has been given the most divergent interpretations by the symphony's numerous analysts.

(No. 9)

There is an "unrest" at the beginning which makes us wonder whether we are listening to the main theme itself or, instead, to an introduction. The more impressive, therefore, is the *fortissimo* outburst of the tutti in the thirty-third measure.

(No. 10)

It proves to be the chief subject itself, although formal objections might be raised. The main characteristic of this theme is the heavy stress on the triplet at the first beat. Its expression is that of indignation. The "lyric" melody is preceded by its counterpoint in the second violins. Thus, the true melody in the first violins works at its first appearance like a counterpoint to the motive in the second violins. This, too, is quite a new vision which appeared to Bruckner.

(No. 11)

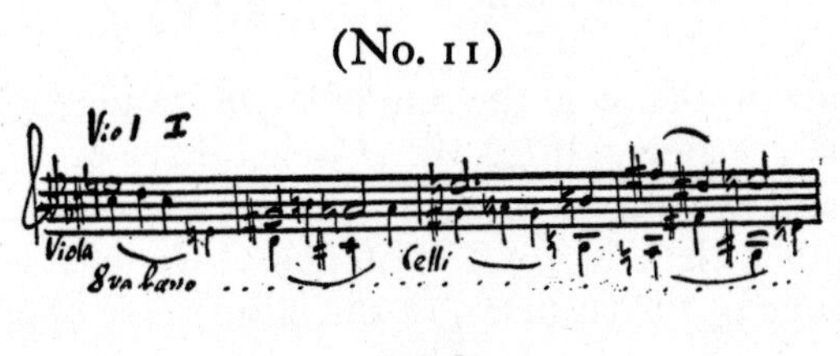

After a general rest the organist Bruckner comes to the fore by soft and solemn harmonies which serve as a transition to the working-out section. Here the recurring principal theme of the First Movement is given the meaning of a counterpoint to Theme No. 9. Up to the Coda, Theme No. 9 and Theme No. 10 battle for supremacy. The very last ending, in C major, dismisses the listener with the prevailing impression of the triplet theme (No. 10).

THIRD SYMPHONY, IN D MINOR

If any specific characteristics can be attributed to the great master works in music, they are an extended inventive imagination and a broad-arched structure, both reflecting the spacious spirit of their creator. The genius thinks over longer spaces than the average composer. This is in keeping with the true character of music as a temporal art. The "latitude" in music, that is, the horizontal melodic line, fills in the passing of time to a greater degree than does the "longitude," that is, the harmony or short-extended phrase, which obviously is of less lasting impressiveness.

I. Moderato con moto

Bruckner's *Third Symphony* has these characteristics of "grandeur" to a greater degree than its neighbor works. Maybe this fact makes the *Third* less easy of approach for the average audience than others in the galaxy of Bruckner's symphonies.

The opening theme in the solo trumpet stands there by itself in lonely majesty. It has the chiseled shape of a statue. It does not aim at continuation; it does not seem to serve any purpose other than its own existence. Two characteristics strike the eye of the reader: (1) the large space of an octave paced through three times within the eight measures of the theme; (2) the triplet which initiates the second portion. Both prove to be germs for later development.

(No. 1)

The horn, joining in, somehow loosens the rigidity of the mood. The organ point on D, which started the work, continues to maintain the tension, which increases with the general crescendo and makes the solution inevitable. The solution is effected by the outburst of the tutti in unison.

(No. 2)

This has been called the "culminating theme." The second violins introduce the lyric phrase with the "Bruckner rhythm" of a triplet plus two quarters.

(No. 3)

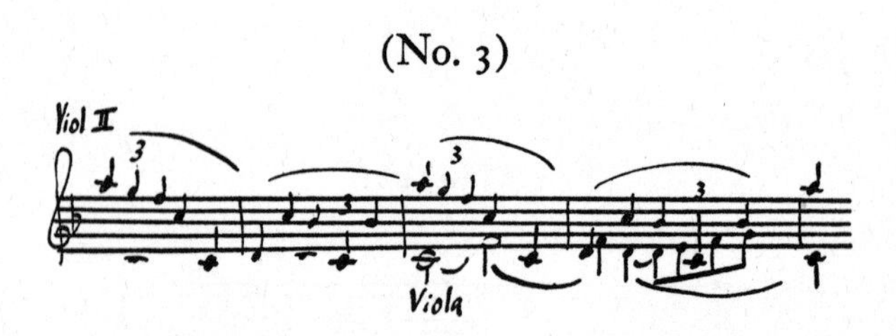

This specific rhythm appears later on in inverted form: two plus three. At the climax of the section, the trumpets intone a short but expressive chorale theme.

A soft cadence in the strings builds the transition to the working-out section. Remarkable in the course of this portion of the work is the tightening of the "culminating theme" by diminution. Since the motion thereby becomes faster, it gains an excitement in expression.

The principal theme performed in triple *fortissimo* and unison stands for the climax of the development. Stretto and inversion follow immediately. The recapitulation is in accordance with the norms the composer set up for himself.

The Coda, starting upon a chromatic *basso ostinato*, is interrupted by soft phrases in the woodwinds. (See the corresponding place in the *Second.*) They end on the diminished seventh of the dominant (A major), followed without transition by the tonic. The principal and the culminating theme, drawn together, close the movement.

II. Adagio

Poco mosso quasi andante

This movement has the tri-partite *Lied* form. The starting melody

(No. 4)

of Classical fragrance houses two elements in itself which prove susceptible of further development. The first (measure 2) is rhythmical in nature. The second (measure 4) is a suspended note which gives rise to strong harmonic modulations. The second melody is different in time (3/4) and in tempo (andante quasi allegretto).

(No. 5)

The bass instruments take it over from the violas. The clarinet joins in, with canonic imitations.

Another theme of Classical attitude appears *misterioso più lento.*

(No. 6)

This section, mainly developing Theme No. 5, is only loosely connected with the main portion of the movement. The recapitulation brings about a climax which is among the most powerful Bruckner ever wrote in an Adagio. The culminating eight measures are interrupted in the middle by a *pia-*

nissimo cadence of pious mood. The Coda dies away in triple *piano.*

III. Scherzo

Vivace ma non troppo

The main constituent of the Scherzo is a whirling motive:

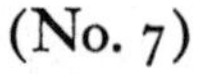
(No. 7)

Very characteristic is the fact that the eight measures of this theme are based solely on the tonic D minor chord. There is not even a hint of harmonic digression. The mere rhythm is expected to work by itself, and it does except in a few measures. The Scherzo leaves the characteristics of the dance far behind. Despite its swift motion, it is heavy in weight. The plunging trumpets and trombones at the end of the climax have Wagnerian power.

The Trio has a gracious dance character:

(No. 8)

It has something of the rustic Austrian *Gemuetlichkeit.* Chains of trills in the violins and violoncelli are of rare occurrence in Bruckner compositions.

IV. Finale

Allegro

A restless chromatic figure in the violins, swiftly increasing, is the introduction to the appearance of the main theme.

(No. 9)

Three trombones and contrabasses proclaim the principal subject, which reminds us harmonically and rhythmically of the irate Wotan in the Third Act of *Die Walkuere*. The full strength of the orchestra is mustered and extended at length. The subsidiary theme is two-voiced: the first violins sing a light-winged melody while the horns and trumpets simultaneously play a chorale of stern character.

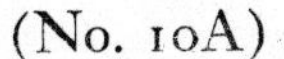
(No. 10A)

(No. 10B)

This section comes to an end in a general rest.

The third theme is a motive in unison:

(No. 11)

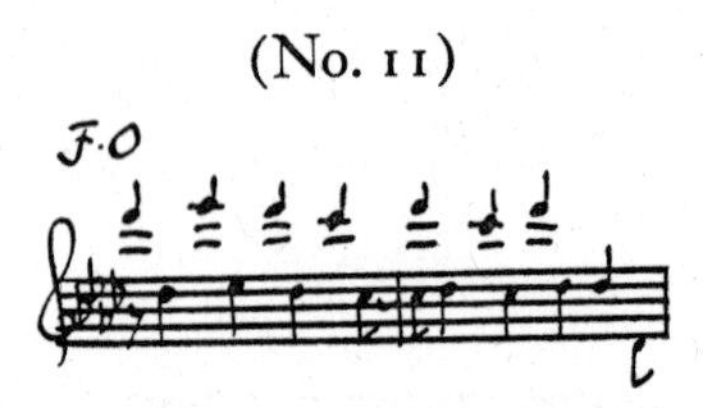

The syncopations in the bass instruments are Beethovian in character. By soft harmonies the wind instruments lead to the development. The basses play a higher part in this portion than they do anywhere else in the work. The inversion of the main theme in the trombones is noteworthy – here the leap of the ascending ninth has a very striking effect. At the end of the working-out part, the opening theme of the First Movement reappears. The recapitulation begins, surprisingly, with the secondary theme (No. 10). The radiant Coda in D major once more re-introduces the trumpet theme, which pleased Wagner so mightily.

FOURTH SYMPHONY, IN E FLAT MAJOR

(Romantic)

"The word 'Romantic' has been used for this symphony in its most popular sense, meaning imaginative, unrestrained, nebulous, and mysterious. Nostalgic reverie is also called 'Romantic' at times and this meaning, too, has been applied to the *Fourth*." I wrote the above years ago in the program for the Nikisch concerts. The interpretation of the work by the great conductors whom I had heard justified my explanation of the title.

Gabriel Engel clearly proves how differently this music can be felt.* He wrote: "The long chain of dark-tinged com-

* In *Chord and Discord*, January, 1940.

positions preceding the *Fourth* makes the radiant sunrise which begins that symphony all the more amazing." Again and again he stressed "joyful upheaval." We must presuppose that the symphony was directed in a rendition very different from that with which I am familiar. It looks as if the only name Bruckner ever chose for a symphony fails to help us in defining its nature. It can be defined no better than the other eight works. All the more do I agree with Engel in his opinion expressed in the same magazine in January, 1939: "In Bruckner's *Romantic* there is heard not the echo of Nature reflected in the soul of a man, but rather the voice of Nature itself."

1. Allegro molto moderato

In fact, the pure atmosphere of Nature surrounds us when we listen to the first theme set forth by that very "romantic instrument" the horn.

(No. 1)

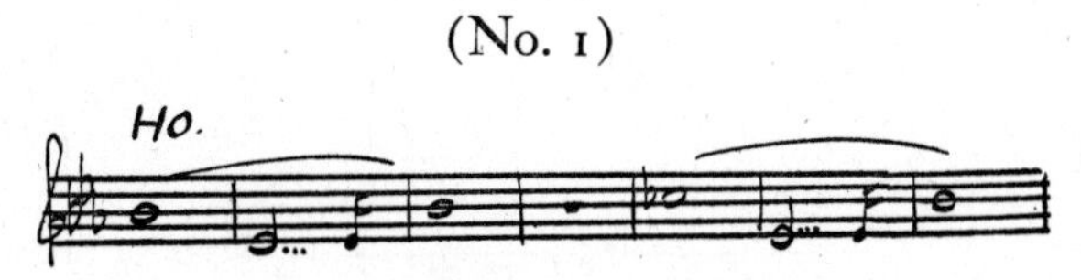

The combination of the high horn tone above the low tremolo in the strings has a particular appeal. It sounds like a call from far away. The musical illustration of Nature by the use of the perfect fifth has long been familiar. The extension of the interval B flat-E flat to C flat-E flat in the second "call" is so striking that the listener hardly becomes aware of the fact that the phrase begins only a half step higher than the first. The character of intervals in music not only is defined by larger or smaller distances but also depends greatly on the way in which the intervals are introduced. The first "call"

is repeated and dies away in the lower register at the end of the last "call." The atmosphere is one of utter calm. Nikisch stressed the chromatic tones of the supporting scale in the contrabasses.

The second theme is represented by the "Bruckner rhythm," which almost came to be a formula in his symphonies. It never fails to be effective as a "motor" factor.

(No. 2)

The following crescendo breaks off at a *fortissimo* in F major. The third motive in the violas is wedded to a graceful counterpoint in the violins, which Bruckner is said to have learned from the *Zizibee* (chickadee). Whether he did or not, it is cheerful in mood and significant in rhythm.

(No. 3)

The motive which immediately follows primarily serves structural purposes.

(No. 4)

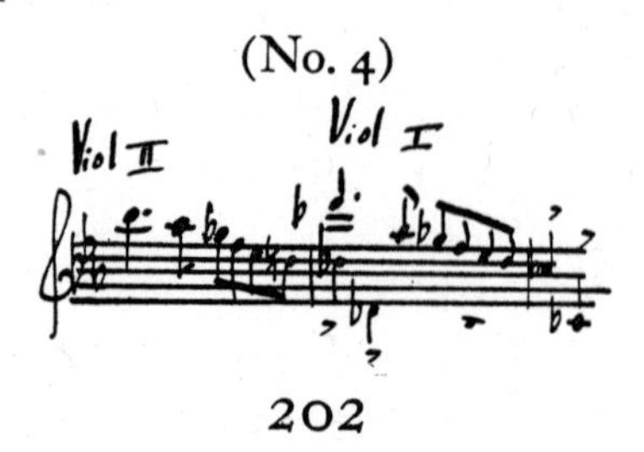

A climax and a chromatic ascent end in a *fortissimo* for the brass choir and a general rest. Softly descending chromatic scales interrupted by the *pianissimo* "call" interpose between the first and second sections. The phrases in the flutes and clarinets cast a poetic, romantic spell. The free suspended note at the beginning of each phrase does not work as a dissonance because of the limpid tone color of the orchestra.

The working-out section starts with the "call" in the horns imitated by the clarinet. The D flat at the beginning of the second phrase can be explained as "Fux's changing note." The harmony in the strings is the dominant of F with a suspended A.

The "Bruckner rhythm" is the stimulating factor in the development, whereas the rhythm of the principal theme reappears transformed into a chorale in the trumpets and the trombones towards the end of this section.

Theme No. 3 in augmented form leads to the recapitulation. The E major at the beginning of the Coda springs from the realm of the Neapolitan Sixth, which dominated Bruckner's harmonic concepts. At the close the main phrase is repeated six times by the brass instruments.

II. Andante

The beginning of the Andante is somewhat epic in character. The long-extended melody in the violoncelli, combined with the funeral-march rhythm in the other strings, sounds like the story of a great man of long ago.

(No. 5)

Lighter colors are given by the motive:

(No. 6)

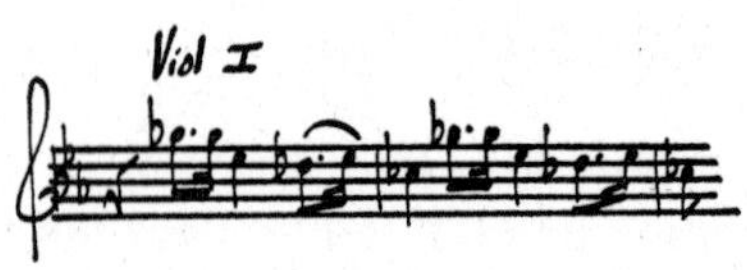

which reminds us of the bird's song (No. 3). The serious mood is soon re-established, by the chorale in the strings. The dotted rhythm of the *Zizibee* has no more than a contrapuntal meaning.

The thread of the interrupted story is taken up by the violas:

(No. 7)

The end of the melody is deeply moving. The bird's song reappears unaccompanied. There is a moment of the most profound loneliness. The development section needs no detailed explanation after what has gone before.

In the recapitulation, the motion surrounding the main theme becomes increasingly vivacious. The climax does not retain the radiant character of the beginning C major but resumes the dim romantic tints. The Coda dies away under the dull beats of the tympani.

III. Scherzo

Vivace non troppo

The original Scherzo of the *Romantic* was replaced by a

new one in 1878 called the "Hunter Scherzo" in accordance with Bruckner's own remarks. The character of "genuine program music" has even been ascribed to this movement in its definitive reading. In fact, the beginning illustrates, almost visibly, the approaching group of hunters.

(No. 8)

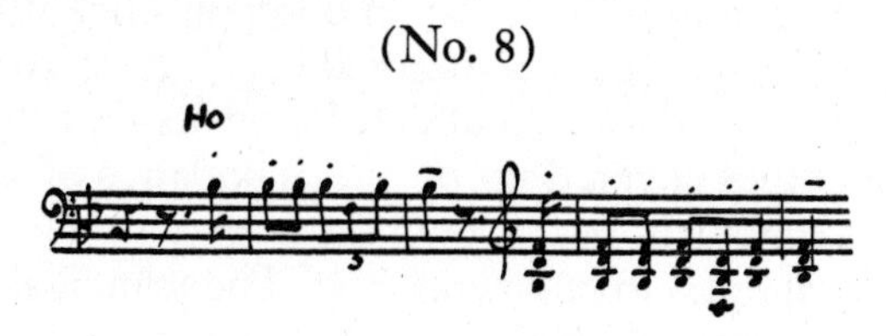

With the solid *fortissimo* of the brass instruments, the hunters seem to come upon the stage.

The secondary theme has a softer timbre:

(No. 9)

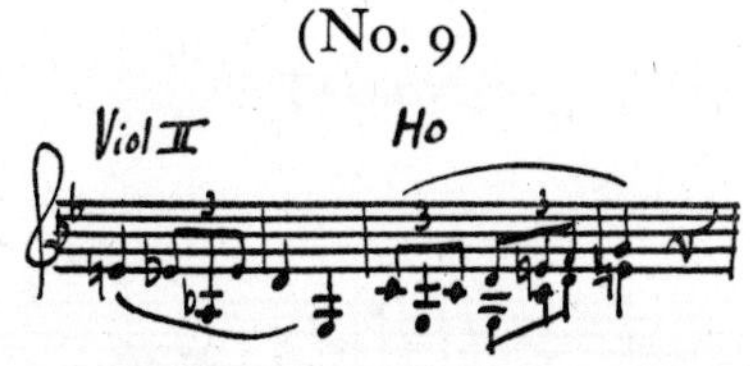

These themes each undergo a separate development.

Trio

In the original score of the Trio Bruckner had written this inscription: "Dance strain during a repast at hunting." The melody illustrates this subtitle clearly.

(No. 10)

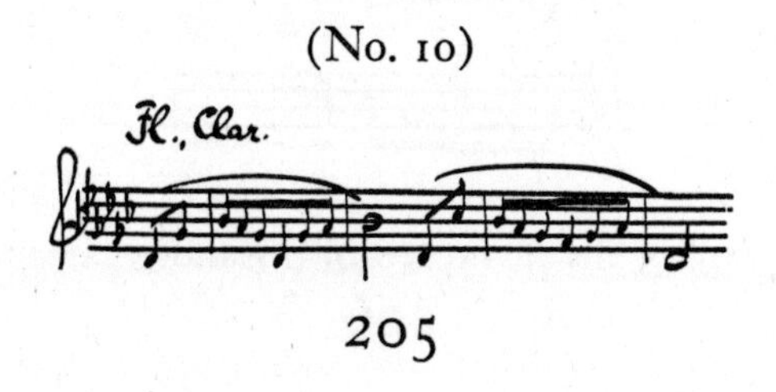

Its basic conception is met again in Mahler's *Second Symphony*, Third Movement.

IV. Finale

Allegro moderato

The Finale is a proof of what an observer once justifiably called "Bruckner's musical insatiability." It is so rich in themes, melodies, motives, and developments that the structure is sometimes covered up by the abundance of material.

The first statement has its own introduction, wherein the main theme appears in embryo shape. The principal subject itself has immense weight and power and is a premonition of the principal theme of the *Ninth*, First Movement. It has the same leap of the descending octave, the accelerating triplets of quarter notes, and the retarding close.

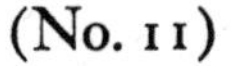

(No. 11)

After a caesura, a "storm and uproar in Nature" are let loose.

(No. 12)

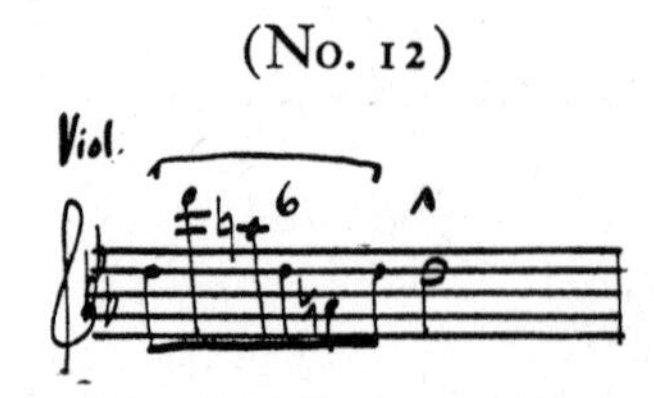

The impetus of the sextuplets of this motive instantly gives rise to a climax, at the end of which the first "call" of the symphony unexpectedly resounds.

The subsidiary theme recalls the somber mood of the Second Movement.

(No. 13)

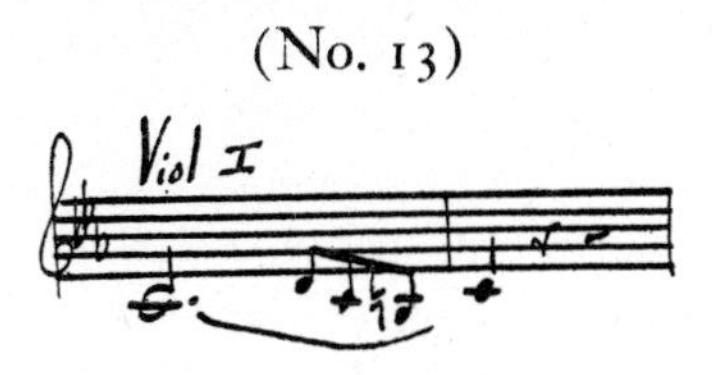

This theme, too, evidently impressed Mahler's creative imagination. There are two more motives of a relieving nature:

(No. 14)

(No. 14A)

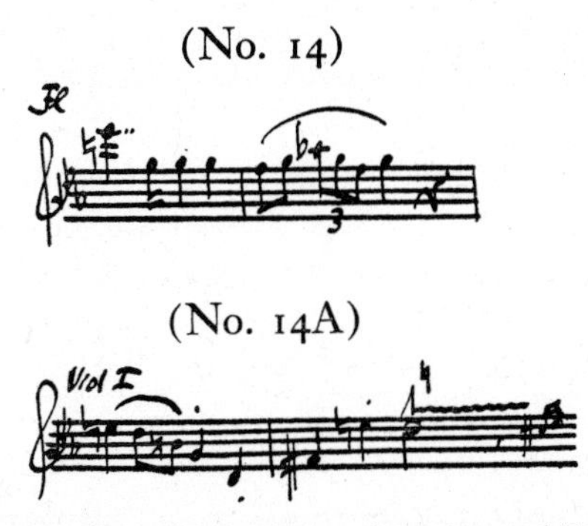

The first section does not end with the exhibition of the structural elements, as is usual, but in its own extended development. Some ideas which are evaluated later in the *Fifth Symphony* are met here. The free fantasy starts, like the opening, in B flat minor, the theme being inverted. The first portion of this section is not long and ends in a general rest. It is followed by the culminating part, for which no climax has prepared the listener. It is a continuous chain of eruptions ending also in a general rest.

Here the recapitulation begins, with the inverted main

theme in D minor. Writers on music differ in their ideas as to the beginning of the last portion. The revised and the original score are greatly divergent at this juncture. One of my reasons for considering it the beginning of the recapitulation is the reappearance of the Scherzo theme. The recall of themes from movements other than the first is generally a characteristic of the very last section.

The Coda begins "quietly." This last indication of the composer's distinguishing trait refers to the motion only. The continuing harmonic transformations decisively distinguish the end of the movement from the typical Bruckner Coda. The last eight measures recall the first theme of the symphony to the listener's memory.

FIFTH SYMPHONY, IN B FLAT MAJOR

Whether a composer works without effort or whether he has to struggle for an adequate expression of his inspiration is of no importance in estimating the work itself. Certainly the divine nature of Mozart's music rests on his apparent ease in composition, his lack of noticeable effort in creating. It raises our spirits. But Beethoven's very human expression moves our hearts and souls no less.

Bruckner undoubtedly belongs to that class of composers whose struggling creative energy is imparted to the listener. The *Fifth Symphony* proves it better than any other of his symphonic works. But although we witness the composer's efforts and share his struggles, we feel relieved when his confident spirit breaks through at the end of the work.

I. First Movement

The First Movement has a thematic substance which includes the sharpest contrast Bruckner ever proferred within the confines of one movement. It is the only symphony he wrote which opens

Adagio

Considering the fact that the theme is to play an important part in the development section, it seems questionable whether we really can call the slow beginning an "Introduction," as has often been done.

Violoncelli and contrabasses start with a pizzicato – one of the outstanding characteristics of the first two movements. The following measures in the strings display the masterly severity of contrapuntal writing. Notwithstanding the calm solemnity, we feel that a surprise is to come. Our expectations are surpassed by the outburst of the orchestra after the first general rest. (No. 1A)

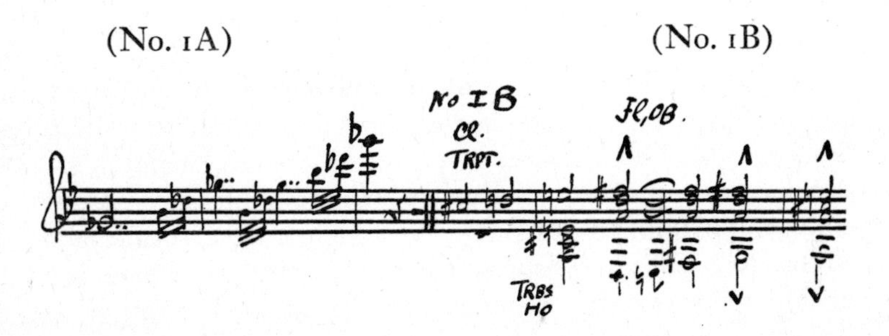

No less striking than the sudden *fortissimo* is the key of G flat after the foregoing long cadence in F major. This deceptive cadence is another often-recurring characteristic of the First Movement. The theme sounds like a challenging signal. The wind instruments answer with a chorale-like phrase. (No. 1B)

After another general rest a climax starts upon the organ point A. This is the first of the numerous organ points, which are additional characteristics of the opening movement. This A receives unequivocal confirmation as the tonic by a powerful cadence which brings the Adagio to an end. With the following

Allegro

the A becomes the dominant of D, and the D changes surprisingly in significance as soon as the main theme in B flat appears.

(No. 2)

This symphony might be called "The Surprise Symphony" with as much justification as the *Second* is called "The Rest Symphony." Theme No. 2 is very peculiar at its first appearance, as far as the key is concerned; the four-measure phrase ends on the dominant of B flat. Now, when we carefully examine the tonal impression left in our ears by this theme, we decide it was not the dominant of B flat major but rather of B flat minor. This certainly is a new surprise. The plain expression of the theme is that of "energy," which in fact works out in the development section.

A pizzicato motive (No. 3A) strongly modulating in itself introduces the melody of the first violins (No. 3B). This pizzicato is somewhat scholastic in character. But as soon as the violins join in with their melody, the theme, now two-voiced, gains archaic fragrance. I wonder whether Bruckner invented both themes simultaneously or whether he added one later in contrapuntal elaboration.

(No. 3A)

(No. 3B)

A very expressive melody in D flat major

(No. 4)

gives rise to a climax at the end of which a unison rhythm appears.

(No. 5)

The most interesting part in the working-out section lies in the measures where the Allegro theme (No. 2) in diminution is drawn together with the rhythm of the "signal motive" (No. 1A). From this transformation a new rhythm of boisterous nature is derived. Two caesuras interrupt its vehement storming shortly before the recapitulation.

In the Coda the trumpets and trombones six times flourish the main phrase of the principal theme in pure B flat major.

II. Adagio

The opening of the Second Movement confronts the conductor with the problem of beating two differing time values or of selecting one theme and leaving to themselves the players who perform the other theme. The strings start a pizzicato motive in 6/4 time.

(No. 6A)

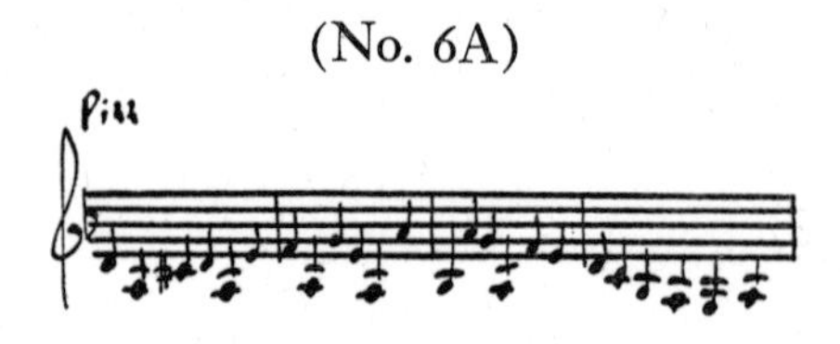

At the fifth measure the oboe enters with a melody in 4/4 time.

(No. 6B)

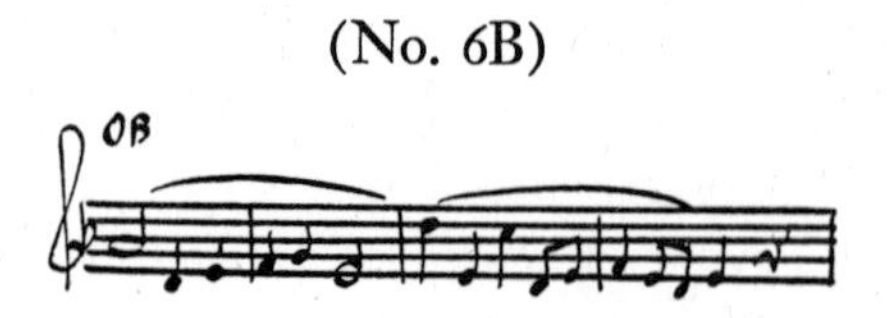

Karl Muck actually used to beat the 6/4 with the baton in his right hand and the 4/4 with his left hand. Nikisch, when

I asked him how he mastered the difficulty, answered: "I always help the group which needs me most." His inborn genius made him unconscious of any "problems" in conducting. I myself beat the first four measures in six and then pass to four, since my feeling of the expressive oboe melody does not permit me to stay on 6/4. The strings easily go on with 6/4 by themselves and even follow the expression of the current melody.

The statement of the first theme has a very delicate, almost fragile, texture. Therefore, the more powerful is the full-sounding and broad melody which follows in the strings:

(No. 7)

In the development of this theme Bruckner makes the orchestra sing incessantly.

The main theme reappears later, surrounded by sextuplets which lead to an excited motion. An unusually long chain of harmonic sequences introduces the last section of the Adagio. The 6/4 rhythm is dissolved into 8/8 in the bass instruments. The bass tuba participates in performing this figure, which widens to the ascending leap of the ninth. The trombones join in and spread majestic solemnity. The weighty and heavy colossus moves slowly on. It is the archetype of gigantic Bruckner music.

III. *Scherzo*

Molto vivace

The opening pizzicato motive of the Adagio starts the Scherzo also. The principal theme

(No. 8)

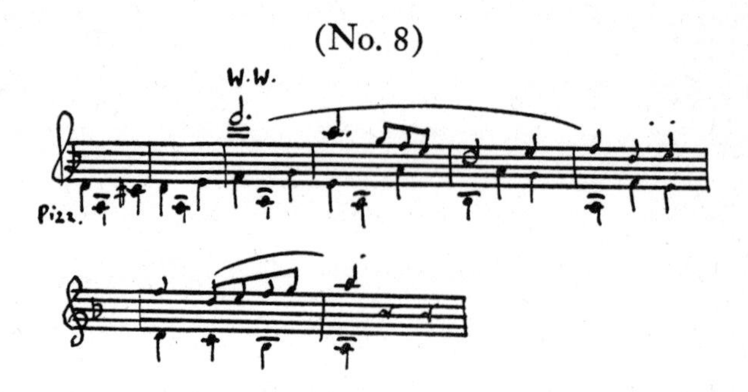

leads to a very short climax, which ends abruptly in a general rest. The subsidiary theme, which follows immediately, is a two-voiced melody of *Laendler* character.

(No. 9)

There are two unusual things in this movement: (1) the thematic development, which extends over a long space; and

(2) the occurrence of phrases of uneven length, which build asymmetric periods of 3, 4, 2, 4, and 6 measures, following each other. It is just this lack of symmetry which gives the Scherzo a singular significance within Bruckner's symphonic works.

The theme of the Trio consists of phrases of six measures

(No. 10)

which are soon extended to eight. With the exception of a few bars, the score here has the subtleness of chamber music. The 2/4 time and the tempo (allegretto) are in cheerful contrast to the Scherzo.

IV. Finale

The Finale also has particular and unusual features: It represents the attempt to combine the form of the sonata with the form of the fugue. This seems to be a contradiction in itself, since the sonata derives its form from a succession of themes while the idea of a fugue is polyphony, that is, the simultaneousness of contrasting subjects. The manuscript score of the movement stresses the sonata form, whereas the revised edition, by numerous excisions, brings the fugue into prominence.*

Before the first subject is introduced, the listener is reminded of preceding events in the symphony: The first measures of the First Movement open the Finale. The solemn calm is not disturbed by the descending octave leap in the trumpet (clarinet in the manuscript) which pre-announces the theme of the fugue. The first phrase of this fugue appears and gives way to the main theme of the First Movement. The phrase of the fugue reappears, followed this time by the Adagio theme. The tension increases. After another and last announcement, the fugue itself is finally set forth by the bass instruments.

(No. 11)

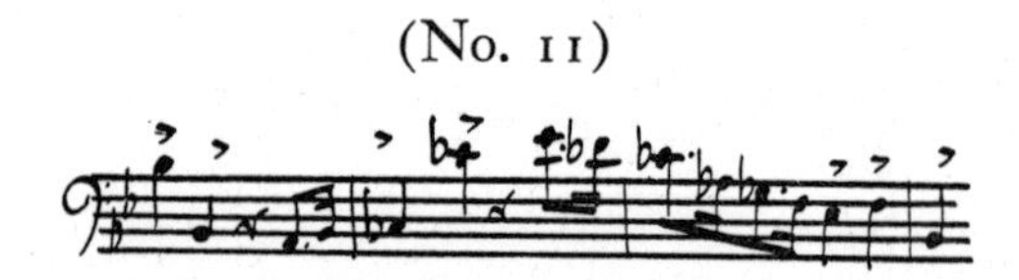

The next theme has the meaning of an episode for the fugue, whereas it stands for the subsidiary theme in the sonata.

(No. 12)

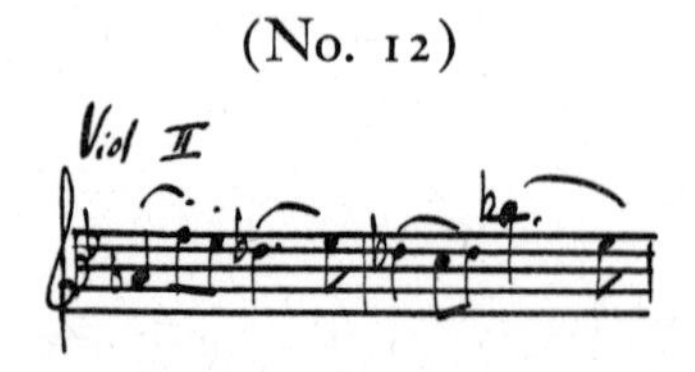

This melody and its sequel abound in fervent expression and

* The different versions of the scores are the subjects of later examination in this book.

are in contrast to the rigid nature of the fugue. The second fugue is based on a chorale-like theme:

(No. 13)

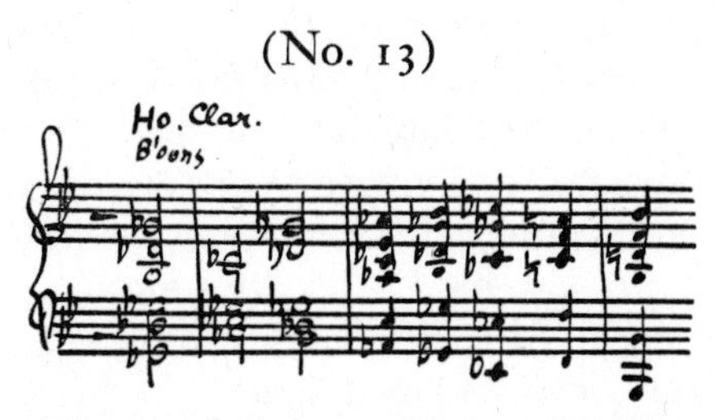

Its harmonic characteristic is the Neapolitan Sixth at the end. Both fugue-themes are later drawn together into a double fugue. The principal theme of the First Movement joins in and is combined with the first fugue-subject. Only a master in orchestration, such as Bruckner, could succeed in maintaining here the transparency of the polyphonic score.

The final climax rests on the augmentation of this theme in the bass instruments. Something extraordinary must inevitably be coming. The inexorably ascending basses together with the relentless crescendo are almost threatening in their force. At the culmination, the theme of the second fugue is played by a special brass-wind choir, while the orchestra performs the first fugue. (This special choir is not indicated in the manuscript.) Four horns join in with the theme of the First Movement. It is one of the most effective Codas in symphonic literature.

Sixth Symphony, in A Major

The *Sixth Symphony* is genuine Bruckner, although certain characteristic features found in the other symphonies are missing. Since they are exactly those features which prevented the popularity of the symphonies, one would assume that the path for the *Sixth* would have been easy. But such was not the case. The *Sixth* remained a stepchild in public estimation. Bruckner loved it all the more.

The old question as to why or wherefore one work becomes popular and another by the same composer does not cannot be examined here. For instance, a master work as sublime as Verdi's *Falstaff* has not become half so popular in Italy as *La Traviata*. The greatest conductors have struggled in vain to win recognition for Peter Cornelius's *The Barber of Baghdad*, although his *Lieder* are sung in every German family. And, of all Mozart's many symphonies, why do we hear only a few, over and over again?

It has been the fate of Bruckner's *Sixth* to meet with such unweighable hindrances and it seems doubtful whether a change can be brought about. And this work is certainly not his longest or heaviest. There is no questioning, no wrestling for expression in it. It is affirmative, assertive, and positive. Moreover, it is original among its original sisters. It proves it from the very beginning.

I. *Maestoso*

There is none of the usual Bruckner mystery in design or in color either – no veil which has to be lifted. The violins start with a clear-cut *leggiero* rhythm; violoncelli and contrabasses join in at the third measure with the really tonal principal theme:

(No. 1)

It is carried on by the motive

(No. 1A)

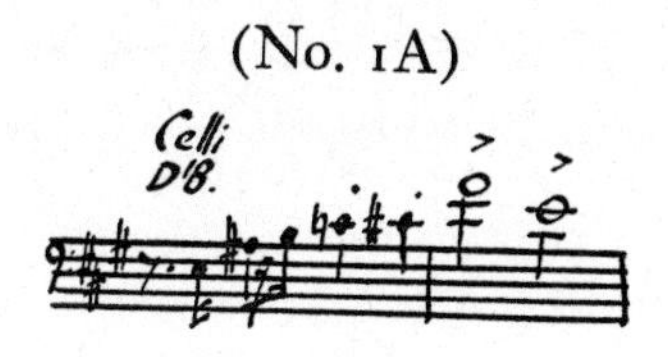

The secondary melody of lyric character is a long chant in the violins, which has an ecstatic leap of the ascending ninth in the fifth measure.

(No. 2)

The delicate aesthete Decsey called it a "female theme," and with a limited amount of justification. The triplets in the violoncelli and contrabasses soon gain importance for the development of this section. They undergo subdivision and lead to poly-rhythmical constructions which are rare in Bruckner's works.

The third motive is only one measure long:

(No. 3)

It is quickly surrendered and gives way to a soft episode, the bridge to the working-out section. Here the principal theme is first presented in inverted form. The motion in quavering triplets goes on through the whole portion and maintains the allegro character of a movement whose main theme does not have this tempo in itself. A general ascent leads to the crowning part of the climax, which has a peculiar meaning in this instance. "For the first time in symphonic literature, the climax of the development and the beginning of the recapitulation coincide."*

The last section publishes no particularly new ideas as to the structure of the movement. The continuity of the triplets is kept up here, too. The orchestration gains new features by the important part given to the trombones and tuba. Their phrases, originating in contrapuntal combination, look strange at certain junctures to the reader of the score. It is not always advisable to render them prominent for the listener.

The Coda, based on the subdominant, displays full radiance.

II. Adagio

Molte solenne

The opening theme is as simple as it is consummate in form and expression.

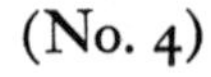
(No. 4)

The oboe joins in with a lamenting and moving phrase:

* Gabriel Engel, in *Chord and Discord*, January, 1940.

(No. 4A)

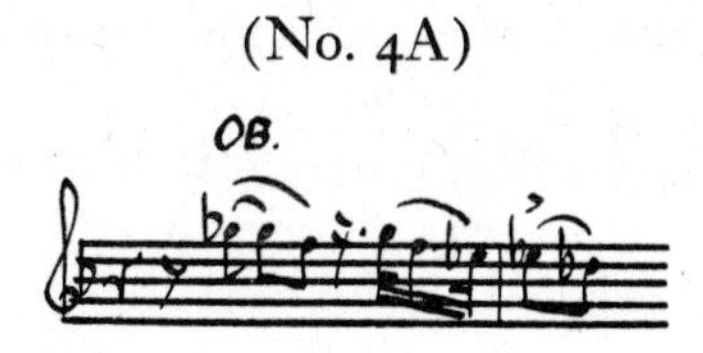

The subsidiary melody is started by the violoncelli and taken up by the first violins.

(No. 5)

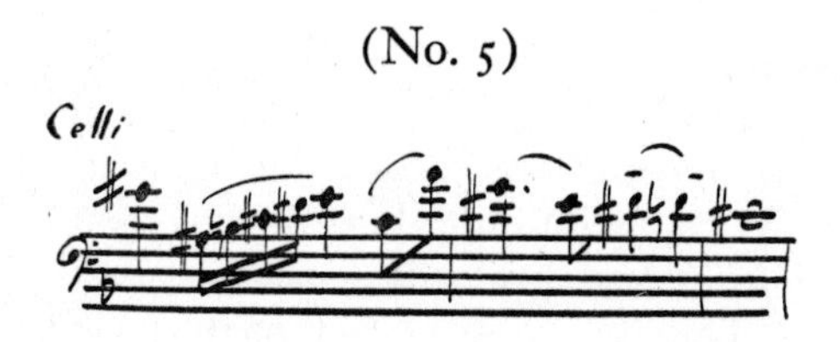

The next theme has a "grave" expression and a Classical air:

(No. 6)

The development is so concise in extent that one is almost tempted to look at this movement as following a scheme other than the sonata scheme. The recapitulation rather resembles a variation in the sense mentioned earlier. On the other hand, the reappearing theme No. 6 gives proof that the symphonic scheme has been observed.

The Coda once more displays Bruckner's unexcelled art in obtaining exquisite tonal effects by the simplest means. Here it is the descending F-major scale in the first violins which brings about a veritable miracle of sound. The unaffected gesture of this phrase discloses the ingenuous spirit of a genius.

III. Scherzo

Con moto moderato

This movement is not a typical Bruckner Scherzo at all. Its texture is woven of fine threads which could not stand any weight. Its most characteristic feature is the lack of a main theme. At the beginning, instead of a main theme, we meet three contrasting rhythmical motives, drawn together from the start. They stay united most of the time throughout the movement.

(No. 7A)

(No. 7B)

(No. 7C)

Though this Scherzo may be less effective than others, it discloses the ideal vision of music. *The lack of material gives the movement weightless character.*

Trio

The pizzicato of the strings alternating with horns provides the Trio with a special fragrance. Woodwinds surprisingly quote the principal theme of the First Movement from the *Fifth*. Some interspersed cadences in the midst of their harmless, playful surroundings recall the great, serious man who wrote this serene music.

IV. Finale

Allegro ma non troppo

The beginning of the Fourth Movement has characteristics similar to those of the *Second Symphony*. The opening theme has the same "unrest." It seems to look for a final point which the theme does not have in itself.

(No. 8)

The end of the phrase on the D minor chord has no harmonic reference to the holding note E in the violas. Rather, it ends in suspension and makes the listener anxious for a solution. A short rhythmical "signal" pre-announces the nearing main theme. It is "very decidedly" set forth by the four horns in unison.

(No. 9)

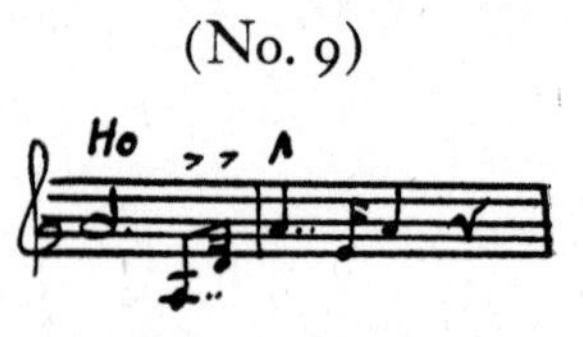

This fanfare is proferred four times, and each time it is followed by heavily accentuated chords in the trumpets and trombones. By boisterous string passages the general tone here is very agitated and *strepituoso.* Bruckner later transferred the substance of this inspiration to the "Aeterna fac cum sanctis tuis" of the *Te Deum.* The two-voiced melody

(No. 10)

is carried on mainly by the strings. After the next climax, the rhythm

(No. 11)

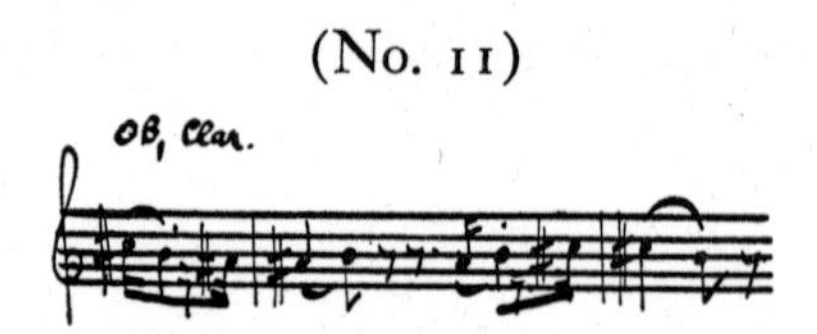

appears unexpectedly, giving way to a new outburst of the tutti. Here we witness the appearance of a unique feature in Bruckner's creation: The trombones are given contrapuntal phrases which have an outspoken "recitative" character. A general rest stops the interesting development suddenly.

The sharply dotted rhythm No. 11 gains predominant

meaning in the following. It is heard also in the short working-out section which starts *molto più lento.*

The recapitulation contains some measures in which the symmetry of periods interferes with the unfolding of natural power. Rhythm No. 11 is now taken up in stretto and by sequences at the same time. The opening violin-rhythm of the symphony joins in, more noticeably for the reader of the score than for the listener. Twice the *impetuoso* motion comes to a standstill by caesuras.

The Coda is marked by continuous reiteration of the principal theme, to which the main theme from the First Movement is added.

Seventh Symphony, in E Major

I. *Allegro moderato*

The opening theme of the *Seventh* is the longest Bruckner wrote in his symphonic works.

(No. 1)

It is the ideal expression of a melody which stands for itself, having its own development, climax, and Coda. At its end we feel as though much time has passed and we have become richer through an unforgettable musical experience. Notwithstanding its twenty-two measures in length, this theme has a natural growth, no elaborate construction being noticeable. In accordance with its specific character, it has less "motor" energy than most of Bruckner's opening themes. Though strongly modulating in itself, it turns back to the dominant of B major, in which key the listener expects the repetition. But the theme reappears surprisingly in the tonic key, which was introduced by an almost unnoticed modulation in the last preceding measure. It is taken up by the high-pitched instruments, which carry on the climax, ending in a *fortissimo* of the tutti.

The next theme is less in contrast with the first than is usual.

(No. 2)

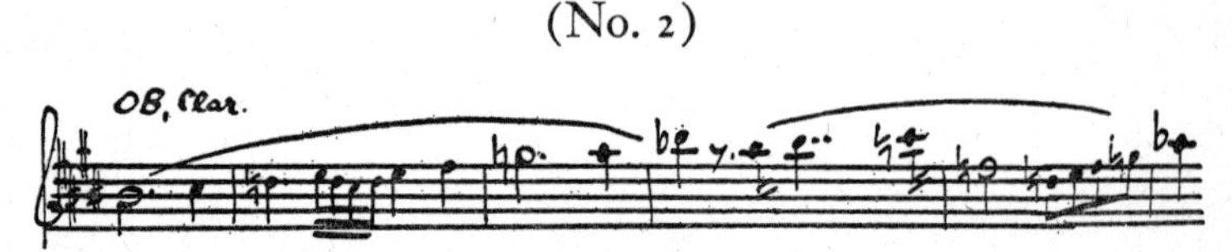

Its main expression does not change in the lengthy development which follows. With its inversion a climax begins on the organ point of F sharp. There is an interesting progression of the parts, which oscillate around the chord of the ninth on C sharp.

The third motive is only rhythmically important and it pushes the motion forward.

(No. 3)

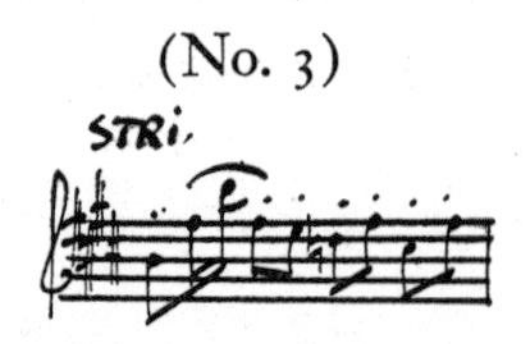

The working-out section starts *molto tranquillo*. Clarinet and imitating oboe take up the main theme in inverted form. Soft trombones augment the restful calm. The climax of this section is built upon a triple stretto in C minor. Elementary force is the characteristic at this juncture. There is no refinement, no elaboration when the Cyclopean blocks appear drawn together. We are reminded of pre-Classic Hellenic architecture and the gigantic lines which give this unadorned art superhuman grandeur. The development portion is comparatively short in extent.

Most remarkable is the Coda, with its organ point of fifty-two measures on the tonic E. It begins with the tenth measure of the principal theme (No. 1) and spreads majestic solemnity. The very last recapitulation of the theme is given to the horns and trombones, and consequently the end is not one of the utmost radiance.

II. Adagio molto lento e maestoso

In this Second Movement Bruckner revealed himself as a real Adagio composer. Though the term "Adagio" is very elastic in meaning, there is no doubt as to the right tempo in this instance. The principal theme bears its tempo in itself. As we have said before, this movement, or at least the last portion of it, was conceived as "funeral music." But its general tone is not that of lament. It has, rather, the character of a mighty musical monument erected to commemorate a great man.

The first three and a half measures are imbued with the dark color of the four Wagner tubas.

(No. 4A)

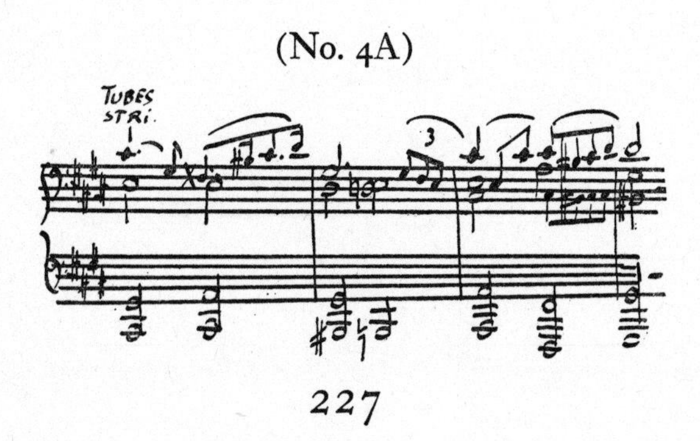

The melody modulates to A major, falling back to the dominant of C sharp minor. We feel as if the attempt to leave the minor key had failed, and for this reason we give ourselves up to a sort of resignation. All the more striking is the unexpected E major in the strings, which carry on the melody.

(No. 4B)

The phrase

(No. 5)

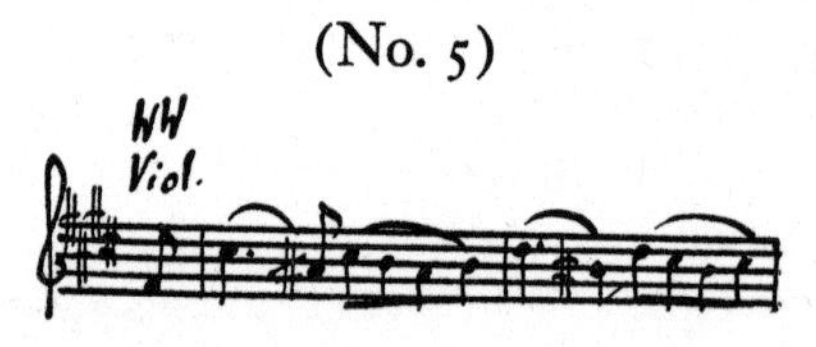

in the first and second violins leads to a short climax followed by a theme which we meet again in Bruckner's *Te Deum* at the words "Non confundar in aeternum."

(No. 6)

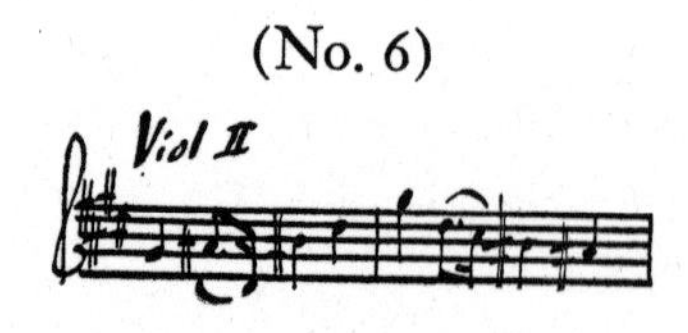

The transition to the next melody, as performed by the brass instruments, renders prominent the tension which is inherent in the nature of the chord of the second.

The secondary section has a cheerful melody in 3/4 time, sung by the violins.

(No. 7)

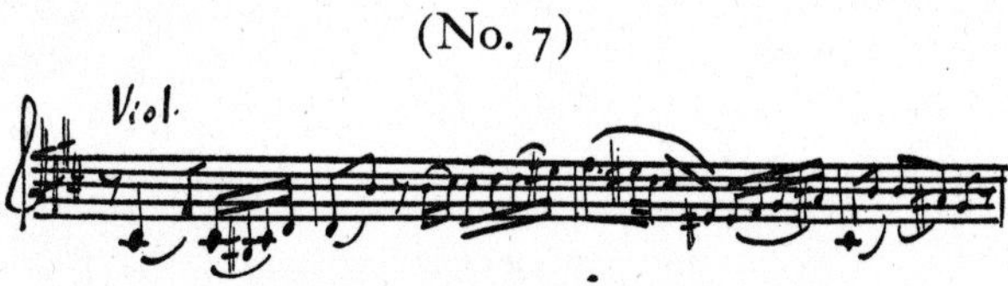

The first phrase of the principal theme, which is then taken up, is developed mainly by harmonic sequences. Special attention should be called to the development of No. 4B, which immediately follows. By the most primitive means – flutes in the lower register and strings – this passage is given a tone color of mystery and softness which is unique in music literature. Only the inner ear of a genius could divine its effect.

The 3/4 motive is repeated, and the main theme reappears for the third time. The climax leads to a triple *fortissimo*, which can justifiably be called "a culminating line." Cymbals and triangles add to the radiance of these four measures, which, by the way, demonstrate the power of C major within an E-major movement. This is very remarkable. The tubas introduce the last portion, which Bruckner conceived immediately after Wagner's death.

The major key at the close does not take away from the music its "funeral" character. The common assumption that major is brighter than minor is valid to a limited extent only. At the time of Johann Sebastian Bach, this feeling did not prevail, as can be proved by many of his compositions which are written in minor and end in major.

III. Scherzo

Vivace

An *ostinato* in the strings, consisting of two eighths and

two fourths, introduces the next movement. The trumpets bring in the main theme, signal-like in character. The clarinet answers with phrases whose distinguishing characteristic is the leap of the seventh. (See the Scherzo of the *Fifth*.)

(No. 8)

The *ostinato* rhythm, with its stress on the first two eighths, displays a power of energy similar to that of the Scherzo rhythm of the *Second*, where this structural idea appeared for the first time. It pushes the motion relentlessly onward. The statement ends on a mighty C-minor *fortissimo*. There is robust, rustic force in the close of this movement.

The kettledrum introduces the

Trio

Poco meno mosso

A *cantabile* sung by the first violins opens the Trio.

(No. 9)

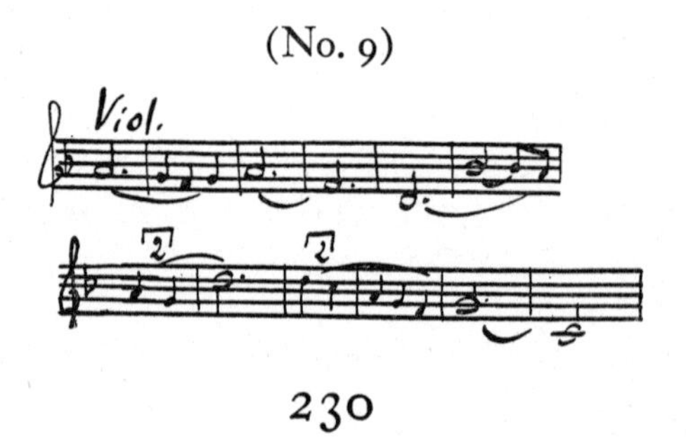

In this melody the well-known "Bruckner rhythm" (two plus three) reappears. The continuing modulations give this movement a questioning timbre. At the end, the naive, bucolic figures of the solo flute re-establish the peaceful atmosphere.

IV. Finale

Allegro ma non troppo

The beginning of the Fourth Movement, unlike most of the other last portions of Bruckner's symphonies, has a very "final" touch. The principal theme, when performed in the right tempo, is both alarming and stimulating. The sharply rugged rhythms of the double-dotted eighth followed by the thirty-second arouse excitement.

(No. 10)

The emphasis in the first four measures lies in the first beat of the second and fourth measures. Then, the up-beat becoming shorter, the following phrase (No. 10B) decreases from two measures' length to one measure's length. Now each bar has its own accent of equal weight. The tightening of the phrase means an intensification of its emotional character.

This theme is remarkable and interesting from a harmonic point of view as well. The progression of the parts makes the listener believe that the harmony in the seventh measure

(10 C) is the diminished seventh on C sharp (with lowered third). He expects its resolution into D or a related key. But by enharmonic exchange, this C sharp assumes the meaning of D flat, as we notice from the following cadence, which stresses the transformation to A-flat major by a *ritenuto*. So this main theme is both emotional and surprising at the same time.

In the score, the second theme looks like an exercise in modulating cadences, but it is replete with majestic calm and full string sound.

(No. 11)

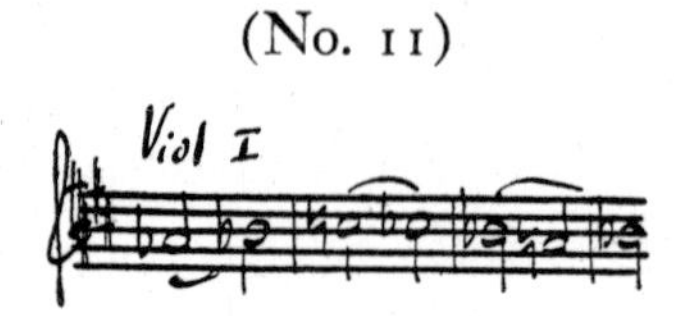

Bruckner was, in fact, a master in creating deep impressions by exiguous means.

This section, somewhat extended in length, is followed by an outburst of the orchestra in unison. No sharper contrast to the foregoing can be imagined.

The first two measures of the principal theme appear extended to four measures. This feature seems unusual to the person who knows that Bruckner as a rule did not change the shape of his themes. The dotted rhythm remains predominating also in the working-out section, which is introduced by a tympani solo. This portion of the Finale ends in a general rest.

One might consider the last foregoing measures the climax of the development section and the beginning of the recapitulation at the same time. The secondary theme, which follows immediately, no longer gains much importance and is suppressed by the reappearing principal rhythm.

The Coda, too, is subdued by this imperious rhythm, which

dominates up to the last eight measures, where the main theme of the First Movement is re-introduced.

Eighth Symphony, in C Minor

Bruckner's own explanatory remarks about the *Eighth Symphony,* as mentioned on an earlier page, were certainly not very significant as far as recognition of the true character of the work is concerned. But they should at least have made the analysts careful in interpreting it. However, they did not. An amazing number of different interpretations are evident in the literature dealing with the composition.

Hans Richter conducting a symphony by Bruckner. Conductor and composer share honors.

Josef V. Woess, the editor of the *Eighth Symphony* for the *Wiener Philharmonischer Verlag*, called it the "Tragic Symphony" because of its "gloomy resignation in the First Movement; the demoniac and fantastic mood of the Scherzo; the solemn grandeur of the Adagio; the belligerent, powerful mood of the Finale, with its gigantic struggle and triumphant victory."

On the other hand, Walter Abendroth ascribes the effectiveness of the work to the "power of metaphysical reality."

There are as many interpretations of the *Eighth* as there are writers about it! All of them tried to find a meaning above and beyond their own powers of expression.

I. Allegro moderato

Mystery is the distinctive characteristic of the beginning. Like a shadow the main theme emerges from the depths:

(No. 1)

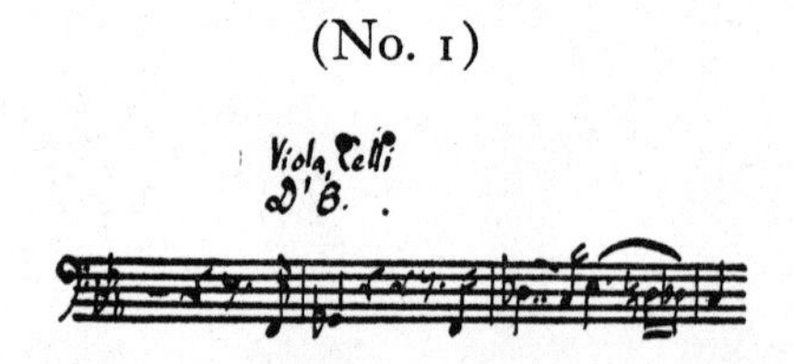

The key is not easy to define. The beginning F is usually held to be the subdominant of C, but the second tone of the theme (G flat) and the further turn of the phrase range into B-flat minor as the subdominant of F. The C at the end of this phrase does not work on our ear like the tonic. The theme runs swiftly through other keys. We do not get an impression of the tonic while the thematic phrases are in the ascent. But when the Bruckner rhythm begins to go down, we feel we are at the dominant of C minor. The tonal agility augments the indefinite and mysterious nature of the theme. When it is repeated *fortissimo*, it assumes an almost threatening expression.

The subsidiary theme appears in G major in the first violins. It is Bruckner's farewell to his favorite motive – two plus three.

(No. 2)

The harmonic richness which adorns this melody is remarkable. A climax of fervent expression ends in a phrase in which the Romantic turn is characteristic.

A short transition performed by the wind instruments brings in the rhythmic motive:

(No. 3)

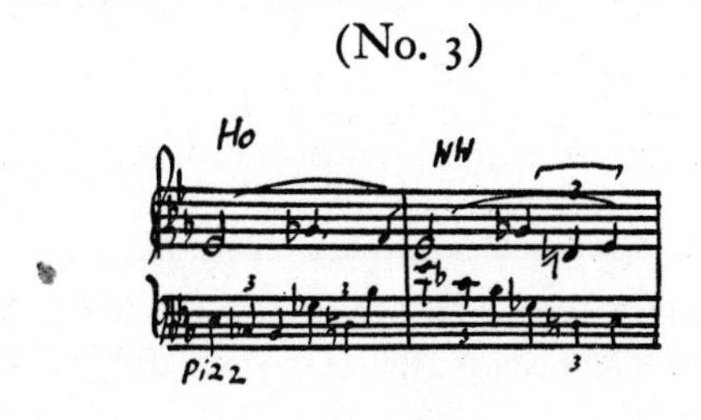

Its triplets are the germ for a new development. The powerful crescendo discharges in trumpet fanfares followed by a peculiar treatment of the opening theme (No. 1). Its characteristic half-step (B flat, C flat) here comes into conflict with the second (B flat, A flat) in the violin tremolo. The effect is striking, even for modern ears.

Calm is spread, all the more, by the following pure E-flat major harmony. Horn and oboe sing the principal theme like a lyric melody. When the Wagnerian tubas enter, all motion seems to have come to a standstill. We are at the beginning of the development section. Augmentation and stretto of the first theme lead to the most daring coincidences of tones (B flat, A flat, A natural, G) at the same time. However, in the careful observance of the fundamental basses, the former Sechter pupil can be recognized.

The climax is reached by the vehement collision of the first two themes, the second in inversion.

(No. 4)

Here is the apex of force and power. The arches of the conflicting two lines are stretched broad. Only a few instruments, so to say, survive the impact. The flute and the low strings mechanically repeat the thematic remainders and the trumpets stay on their main rhythm with inflexible monotony.

The recapitulation starts unnoticed in the first oboe, while the flute is executing a melodic particle from the first theme. In no other symphony has the composer welded the sections together as perfectly as here.

The Coda has its own motive:

(No. 5)

It is drawn together with the principal rhythm of the first theme in the horn and trumpets. This rhythm dominates to the end. Gradually it dies away in the violas.

II. Scherzo

Allegro moderato

A motive one measure in length represents the thematic material of the Scherzo.

(No. 6)

It is also the basic material for the increase in dynamics, no other resources having been used. It gains steadily in might and power. Repetition in music, which can easily grow wearisome when used to the full, becomes a means of intensified expression in the hands of a genius.

Trio

Poco andante

Here, in this Trio, Bruckner used the harp for the first time. Adopting this instrument required a good deal of resolution on his part because of its "luxurious" tonal character. The melody is one of Bruckner's most felicitous inspirations:

(No. 7)

The score has a perfect and consummate transparency. The atmosphere is one of heavenly serenity. The melody does not aim at a goal but, rather, rests in itself. The hard-laboring Bruckner has disappeared. The close of the movement has the grace of Raphael.

III. Adagio

Solenne, largamente ma non troppo

The ground upon which the main theme develops is a dark-tinged D-flat major chord of indistinct motion. Under Nikisch's baton these two introductory measures kept their blurred, mysterious design, for he did not try to bring any rhythm to prominence here. His conception of the string introduction to the slow portion of the love-duet in *Tristan and Isolde* was the same.

Three different elements are the constituents of the Adagio theme: The first four measures, with the sudden change from major to minor, have no direction in themselves. The tension arises the very moment that the organ point on D flat in the basses becomes the fundamental of the chord of the ninth, wanting a resolution. Nine measures later the veil is torn; the whole orchestra soars into high regions in the bright chord of A major.

(No. 8)

The melodic flow goes on in the strings. United with the harp, the strings end the first statement by spheric harmonies.

The whole section is repeated in a changed key. The next melody once more shows why violoncellists love to play Bruckner's symphonies. It is a long-spun chant in the best-sounding registers of their instruments.

(No. 9)

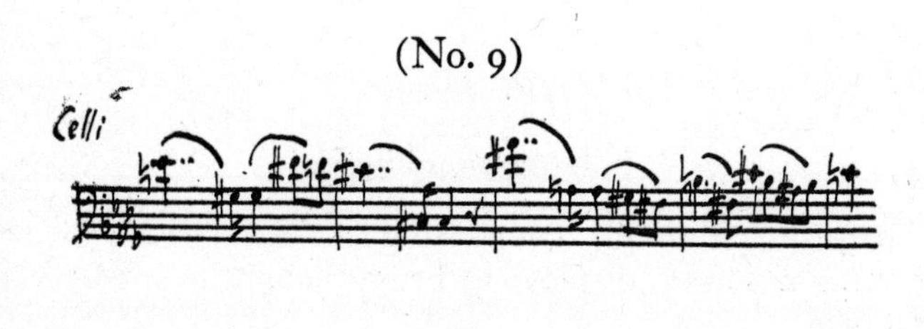

They lead the development, which is interrupted once by a contrasting phrase in the tubas:

(No. 10)

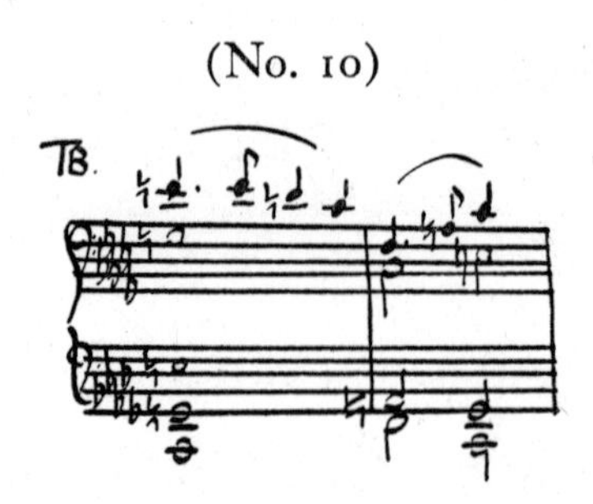

There is a short episode in 3/4 time, built on the first motive of the cello melody. The whole thematic material is exhibited once more. This portion has the characteristics of the development section rather than of variations, as has sometimes been asserted. Most remarkable is its close, where the first violins take up melody No. 9 and the solo violoncello joins in with a phrase which ends in dreamy forlornness.

Thereupon a long-extended climax begins, a climax which has a radiant culmination in the third portion of the principal theme. The Coda, too, is as long as it is fervent in expression. At the very end, the tubas announce in advance the opening rhythm of the following movement.

IV. Finale

Solenne non allegro

The principal theme, contrasting to the nervously twitching string rhythms, displays its heavy weight in the brass instruments.

(No. 11)

It starts on F sharp (that is, G flat), the subdominant of the key of the Adagio. It turns to D-flat major, emphasized by trumpet fanfares. The phrase is repeated, this time modulating from A flat to E flat, and thereupon only the ending phrase makes a clear statement in the definite key of C minor, reiterated by the irresistible power of the cadence. The following general pause is felt as a needed rest here, after the exhausting effort of the opening.

The subsidiary melody has ardent fervor:

(No. 12)

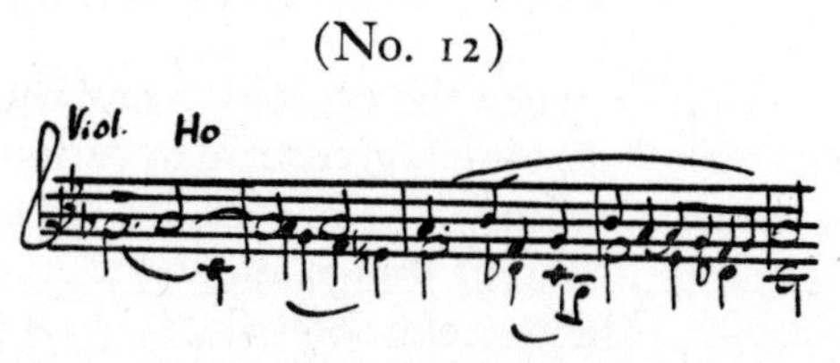

It reaches its apex by an ecstatic and passionate flight of the first violins alone. Although the tone volume is obviously much inferior to the foregoing, the inner expression is rapturously forceful.

The following rhythmical motive

(No. 13)

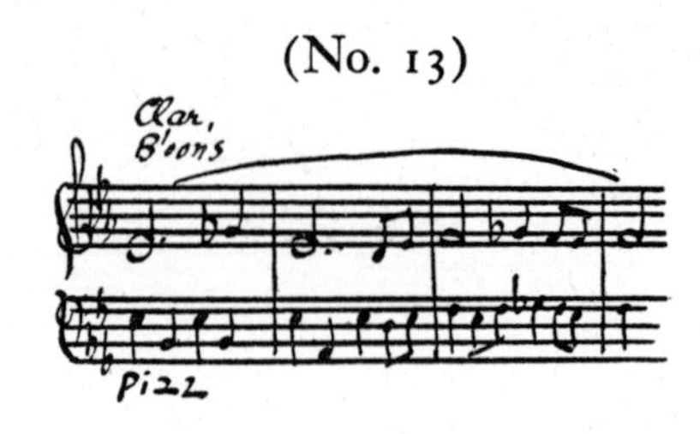

gains active importance for a mighty climax, which is interrupted by solemn, calm harmonies

(No. 14)

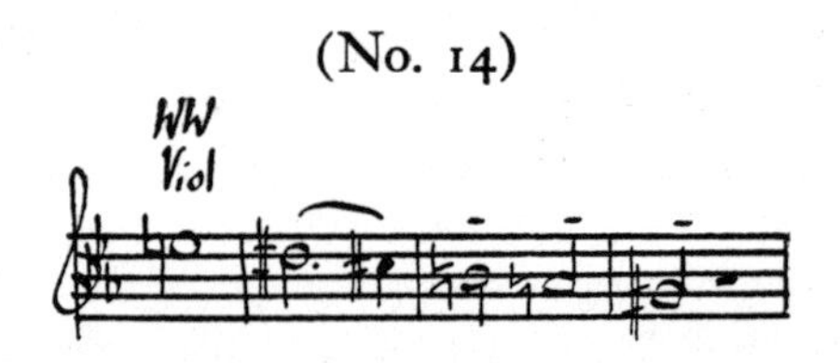

and is then taken up by the whole orchestra. The *ostinato* in the strings is strongly supported by the tympani, which here play an exceptionally important part. At the same time, the rhythm of the opening theme of the work (No. 1) reappears in the brasses.

The connection between the exposition and the working-out section is so close that it has given rise to various interpretations as to what constitutes the border line between them. Eye and ear tell us different things about the starting point of the next section. I believe the three flutes close the exposition with the main theme. Then the inverted melody No. 14 begins the development, which is based mainly on the principal theme combined with the rhythmical motive. A triplet-rhythm introduced here proves temporary in meaning. Nor do new counterpoints at this juncture gain the importance they have in other symphonies. By its power, the main theme overcomes all other ideas which emerge.

In the recapitulation, the dotted rhythm of this theme dominates and brings about an almost dramatically vehement outburst of the tutti. This is the culmination of unfolding power. Towards the end of this section the trumpets and trombones sound the opening theme of the symphony.

The beginning of the Coda, following upon a general rest, is majestically calm and solemn. Towards the end, the horns intone the Scherzo theme enlarged to 4/4. The trombones join in with the principal theme of the First Movement, while the horns change to the theme of the Adagio. At the close, the main themes of all four movements appear, drawn together.

Ninth Symphony, in D Minor

"Bruckner's custom of interspersing quotations from earlier works among his symphonies is particularly noticeable in the *Ninth*. Thematically, the Adagio constitutes, in a manner, a survey of Bruckner's life work, and an intended one."

Even if these quoted opinions of Woess had more substantial reference to the corresponding measures in the Adagio, his assumption that Bruckner really intended to present a survey would not be convincing. While the master was working on the last movement, he did not cast his eye backward. He worried about the fate of his work, since he felt that his own was sealed. At the end of the Adagio, the flickering violins and the dark-tinged tubas convey the picture of the deeply absorbed composer writing the last pages with a trembling hand. This time Bruckner tells us a story – the story of his end.

Anton Bruckner

I. Solenne

Misterioso

The symphony opens, like others, with a tremolo; but here the open strings in unison with the low woodwinds give the D a somber timbre. The first phrase, proffered by eight horns, rises from D to F.

(No. 1)

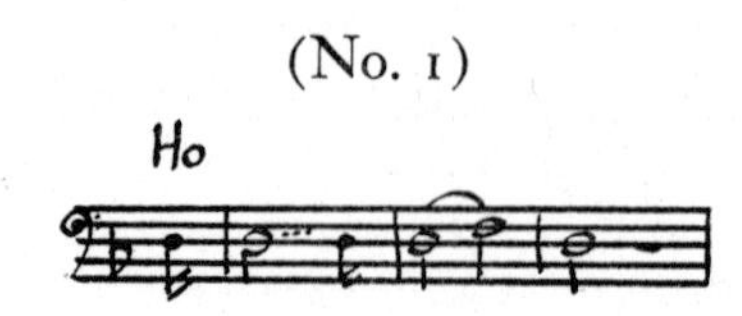

The second phrase attains the A. These two phrases have so important an air that Walter Abendroth is right when he speaks of the "creation" of the third and the fifth. As is the following, both of them are pulled down to the tonic as though it had magic power. A mysterious calm lies over the beginning. Suddenly the D splits into its two neighbor tones (D flat and E flat). The horns, now unhindered, perform the first ascent.

(No. 2)

This has been called the "basic theme" because of its significance for the First Movement. Distorted harmonies give the melodic figures in the violins a morbid expression. The leap of the octave, foreboding the main theme, starts the first climax. Harmonies of strange opalescence (chords of the second with free suspensions), chromatically rising aloft, bring in the dominant. The full complement co-operates in introducing the main theme, which makes its appearance in a *fortissimo* unison.

(No. 3)

Three times it plunges like a cascade from the higher to the next lower level at the distance of one octave. Never before did a theme extend over spaces so wide. A further characteristic is the triplet (in the fourth measure of No. 3). Its pushing effect is neutralized by the heavy three quarters in the sixth bar. (See the main theme of the Finale, *Fourth Symphony*.) The center of the theme is the lowest tone, E flat, which bears the heaviest emphasis in the phrase. This is both remarkable and unusual. The ending portion (No. 3B) of rather constructive nature resolves unexpectedly into major.

The transition to the next section develops on the organ point of D.

The two-voiced secondary melody in A major is chanted by the first and second violins.

(No. 4)

This warm-timbered song culminates in the C-major phrase:

(No. 5)

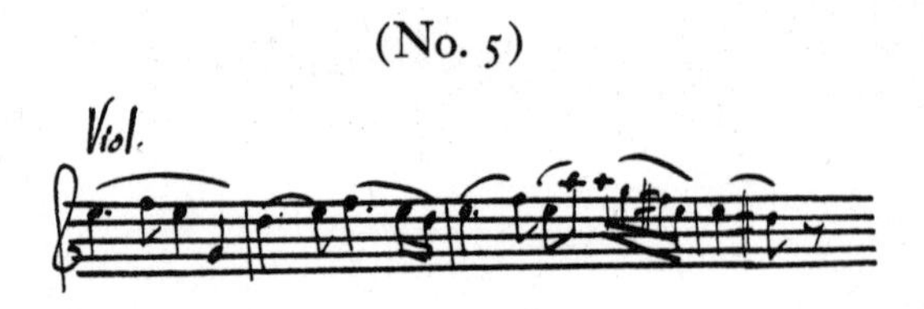

The third motive is heard first in the oboe, imitated by the clarinet, flute, and horn. It appears in inversion before it is published:

(No. 6)

Marked counterpoints in the horns, especially the triplet in No. 6A, gain importance only later. Here they serve the purpose of rhythmical contrast. If the conductor emphasizes

(No. 6A)

them too heavily, they interfere with the majestic magnitude of the main motion, which impresses the listener by its uniform continuity.

The beginning of the working-out section is based on the opening motive (No. 1). The same mysterious calm makes itself felt, a calm torn by the splitting basic theme.

The recurring main theme on the tonic does not mean the recapitulation, as sometimes has been thought. The 4/4 portion which follows upon the thrice-appearing main theme proves that the development section is still going on. It has its own heavily marching rhythm, taken from No. 1:

(No. 7)

All the means customarily used in this section, such as inversion, diminution, and stretto, are used here. At this juncture, the triplet in the conflicting horns (No. 6A) becomes the acting factor. The general ascent gains a superhuman weight. At the *fff* summit in F minor, the leap of the descending octave appears enlarged to that of the tenth.

Here, at the unfolding of extreme force, the climax of the working-out section and the beginning of the recapitulation coincide. (See the *Sixth Symphony*, First Movement.) A general rest of exhaustion follows. The immediately ensuing triplets on the pedal point on A correspond perfectly with the transition to the subsidiary melody in the exposition.

The recapitulation ends in a long hold in the horns. Woodwinds, violins, and the brass choir, following each other, proffer a chain of cadences which introduce the Coda. Here the breadth of design is almost oppressive. The ending phrase of the main theme now initiates the last general crescendo. Trombones and woodwinds take up the basic theme. Trumpets repeat the phrase half a step higher. This does not mean an accumulation of two degrees, as has been asserted. Rather, the trumpet phrase springs from the Neapolitan Sixth, drawn together with the tonic. Its association with the main theme brings in the close of the movement.

II. Scherzo

Mosso vivace

The harmonic dress in which the fundamental idea is first exhibited differs greatly from the definite statement.

(No. 8)

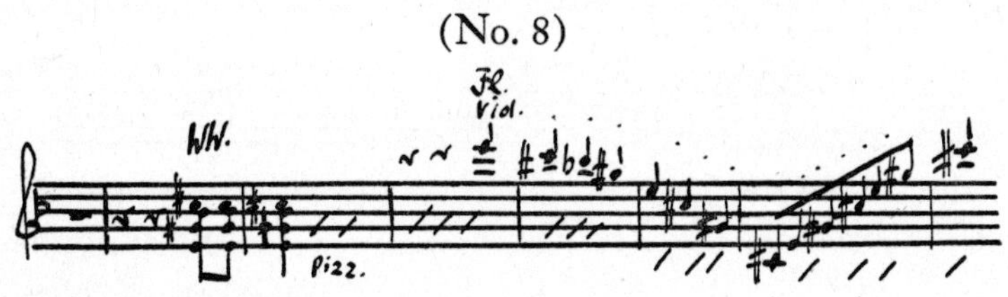

At the first hearings of the work this harmony was a hard nut to crack, even for the experts. In fact, the C-sharp minor chord broken into eighths looks foreign to the tonic D. But it is nothing but three tones picked out of the diminished chord of the seventh of D minor (C sharp, E, G sharp, B flat). The characteristic of a diminished seventh chord, that is, its three minor thirds, become unrecognizable here because of the raised G. The following holding note in the trumpet is the leading tone — C sharp, on which the most varying light is thrown from its surroundings. The definite form of the main theme is again peculiar in a harmonic respect: Here the chord described above is drawn together with the tonic D in the basses:

(No. 9)

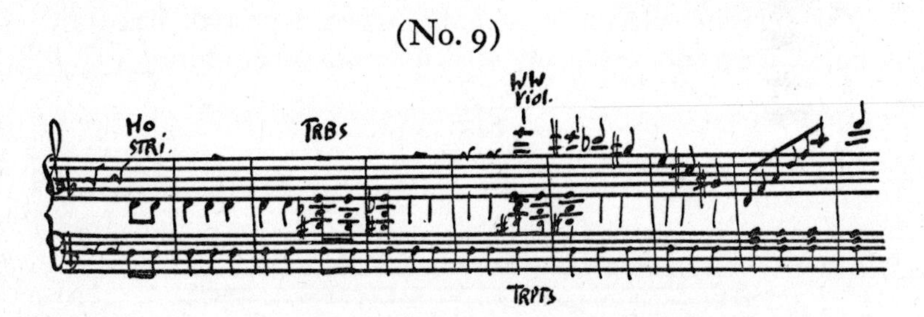

The development receives specific impetus by the augmented broken triad. The subsidiary theme has something of a dance character, although it is not a dance of human beings that we are observing.

(No. 10)

Simple ingenuousness and consummate artistry alternate in this Scherzo, built up of large ashlars.

Trio

The Trio, departing from the customary slower tempo, has a very swift motion and something of French brilliance:

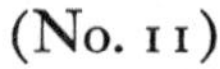

The fervent subsidiary melody, when repeated, has tone colors we do not see in any of Bruckner's other scores.

(No. 12)

III. Adagio

The Adagio is an interposition between sonata and rondo form. The ascending ninth at the opening has retained its striking effect even down to our own day. The violins seem to take leave of the earth. The dissolution of the chromatic progression into the radiant D-major triad is related to the ending phrase of the Adagio theme in the *Eighth*.

(No. 13)

When the first phrase appears *fortissimo* in the horns, the effect is no less striking than at the beginning, but here it is because the ninth (G sharp) is not the top note but lies lower than the seventh (E).

(No. 14)

If we had not been told that the composer called the following scale-like melody in the horns and tubas his "farewell to life," we would think the melody an abandonment on the creator's* part to the spell of sound. The hitherto static nature of the movement is altered by the next melody in the strings:

(No. 15)

Woodwinds answer in light colors. The ensuing phrase, again in the strings, has Classical purity and grace.

Out of the great number of noteworthy items in the recapitulation, we may mention, first, the encounter of the main theme in the violins with its mirrored reflection in the flute. The resulting friction between B sharp and D is an unforgettable and unique impression. Second, the peculiar fragrance of the main theme when it appears in the basses. Several general rests threaten to deprive the development of its cohesion. But the music as it becomes more and more unearthly seems no longer to be subjected to human rules and norms. Towards the end, it hovers in other spheres. The material texture is dissolved into a few tiny threads. A short reminiscence of the Adagio of the *Eighth*, perhaps put down unconsciously, and the last tones of Bruckner's music dies away.

* In *Le Courier Musical*, 1909, William Ritter wrote as follows: "Il y a dans les symphonies de Bruckner des pages entières, superbes du reste, où la musique est là par ivresse d'elle-même, pour la joie du maître à faire de la musique . . . et non pas parce qu 'un plan de symphonie . . . l'exigeait et le comportrait."

CHAPTER XIII

THE STRING QUINTET, IN F MAJOR

IT WAS quite characteristic of Bruckner that he wrote his first and only piece of chamber music when he was fifty-four. If it had required firm resolve on his part to write symphonies without any training in symphonic composition through previous works of a smaller size, the writing of a string quintet entailed certain dangers, for he had created five great symphonies yet had no experience at all in the new field of chamber music. Decsey makes the following criticism of the work: "In this composition the symphonist prevails over the composer of chamber music, who manipulates the five instruments as though they were an orchestra."

The question as to what the true style of chamber music is can be answered from different standpoints. Here I shall emphasize only one side of the matter. The palette of the composer of this kind of music has, of course, only a limited number of colors which he can give to his ideas. His creative imagination will not be restricted thereby but, rather, stimulated towards a sort of invention determined by the available means. Ideal chamber music is born out of the spirit of a few instruments which, alternating in solo and ensemble playing, prove that tone volume and variety in tone color are secondary means of expression in music. The greatest power of expression rests on other factors in keeping with the specific nature of music.

Although one can hardly say Bruckner was a born chamber-music composer — the single piece of chamber music, the *Quintet*, denies it — Decsey's criticism does not seem fully justified. The beginning of the First Movement (Moderato) was conceived in the very mood of chamber music. No other body could render the principal idea as well as those five string instruments. Noteworthy is the fact that in this composition the "rhythmical motive" stands in second place, where the "lyric theme" appears in the symphonies. It was necessary for Bruckner to place it there, for the third theme is not sufficiently contrasting to the first. The rhythmical motive is developed at unusual length, but the structure of the movement is in accordance with the customary Bruckner scheme.

The Scherzo which follows was not conceived through orchestral imagination either. It maintains a graceful mood, the main theme being contrasted to a counterpart of *Laendler* character.

The crown of the work is the Adagio. Its principal theme is immediately soul-stirring. The secondary theme is substantially nothing but an inversion of the first. But what a difference in expression is attained by this simple treatment! The third theme does not appear until much later.

The Finale has, in truth, some inspirations which are not quite in keeping with the idea of chamber music. Its first theme, on an organ point, though lively, is not impressive in nature. The characteristic motive of the *fugato* as well as the general rests remind us of the composer of the *Fifth Symphony*. It had been finished only two years earlier.

THE CHORAL WORKS

It was when he was about forty years old that Bruckner began to write the symphonies which the world knows as his lifework. All through his life, however, he was busy composing choral music. Auer catalogued 86 compositions for chorus, half of them religious in character. Little of Bruckner's secular vocal music is widely known, although works like the *Germanenzug* and *Helgoland*, his last finished composition, house many significant details which should serve to make the completeness of his creativeness apparent.

Not all the compositions of our great masters are equal in merit, as far as their absolute value is concerned. But even in the less prominent works there is at least one phrase or some other feature which clearly betrays the genius of the author. This is true in most of those Bruckner choral compositions which do not rank with the great sacred works. One reason for their lack of popularity is to be found in the texts. They are not equal to the music. If some biographers really believed Bruckner's lack of general learning a good thing for his particular kind of genius, the fact just stated proves them mistaken. His lack of interest in all matters of general culture except music left his sense of discrimination undeveloped. So he selected texts which not only were inferior to his own level but did not kindle his imagination to the same extent as did religious subjects.

The sacred compositions are eminent tests of his creative power, which was primarily devoted to serving the liturgy of the Roman Catholic Church. The Church should call her greatest composer-son of the last century to the memory of her congregations more frequently than she has heretofore.

The three Masses – in D minor, E minor, and F minor – and the *Te Deum* are the peak of Bruckner's sacred compositions. Here not only does his own individual religious feeling display itself but the fundamental idea of the service – Christ's sacrifice for humanity – is felt through music of high and illustrative inspiration. We witness the absorption of the congregation into the hallowed procedure, the trembling at the invocation of the Lord in the Kyrie, the ecstasy in the Gloria, and the gratitude and longing for peace of soul in the Agnus Dei.

Bruckner's long experience as a composer in the field of sacred music made him an accomplished master when he wrote these three Masses. Ease in writing is noticeable here and it alters the portrait of the composer whom we have seen striving for expression throughout nine symphonies. And yet it was the symphonies that made him the great Bruckner, the symphonies which proved him to be singular and original. As a composer of Masses he was just the great successor of great ancestors in music. As a faithful believer he would never have ventured to introduce reformative ideas into Church music. "The man who would dare to do this would have to pick up the threads knotted by Franz Liszt."*

Among the Masses, the *Mass in E Minor* occupies a special position. "It stands alone, apart from the world, a pure church building. Its color is the white of the altar. . . its only ornament is the purity of that style which lifts the soul in the *Missa Papae Marcelli.*" The *Mass in E Minor*, in fact, is the only one of Bruckner's Masses with something of Palestrina's style. He did not make this archaic style a manner, as is noticeable in neo-Italian compositions of recent date. The relapse into a style of the past has never convinced me of its vitality. Rather, it emphasizes our remoteness from a period long past.

Bruckner's contrapuntal writing appears in a new light in the *Mass in E Minor*, which has always been a subject for admiration on the part of musicians. It has the genuine vocal style, the eight-voiced sections demonstrating true polyphonic inspiration. Only wind instruments support the singers. The center of the work is the Sanctus, beginning with a canon. This canon, during its course, undergoes the short development of a fugue, whereby the score becomes rather complicated. Like all Bruckner's vocal compositions, it requires a good deal of training to perform it. His vocal compositions make the greatest demands on the human voice. The inventive ideas in them often spring from instrumental imagination in about the same way as they do in Beethoven's *Missa Solemnis*.

* Rudolf Louis, page 176.

The *Mass in E Minor* proves its liturgical nature and purpose by the omission of the opening words "Gloria in excelsis" in the second section and of the "Credo in unum Deum" in the following part. Those words are supposed to be pronounced by the officiating priest. Even Bruckner's flowing creative imagination appears subdued in this work for the sake of an almost ascetic style.

Both the other Masses are very much "nineteenth century," primarily because of their rich orchestral dress. One might at times recall reminiscences of Wagner, if those short phrases which occasionally remind us of *Tristan and Isolde* and *Parsifal* had not been written down long before Wagner published them. The two works vie with each other in inventive power. The Kyrie in the *Mass in F Minor* has more of an inner connection with the words than has the *Mass in D Minor*, which, on the other hand, is richer in thematic substance. A characteristic of the latter is the ascending scales harmonized in a manner which must have appealed to Teacher Kitzler. Surprising in both Masses is the swift movement at the words "et in terra pax" in the Gloria. It is hard not to think of Bach's interpretation of these words in his *B Minor Mass*. The "Amen" of the Gloria is a fugue in both the *Mass in D Minor* and the *Mass in F Minor*. The Gloria in the *Mass in E Minor*, however, surpasses both of them in originality.

An unfamiliar trait in Bruckner's music is the dramatic expression in some portions of the Credo in the *F Minor Mass*. It begins with the "Credo in unum Deum," omitted in the other two Masses but here proclaimed vigorously. The following musical illustration of the "visibilium omnium et invisibilium omnium" possesses a power which almost recalls Verdi in his *Missa da Requiem*.

It was in these mysterious passages more than anywhere else that Bruckner excelled his predecessors. The finishing fugue is interrupted by eight "Credo" calls of the chorus which stand like pillars of granite in this art-permeated structure. The heavy beat on the second syllable of the word "Credo" looks stranger to the eye of the reader than it sounds to the ear of the listener. Noteworthy in both scores is the *piano* at the words "non factum, consubstantialem Patri." One is tempted to assume the composer desired to point to the mystery surrounding that basic doctrine. The illustrative effect of the long orchestra crescendo on a tympani roll introducing the "et resurrexit" in the *D Minor Mass* is rather naive in nature. The more significant, therefore, is the daring harmony in the following "et ascendit in coelum" and its resolution into the plain chords at the "sedet ad dextram Patris." The last repetitions of the "non erit finis" in the *F Minor Mass* have a special fragrance, for the high woodwinds and the voices in the low registers result in a very delicate tone color. The Sanctus which follows does not display the same amount of inspiration in either the *F Minor Mass* or the *D Minor Mass* as it does in the *E Minor*. There was no vision at work when Bruckner wrote this section.

The introducing melody of the Benedictus in the *F Minor Mass* can be called, without exaggeration, one of Bruckner's most felicitous and blessed inspirations. The violoncello, the bearer of so many noble ideas in the symphonies, publishes the long-spun chant here too. The Benedictus of the *D Minor Mass* cannot compare with it. Several utterances of the same idea with an identical amount of power of expression are rare in music. Interesting at this point is a short Intermezzo in which the horn, introducing the "Hosanna in excelsis," presages the future composer of the *Fifth Symphony*.

The Agnus Dei of the *D Minor Mass* is the greater one as to design and proportion. Like the beginning of the Finale in a Bruckner symphony, it does not hint that the end of the work is near. The opening descending scale in unison has been said to resemble Wotan's spear motive, although the rhythm is decidedly different. The scale belongs to Bruckner's indispensable technical equipment as well as to that of many other great composers. Although Bruckner employed it abundantly, he did not give it the significance it has been given in the Prelude to the *G Minor Organ Fugue* by Bach or in the Introduction to the *Don Giovanni* Overture, where its dramatic meaning has been discovered, or in the *scala enigmatica* by Verdi, where the aged composer of *Falstaff* seemed to be concerned with contrapuntal experiments.

Bruckner's predilection for taking over themes of earlier sections into the Finale, as evidenced in his symphonies, is noticeable to a slight extent in the Agnus Dei of the *D Minor Mass,* where some ideas of the Kyrie are again intimated. In the Agnus Dei of the *F Minor Mass* there can be no uncertainty about the composer's intention to quote what he earlier had expressed. He evidently considered this idea a helpful element in the completion of the form. Here in the Mass it is movingly reminiscent in effect when phrases from the Kyrie and the "Amen" fugue reappear, changed in nature and expression.

TE DEUM

Briefly, one might say that of all Bruckner's sacred music the *Te Deum* has the highest sustained tension. Because of its concentrated dynamic power and lapidary style it has been called the *Bauern Te Deum* (Peasants' *Te Deum*).

The missing third in the opening harmony does not denote mystery, as it does in the symphonies. Any major or minor third here would mean narrowing the universality of this monument *aere perennius* (more lasting than bronze). Even the softer portions keep up the exultant and excitedly vibrating tone. There is no abandon to musical meditations.

The first section is utterly concise in form and expression. Remarkable is the effectiveness of the unison. It seems to tell us: All people on earth speak the same idiom when they praise God.

The following "Te ergo quaesumus," though quite different in nature, is not inferior in power of expression. The unexpected leap (C to A flat)in the tenor melody is completely stirring. In the "Aeterna fac cum sanctis Tuis" the word "Aeterna" seems to be illustrated by the relentless motion in the strings. The "Salvum fac populum Tuum" takes up the melody from the "Te ergo." Thereupon follows the opening idea of the work, at the words "Per singulos dies benedicimus Te." The main part of the "In Te Domine speravi" is built upon a fugue which, according to information from his pupils, caused Bruckner much hard labor. The result was an achieved masterpiece in this form, a form by which the improvising organist Bruckner had so often astounded his listeners.

The last section, "Non confundar in aeternum," proves that a climax overtowering the first "Te Deum laudamus" was actually possible. It becomes a fact, not by external means such as tempo or increasing tone volume but, rather, by an immense intensification of the inner forces of music. Nothing can impress us more than the *subito piano* in the last ascent or the long holding notes in the soprano beneath which strange progressions are mysteriously developing. They discharge in combinations of tones which are far beyond the customary Bruckner harmony. Here the master must have been in a state of rapture.

PART V

MANUSCRIPT AND REVISED SCORE

A BRUCKNER PROBLEM OF RECENT DATE

CHAPTER XIV

WITH the increasing popularity of Bruckner's music the "Problem Bruckner," deeply rooted in both works and personality, seemed to approach a solution. The great interpreters had created a style of rendition which set up a firm Bruckner tradition. Friends and followers were relieved and looked forward to undisputed triumph. Yet, more than thirty years after the master's death, with the initial publication of the original scores, which differ greatly from the editions previously used, a new problem of unexpected weight arose. We were confronted with the question of keeping to the successfully tested versions or of following the new trend, which claimed exclusive rights to Bruckner's true wishes as to the different readings. The question stirred up musicians, conductors, and music lovers to so high a pitch that the success of the Bruckner movement was almost menaced.

It had always been common knowledge that the printed scores contained many alterations, most of which originated in experiences gained through performances of the works. The two Schalk brothers and Ferdinand Loewe had, in fact, extended their concern for Bruckner's works to an unusual degree. They had made excisions as well as changes in orchestration wherever they considered them necessary for easier understanding and better reception on the part of the audience. Generally speaking, they did a wonderful job and deserve the greatest gratitude from all who look at their work with an unprejudiced eye. It certainly required high resolve on their part, since, being faithful and conscientious disciples of the master, they solicitously respected his wishes. Their only desire was to help Bruckner, who, as a matter of fact, enjoyed their support and gave his willing consent to the alterations. He knew why he allowed their co-operation and why he asked for it.

There are documents which most convincingly show Bruckner's desire for help, even from those who did not belong to the "Bruckner circle" and were not so well acquainted with his ideas as were the Schalk brothers. In letters to Felix von Weingartner, who came from Liszt's headquarters, Bruckner repeatedly expressed full confidence in whatever the conductor would hold to be opportune for the first performance of the *Eighth*. It has been objected that Bruckner permitted those changes only temporarily, expressing the hope that the works would later be given in their original form. But we find remarks like these of rare occurrence. Bruckner himself expected only friends and connoisseurs to listen to the unrevised editions, even in the future.

We have performed the printed scores for decades, considering them sacrosanct. And now we are asked to abjure our faith. If we were told that one of the Gospels is not authentic but, rather, apocryphal, would we cease believing in what two thousand years of Christianity has held to be the truth?

Those who think a strict observance of the composer's indications the only right way for performances will, of course, prefer the manuscript to the revised score, although Franz Schalk, who lived in the closest contact with Bruckner, denied that the manuscript always represented the master's final ideas on the definite form of his symphonies. They overlook the fact that a composition once detached from its creator has a life of its own and a right to interpretation defined only by its specific needs. This is the unprejudiced point of view and the only real support for the work.

It clearly is not right to interpret a piece contrary to the clearly expressed indications on the score. But many composers, especially the Classicists, did not give more indications than are sufficient for a general basis of interpretation. Try to perform *The Magic Flute* according to Mozart's scanty directions and you will soon see they do not suffice for an impressive rendition. As Purists should remember, music notation cannot deny its origin in *neumes*. I never will forget what Richard Strauss told me immediately after he had conducted a wonderful performance of the *Jupiter Symphony*. "Keep this in mind," he said, "whenever you plan to conduct a Mozart symphony, write everything you want played by the orchestra into every player's part. It is essential." Those words from a fellow composer of Mozart have been my motto in my career as a conductor.

Even adding a crescendo or a diminuendo is a break, in principle, with the inviolability of the score. Once the barriers are removed, nothing but the conductor's background, education, and control of style are the deciding directives for the performance. Moreover, the director's re-creative imagination is required for making the printed hints living music.

Here are two instances of extensive alterations in Classical scores by two of the greatest musicians I ever met: In one of the recitatives in *The Marriage of Figaro*, Gustav Mahler introduced four solo celli. It is not advisable to imitate him in this, but one should recall his meticulous conscientiousness, an ideal for a generation of conductors, which nevertheless did not deter him from upsetting the Mozart style. Karl Muck had the woodwinds, and sometimes the horns, doubled for playing Beethoven's symphonies. He thought it the obvious thing to do, since the strings in the modern orchestra outbalance the wind instruments. The result was striking in certain instances and had, to be sure, something of the Berlioz timbre. But America as well as Europe acknowledged Muck as one of the most faithful in observing Classicism.

Mozart and Beethoven could not protect themselves from

these alterations as Bruckner might have done, had he so desired. But he did not. He loved the Schalks and Loewe and let them work for him. He did not have too many friends to foster him as they did. It has been said that his indulgent and complaisant nature led him to yield to their suggestions. But everyone with a knowledge of the patriarchal relations existing between Bruckner and his pupils will acknowledge that the authority he enjoyed in their estimation would never have permitted an undesirable change in a score. Friedrich Klose, who for a period of years was present at many meetings of Bruckner and his friends and pupils, never noticed any disagreements over the arrangements of the scores. "Bruckner was not the man to whom they could do violence... There is a touch of the comic in seeing him depicted nowadays by a romantic fancy as personified devotion to the will of others."*

The most censure was directed at the numerous changes in orchestration, as evidenced by a comparison of the original with the revised scores. Referring to the partitura of the *Ninth*, Auer says: "The rough Bruckner has become elegant through Loewe." Loewe was nicknamed "Berlioz" by the master, according to Auer, who could not refrain from admiring the conductor's skill in revising the *Ninth*.

An article in the *Muenchener Zeitung*, 1932, reads as follows: "The true Scherzo (of the *Ninth*) has not a trace of sparkling froth; rather, it stands with solid, pithy bones on the soil of the Upper Austrian homeland." To bring the Scherzo of the *Ninth* into any relationship with that lovely little country shows a complete misunderstanding of the inner proportions of this gigantic music.

The criticism of the revised scores found its most concentrated expression in the assertion that "the Bruckner orchestra has thereby been transformed into a Wagnerian orchestra

* *Deutsche Musikkultur*, 1936-1937.

of Romantic timbre, which is not in keeping with the composer's true ideas on instrumentation." The definition of a "Romantic orchestra" has never been formulated. The term apparently refers to a sound fuller and smoother than that in the Classical period and, especially, to the abundant employment of the horns, which in the second half of the last century acquired about the same meaning as the pedal on the piano. I do not see how a composer as Romantic as Bruckner could be harmed by a "Romantic orchestration," if there is any such thing. As to the "Wagnerian timbre," it is the introduction of the tubas, more than anything else, which reminds us of the Master of Bayreuth. But these instruments are called for in the original as well as in the revised scores, and Bruckner was as proud of this innovation as he was of other Wagner reminiscences, such as the harmonic turns in the *Te Deum* which he had consciously taken from *Goetterdaemmerung*. Not everyone would dare venture it, according to his thinking.

The orchestrations in the two editions are not so fundamentally different as we have been led to believe. At least, they are not to the ear of the average listener. As a matter of fact, Bruckner preferred the contrasting tone-color to the mixed one. This is consistent with his tendency to contrast in music in general. The sound of organ stops, pushed or pulled, often guided the scoring hand of the symphonist Bruckner. That brought about a clarity and transparency in texture which renders the inner parts especially prominent. Here the question arises as to whether the utmost clarity throughout Bruckner's music is for the best. Unmixed color entails a certain danger to the rendition of works like Bruckner's, in which symmetry and sequences play so important a part. To my mind, this straight-lined music needs the utmost variety in color.

One of the main aims of the revisers, as evidenced by a comparison of the original and revised scores, was the support of the strings in the low registers. We see that numerous wind instruments have been added to "help" the low strings. But this support can gain a significance higher than mere dynamic importance. An example will illustrate my meaning: At the opening of the *Fifth Symphony*, First Movement, third measure, the original score calls for the strings only, whereas the revised edition adds the bassoon in order to stress the melodic phrases in the violas. The conductor who desires to keep the entire introduction mysterious and who does not want to emphasize this phrase will follow the manuscript. But if he wishes to make the beautiful phrase prominent, he will have the violas play louder, thereby disturbing the general soft tone of the introduction. Following the revised partitura, he can keep up the *piano* throughout. The listener will hardly hear the co-operating bassoon. It serves its purpose unnoticed. One must admit the revisers did a very tasteful piece of work.

Of greater importance are the alterations which entirely suppress the strings and substitute wind instruments in their place. Bruno Walter recently called my attention to the potential change of tempo which might arise from these arrangements. In the Scherzo of the *Ninth*, eleventh measure, the composer scored the thematic figure of descending eighths for violoncelli pizzicato. Walter considers this pizzicato an unmistakable hint for a very moderate tempo, since it can be played with only a limited amount of speed. But then the secondary theme (No. 10 in the analysis of the *Ninth*) will be affected by this rather slow tempo and subjected to something like a *Laendler* motion, which, however, is foreign to its nature. The experienced and adept orchestrater Loewe solved the difficulty by giving the passage to the bassoon. He no doubt had found out the right tempo from the master himself and took suitable steps to have it observed.

As mentioned earlier in the analysis of the *Fifth Symphony*, the brass choir at the end of the Finale was not scored by the composer but added by Schalk for the first performance in Graz. Bruckner could not attend the première but he approved this support for the orchestra. So the conductor had authentic authorization for his step. As a matter of fact, the huge preceding climax has prepared the listener for the apex of the Finale and therefore the outburst of the brass choir comes in quite naturally at this juncture. Not only is it very Brucknerian in effect but it never fails to transport the audience by means which, after all, are in line with the entire development of the Finale.

The addition of wind instruments in general was not made indiscriminately nor because of the reviser's mere desire to increase the tone volume. Loewe, who edited the *Ninth*, had extremely sensitive ears, as we see from the following. At the letter G in the Adagio of the *Ninth*, a long ascent begins, led by violins and also violoncelli and contrabasses. Here the two scores do not differ in any way. The editor obviously was quite conscious of the particular ghostlike effect of the unsupported bass instruments. That is why he made no changes here.

All alterations in orchestration, as important or unimportant as they may seem to be, are irrelevant when compared with the numerous excisions, most of which the editors did *not* indicate in the scores. It was not until the manuscript scores were published that we learned to what an extent cuts had been made. As a matter of fact, there are a great number of them.

Cuts are generally one of the most unpleasant and precarious problems the conductor has to face in his career. They cannot be discussed at length in this book. We must stress the fact, however, that works of all periods have been subjected to "surgical operations" of the kind. Even Mozart's operas, which do not "suffer" from excessive length, are not produced in their complete forms. There are arias in the original version of *The Marriage of Figaro* which you may never have heard at all, and the final sextet in *Don Giovanni* is often omitted although the major triad at the close of the death scene was never conceived as the final chord after the foregoing minor. (It was introduced only as the dominant of the following G major.) We have heard Weingartner cut the partitura of the *Ring* to an extent which aroused downright indignation, and that not only among the Wagnerites. Bach's *Mass in B Minor* and the *Passions* are given in their complete forms only on special occasions, such as music festivals.

The reasons for treating musical works in this fashion fluctuate between the most distant boundary lines, such as sincere artistic conviction on the one hand and external incidental circumstances on the other. The imperturbable Gustav Mahler omitted the aria of Rocco in *Fidelio* because he felt it interfered with the atmosphere of that part of the first act. During the World War, the great Wagner operas were forced to undergo the most drastic cuts on German stages because, had they been produced in their entirety, the audience and the artists would have missed the last bus, which left rather early, in keeping with traffic regulations imposed by war emergencies. The cuts did not affect the listeners' enthusiasm.

The task of the conductor becomes especially difficult when he believes the work would have a bigger success if it were cut and the composer, on the other hand, opposes him. The popular opera *Tiefland* could not have been kept in the repertory of the German theaters if extended excisions had not given it vital force.

Coming back to Bruckner, surely the proportions of the symphonies, which had originally alarmed conductors and audiences alike, can no longer be considered reasons for cutting. The directors who actually make them should not be condemned on principle, as they often are. Their reasons are merely psychological. As mentioned earlier, the contrasts within a Bruckner movement are the sharpest to be found in symphonic literature. Not only the character but also the motion of the different themes and other constituents are utterly conflicting. This conflict, supported by frequent general rests, certainly arouses the listener's interest and tension during the exposition. But when the heterogeneous elements reappear in unchanged separateness and isolation in the recapitulation, the momentum of *surprise* cannot be as effective as it was at first. This reaction is in full accord with general psychological experience. It becomes especially noticeable at the place where the secondary "lyric" melody, with its decreasing motion, recurs. Even unconsciously, the listener has expected the conflicting ideas to be reconciled by the foregoing development, but now he sees them re-emerging in their original antagonism. Yet manifold impressions are no match for the intensification of a single impression, especially in the temporal art of music. So the listener's tension may be slightly loosened at this juncture and some "lengthiness" may be felt. As a consequence, the question arises for the conductor whether to yield to or to resist the listener's feelings. If he resists, he will have to place less stress on the idea of contrast, for the reasons outlined above. Maintaining the fundamental tempo, even at the expense of expression, will help him in welding the divergent elements together.

Of all conductors, Arthur Nikisch, the first Bruckner apostle, made the most extended cuts. Furtwaengler preferred numerous excisions of smaller size at the time he used the revised scores. Muck and Sigmund von Hausegger did not cancel one bar.

The First Movement of the *Eighth* and the First Movement of the *Ninth* have always been kept intact. This should be a matter for reflection! When Bruckner entrusted his work to the Schalks and Loewe, he was conscious not only of their familiarity with his innermost wishes but also of their abilities as outstanding musicians. It must be acknowledged that they worked with exquisite delicacy and unlimited enthusiasm for their master's cause, not only sacrificing an enormous amount of their time but also exposing their reputations to undue criticism. It is deplorable that they earned everything but thanks from certain zealots. "One can hardly picture the 'honorary' epithets bestowed on them. Forgers and imposters they have been called. They were stamped as criminals in art." Friedrich Herzfeld, who wrote these words in the *Allgemeine Musikzeitung*, 1936, is quite justified in saying that nobody has the right to abuse the Schalks and Loewe, whose efforts for the Bruckner cause cannot be overrated. The critic who abuses them comes *post festum*, when things are over. I believe artistic motives alone should be the criterion in deciding which edition to use. But to make the matter one of character is wrong and rather disagreeably distasteful.

The *Musikwissenschaftlicher Verlag* of Vienna, under the editors Robert Haas and Alfred Orel, has the great merit of having started the Complete Critical Edition of Bruckner's works, with the support of the *Internationale Bruckner Gesellschaft*. As far as we have been able to find out, the publications from 1932 to the present include the *First*, *Second*, *Fourth*, *Fifth*, *Sixth*, and *Ninth* symphonies. *Vier Orchesterstuecke* and the *March in E Flat Major* have also been released. The following vocal compositions likewise have been published: *Requiem in D Minor*, *Missa Solemnis in B Flat Minor*, and the motet "Christus Factus Est." The editors' critical remarks about the different versions of the scores testify to an amazing amount of research work and they offer the Bruckner student a notable opportunity to look deeply into the composer's creative processes.

"The poor schoolmaster's son" is again keeping the musical world busy.

THE END

APPENDIX

CHRONOLOGY

BRUCKNER'S LIFE AND PRINCIPAL WORKS

1824	September 4th: Anton Bruckner born at Ansfelden
1835	*Pange Lingua* for mixed Choir
1835–1837	Studying music with his cousin Weiss
1837–1840	Chorister in St. Florian
1841–1843	Asst. Teacher in Windhaag
1843–1845	Asst. Teacher in Kronstorf
1844	Choral Mass for Maundy Thursday

* * * * *

1845	Teacher in St. Florian
1846	Five *Tantum Ergo* for mixed choir
1848	Expectant organist at St. Florian
1848–1849	*Requiem* in D-minor for soloists, chorus & orchestra
1854	*Missa Solemnis* in B-flat minor for soloists, chorus & orchestra

* * * * *

1856	Organist in Linz
1858–1861	Trips to Vienna to study with Sechter
1861–1863	Studying with Kitzler
1863	*Overture in G-minor*
1863	*Symphony in F-minor*
1863–1864	*Symphony in D-minor*
1864	*Mass in D-minor*
1865	Bruckner meets Richard Wagner in Munich
1865–1866	*First Symphony* in C-minor
1866	*Mass in E-minor*
1867	Suffering from nervous break-down
1867–1868	*Mass in F-minor*

* * * * *

CHRONOLOGY

1868	Teacher at the Conservatory in Vienna and expectant organist at the Hofkapelle
1869	Organ recitals in Nancy and Paris
1871	Organ concerts in the Albert Hall and Crystal Palace, London
1872	*Second Symphony* in C-minor finished
1873	*Third Symphony* in D-minor, revised '76-'77 and '88-'89
1873	Bruckner calls at Wagner's in Bayreuth and dedicates the *Third Symphony* to him
1874	*Fourth Symphony* revised in '77-'80 and '88-'90
1875	"Lector" for Harmony and Counterpoint at the University of Vienna
1875	*Fifth Symphony*
1877	Fiasco of first performance of *Third Symphony* in Vienna
1879	String Quintet
1880	Journey to Oberammergau and Switzerland
1879–1881	*Sixth Symphony* in A-major
1882	Bruckner meets Wagner for the last time at first presentation of *Parsifal* in Bayreuth
1881–1883	*Seventh Symphony* in E-major
1883–1884	*Te Deum*
1884	First performance of *Seventh* in Leipzig under Arthur Nikisch's baton lays the foundation of Bruckner's world-wide fame
1885	Walter Damrosch presents the *Fourth Symphony* and Anton Seidl the *Third Symphony* in New York
1884–1886	*Eighth Symphony*
1892	*The 150th Psalm*
1891–1894	First three movements of the *Ninth Symphony*
1896	October 11th Bruckner dies.

BIBLIOGRAPHY

ABENDROTH, WALTER, *Die Symphonien Anton Bruckners*, Eduard Bote & G. Bock, Berlin, 1940.

AUER, MAX, *Anton Bruckner, Sein Leben und Werk*, Musikwissenschaftlicher Verlag, Vienna, 1934.

BRUNNER, FRANZ, *Dr. Anton Bruckner, Ein Lebensbild*, Linz, 1895.

Chord and Discord: A Journal of Modern Musical Progress, The Bruckner Society of America, Inc.

DECSEY, ERNST, *Bruckner, eine Lebensgeschichte*, Max Hesse, Berlin, 1919, 1930.

ENGEL, GABRIEL, *The Life of Anton Bruckner*, Roerich Museum Press, New York, 1931.

GOELLERICH, AUGUST, *Anton Bruckner: Ein Lebens- und Schaffensbild*, G. Bosse, Regensburg, 1922-1936.

GRAEFLINGER, FRANZ, *Bausteine zu Anton Bruckners Lebensgeschichte*, Munich, 1911.

HAAS, ROBERT MARIA, *Anton Bruckner*, Akademische Verlagsgesellschaft, Potsdam, 1934.

HALM, AUGUST, *Die Symphonien Anton Bruckners*, Munich, 1914.

HEBENSTREIT, JOSEF, *Anton Bruckner*, 1937.

KLOSE, FRIEDRICH, *Meine Lehrjahre bei Bruckner*, G. Bosse, Regensburg, 1927.

KURTH, ERNST, *Bruckner*, Max Hesse, Berlin, 1925.

LOUIS, RUDOLF, *Anton Bruckner*, Georg Mueller, Munich and Leipzig, 1905.

OREL, ALFRED, *Anton Bruckner: Das Werk – der Kuenstler – die Zeit*, A. Hartleben, Vienna, 1925.

SINGER, KURT, *Bruckners Chormusik*, Deutsche Verlags-Anstalt, Stuttgart and Berlin, 1924.

STRADAL, AUGUST, *Erinnerungen an Anton Bruckner*, Neue Musikzeitung, Vol. 34 (Nos. 7,9) 1913.

TESSMER, HANS, *Anton Bruckner*, G. Bosse, Regensburg, 1922.
WETZ, RICHARD, *Anton Bruckner, Sein Leben und Schaffen*, Reclam, Leipzig.

* * * * *

Anton Bruckner, Gesammelte Briefe (FRANZ GRAEFLINGER, ed.), new edition, MAX AUER, ed.

INDEX

Index

Index

INDEX

Index

Index